4 MAR 1991

Youth

N 1983

1987

Justice

Compiled by a Working Party on the Young Offender in Ireland, Department of Social Administration, University College Dublin.

Helen Burke, Chairperson, Department of Social Administration, Combined Departments of Social Science, U.C.D.

Claire Carney, Chairperson, Department of Social Work and Applied Social Studies, Combined Departments of Social Science, U.C.D.

Geoffrey Cook, Lecturer in Social Administration, Department of Social Administration, Combined Departments of Social Science, U.C.D.

Geraldine Cullen, B.Soc.Sc. student, 1975-78; now working as Development Officer, National Social Service Council.

Patricia Daly, Dip.Soc.Admin. student, 1978-79; now working as Social Worker, Eastern Health Board.

Mary Goode, B.Soc.Sc. student, 1976-79; now working as Probation and Welfare Officer, Department of Justice.

Mary Harding, Dip. in Applied Social Studies student, 1978-79; now working as Social Worker, Adolescent Service, Cluain Mhuire Family Centre.

Mary Horkan, Lecturer in Social Administration, Department of Social Administration, Combined Departments of Social Science, U.C.D.

Ciaran Kennedy, Dip. in Applied Social Studies student, 1977-78; now working as Senior Probation and Welfare Officer, Department of Justice.

Judith Leetch, Dip. in Applied Social Studies student, 1978-79; now working as Probation and Welfare Officer, Department of Justice.

Maeve McMahon, B.Soc.Sc. student, 1974-77; now working as Development Officer, Catholic Youth Council.

Aideen O'Connor, B.Soc.Sc. student, 1975-78; now working as Research Assistant, Mental Health Section, Medioc-Social Research Board.

Valerie Richardson, Lecturer in Social Work, Department of Social Work and Applied Social Studies, Combined Departments of Social Science, U.C.D.

Máire Stedman, B.Soc.Sc. student, 1976-79; now working as Social Worker, Child and Family Centre, Mater Hospital.

Mary Whelan, Lecturer in Community Development, Department of Social Administration, Combined Departments of Social Science, U.C.D.

Legal Readers Paul Gallagher, Barrister-at-Law; Dermot Kinlen, Senior Counsel; Paula Scully, Solicitor.

Because students, both undergraduates and post-graduates inevitably move in and out of University in the course of two years, some of those who participated for a time are not listed here. This comprises 'the hard core' of the Working Party that produced the book.

Youth
and
Justice

Young Offenders in Ireland

By a Staff-Student Working Party
Dept. of Social Administration UCD.

Edited by Helen Burke
Claire Carney
and Geoffrey Cook

Research by
Maeve McMahon

turoe PRESS

© Helen Burke,
   Claire Carney,
   Geoffrey Cook, 1981.
ISBN 0 905223 24 1

Design: Hugh Donoghue
Photo: Conor Kelly
Typesetting & printing:
Cahill & Co.
Published by Turoe Press Ltd.,
P.O. Box 1113 Baldoyle,
Dublin 13, Ireland.

INTRODUCTION AND ACKNOWLEDGEMENTS

This Working Party developed from a meeting of students, graduates and staff of the Department of Social Administration, University College, Dublin, that took place in May 1978. At that time there was considerable controversy about the government's decision to set up a closed detention centre for boys in Loughan House, Co. Cavan. The meeting decided to work together to produce a document that would put together in one volume information on the young offender in Ireland. That document has since grown into this book. Our goal was a simple one: that policy making for children and young people in trouble with the law should grow from a sound knowledge base. By writing this book we hoped to contribute to that knowledge base.

To achieve this goal in practice is far from easy. We recognise that there is considerable pressure on policy makers 'to get trouble makers off the streets', 'to punish delinquents', 'to protect the public', in effect to 'do something'.

What we have tried to do in this book is to examine in some depth the problem of the young offender in our society, with its values and structures of which we are all a part. The book opens with an attempt to quantify the extent of juvenile crime in Ireland and to relate Irish crime statistics to other important social and demographic trends, such as the growing population and high unemployment rates in this country. Irish research and official reports on young offenders are reviewed and the need for much further research in this and related areas is stressed. The juvenile court system in this country is compared with the English and Scottish systems; likewise the dispositions available in each of these three jurisdictions are examined. The Working Party studies the various types of residential provision for young offenders in Ireland ranging from prison through to open facilities. Drawing on research from abroad and our own experience here in Ireland, some basic questions about residential care, such as its function in modern society, its varieties, its effectiveness and its staffing needs are addressed. Community-based services, particularly those relevant to young people, are discussed and information is given on recent developments, such as the Neighbourhood Youth Projects and the Youth Encounter Projects. From community-based services the book turns to the wider issues involved in building better communities and a more equitable society; for the Working Party sees the problem of juvenile crime as primarily a by-product of human tragedy and inequality in our society. Throughout the book we have tried to draw conclusions from our analysis of the data. We have also made several recommendations. Most of our recommendations are broad rather than detailed; they tend to concentrate on the principles and innovative ideas that we believe should guide policy for children and young people.

All the time we have been working on this book we have been conscious of our limitations as a group of volunteers embarked on a difficult

v

task. We did not have the money to engage in primary, survey-type research; instead we drew on existing sources of data, on personal interviews and on observation studies carried out by members of the Working Party. We have also been very much aware that the 'Task Force on Child Care Services' appointed by the Minister for Health in 1974 has been working on a somewhat similar and more exhaustive task. Obviously, we have left to the Task Force the detailed job of formulating the precise shape of new legislation for children in Ireland in the 1980s. However, we believed that the more research done in this rather neglected and unpopular area the better; the more informed debate that research can arouse the more chance there is of sound development in the field of child care, young offenders, their families and communities. As a group of people working in social administration and social work as either academics, researchers or practitioners, we felt we had something constructive to contribute from our particular perspective as social scientists. We know we do not have all the answers but we hope we have clarified some of the fundamental questions that surround the issue: 'Youth and Justice'.

Helen Burke, PhD

Chairperson of the Working Party,
Department of Social Administration,
Combined Departments of Social Science,
University College, Dublin.

June 1980

The Working Party wishes to thank most sincerely all those people, too numerous to mention by name, who helped in a variety of ways in the preparation of this book: the students, graduates and colleagues who brought the Working Party into being; the people who gave generously of their time in collecting information and writing up material; the people who attended meetings and commented on the various drafts; the colleagues in the field and in government departments who willingly gave the benefit of their expertise.

We wish to acknowledge the help of the Committee for Social Science Research in Ireland who gave a grant of £1,000. This grant enabled us to employ Maeve McMahon for a period of five months. Without Maeve's work as research assistant it is most unlikely that this book would ever have been written, so we wish to express to the Committee for Social Science Research and to Maeve our very special thanks. We also want to acknowledge help received from Comhairle le Leas Oige, The Eastern Health Board and Allied Irish Banks.

Thanks also are due to University College, Dublin, for providing accommodation and back-up facilities. We are particularly grateful to our colleagues in the Combined Departments of Social Science for their tolerence and their help particularly to Dorothy Connolly, Ann O'Dwyer and Colette O'Beirne, to the students who helped generously with different tasks, and to Anne Coogan who typed the final manuscript.

We are grateful to our publisher, Turoe Press who have brought this book from its academic groves into the arena of public debate.

CONTENTS
I.   Statistical Background to Juvenile Crime

II.   Research on the Young Offender in Ireland

III.   Juvenile Justice Systems in England, Scotland and Ireland

V. Residential Care in Ireland

VI. A Community-Based Approach

Appendices

Selected Bibliography

Index

I. 'Statistical Background to Juvenile Crime*

'If economic and social conditions bear an intrinsic
association with the nature of officially recorded
crime, a shift in societal conditions ought to be
followed by a shift in the crime statistics.'[1]

In this first chapter, statistics on juvenile crime in Ireland are
examined in the context of some of the trends in society that
have a bearing on juvenile crime. First of all juvenile crime[2] is
just part of the overall body of crime committed in a country,
so general crime statistics are examined. But as no crime takes
place in a social vacuum, then other 'societal conditions' such
as growth in the population, in urbanisation and in unemployment are also discussed. The purpose of the exercise is to try
to understand juvenile crime not as an isolated phenomenon
but as part of the changing and complex society in which we
all live.

An increase in recorded crime
In Ireland since 1961 official crime statistics reflect what can
only be described as a vast increase in the number of offences
recorded by the gardaí. Not only have crime rates soared but
there has been a corresponding expansion in the number of
police, court cases, welfare officers and all that is involved in
a growing criminal justice system. Table 1.1 shows the growth
in the total number of indictable crimes recorded since 1961.

Table 1.1
Total Number of Indictable Crimes Recorded 1961–1978

	1961	1966	1971	1976	1977	1978
Total indictable crimes recorded	14,818	19,029	37,781	54,382	62,946	62,000

Source: Garda Commissioners' Annual Reports on Crime

Table 1.1 indicates what might be interpreted as a vast increase
in the amount of crime in Irish society. However, the reality
is not as clear cut as this simple table would suggest. A number
of factors and social processes need to be identified and ana-

*Editor: Dr Helen Burke; Research: Maeve McMahon, assisted by Patricia Daly and
other members of the working party.

lysed before any comprehensive account of a growth in crime figures can be given–these include factors such as the extent of unrecorded crime, and the strength, deployment and effectiveness of the police force, as well as trends in population, urbanisation, industrialisation and unemployment. Obviously an in-depth analysis of the structural changes that have taken place in Irish society in the course of the past twenty years was beyond the scope of this book; however, some of the more important trends are examined in this chapter, starting with the difficult problem of unrecorded crime.

Unrecorded crime
Table 1.1 shows that almost 50,000 more indictable crimes were recorded in 1977 than in 1961. However, the existence of unrecorded indictable crimes must also be taken into consideration. Various research studies of non-detected, self-reported crime indicate that a large proportion of crime is neither reported nor detected. For example, West and Farrington in *The Delinquent Way of Life,* a longitudinal study with a sample drawn originally from a working-class area of London, have shown this to be the case.[3] Research studies further afield have also had similar findings, for example by Erikson and Empey[4] in the United States and by Elmhorn[5] in Sweden.

Many factors affect the number of crimes which are recorded. These include changes in the numbers and deployment of gardaí, not to mention the response of the individual garda to a given situation. For example, in the case of a street brawl the particular garda on the scene may be more concerned with restoring peace than with pressing a charge against one or other of those involved, whilst another garda might have his priorities in the reverse order.

Thus, it is obvious that interpreting crime rates such as those in Table 1.1 must be done cautiously. It is a theoretical possibility that the number of unrecorded crimes was higher in 1961 than in 1977, in which case the growth of crime is not as large in reality as would at first appear. On the other hand, there may have been more unrecorded crimes in 1977, in which case the growth in crime would be even larger than appears in Table 1.1.

Population trends
'Trends in the number of births and deaths, changes in the proportions in various age groups, patterns of migra-

2

tion, both internal and external, all affect both the economic and social environment'.[6]

The population of the Republic of Ireland grew from 2,818,341
in 1961 to 3,364,881 in April 1979.[7] This rate of growth is
unparalleled in Europe. Most recent projections estimate that
the population will rise to 3,486,000 by 1986. This figure
represents an increase of approximately 10% of the total
population in the decade 1976-86.[8] However, given the 1979
census figures cited above, these projections appear to be on
the conservative side.

The Irish population is a relatively young one. While in the
EEC as a whole just over one-third of the population is under
25 years, in Ireland almost half of the population comes into
this age category. Dr David Rottman, in his report for the
National Economic and Social Council, states that although
'. . . increases in the size of the total population are important,
criminologists have long argued that what is crucial is the
expansion or contraction of that population group held to be
most prone to involvement in crime – males between the ages
of 15 and 24.'[9]

Rottman has also stated that the number of males in the 15
to 24 age group in Ireland increased by 6.75% between 1951
and 1971, while the increase for the population as a whole was
only 0.6% for the same period. He goes on to say: 'Those same
years also witnessed a decline in the rate of emigration, an
increase in the marriage rate, and a lowering of the average
age at marriage. Together these trends suggest that the
increase in the proportion of the population represented by
young males will be magnified in the years ahead.'[10] The
growth in the population of Ireland, particularly the growth in
the age group of 15 to 24 year olds, has therefore an important
bearing on the incidence of crime in the country.

Urbanisation

'We believe that the environment has a big influence on
the behaviour of youth and on their needs and activities.[11]'

Not only have there been changes in the age structure and
growth in the size of the population of the Republic but there
has also been a shift in the geographical distribution of the
population itself. According to the 1961 census 44% of the
population were living in urban areas. By 1971 this figure had

risen to 53%.[12] Ireland has been undergoing a process of urbanisation more evident in some areas than in others.

The usual trend in Western societies is for statistics to show the vast majority of offences occurring in urban areas. Ireland is no exception as Table 1.2 shows. As can be seen from this table the trend of urbanisation between 1961 and 1971 has been paralleled by an increase in the percentage of reported crime in urban areas. As Dublin is the most densely populated urban area in the Republic, it is relevant to examine the percentage of offences recorded there (see Table 1.3).

Table 1.2

Percentage of Indictable Crimes Occurring in Urban Areas in Ireland

Year	Per Cent Urban
1961	62.1
1966	70.3
1971	72.4

Source: NESC, No. 25, op.cit., Table 9.7 (partial reproduction). The term 'urban' includes the Dublin Metropolitan Area, and the city districts of Cork, Limerick, Galway and Waterford. In 1964 the Dublin/Wicklow Garda Síochána Division was abolished, with the bulk of its territory being added to the Dublin Metropolitan Area Division. Statistics from 1964 onwards reflect this change in DMA Divisions boundaries.

Table 1.3

Indictable Offences Recorded

Year	Per Cent in Dublin Metropolitan Area	Per Cent in Rest of the State	Total Indictable crimes recorded
1961	52	48	14,818
1966	59	41	19,029
1971	61	39	37,781
1976	54.9	45.1	54,382
1978	56.5	43.5	62,000

Source: Garda Commissioner's Annual Reports on Crime. Again it should be noted that the Dublin Metropolitan Area was extended in 1964 and 1973.

Significantly, it may be noted that a disproportionately large amount of indictable offences are recorded in the densely populated Dublin Metropolitan Area. Dr David Rottman has described the urban nature of crime generally found in Western

4

societies and has tentatively explored factors relevant to the growing percentage of indictable crimes occurring in urban areas in Ireland.[13] Rottman relates the nature of crime to economic and social conditions in society, including modernisation, industrialisation and urbanisation. Concerning crime in urban areas he states:

> While crimes against the person are often as common in rural areas as they are in urban areas, crime against property has traditionally been a city phenomenon. The scale of urban life, the lack of cohesion in the urban family, and the anonymity of the city all make for more freedom on the part of the individual. Along with increased opportunities for committing crimes, both in terms of freedom from control and of temptations, urban living generally brings a heightened reliance on the police as the arbiter in disputes and as a source of assistance .... As material goods accumulate and become more widely available, the opportunities and the potential rewards for offences against property increase. The numbers of television sets, motor vehicles, radios and like commodities have expanded far more rapidly than measures aimed at safeguarding them against theft. Similarly, the use of cheques and credit cards has grown dramatically in recent years, opening new vistas for the unlawful acquisition of money and property.[14]

Given that Rottman associates crimes against property with urban areas, it is relevant to examine crime statistics to see if the trend of urbanisation in Ireland has been accompanied by a growth in both the number and percentage of crimes against property. From Table 1.4 it is obvious that offences against property have vastly increased both in numbers and per 10,000 of population. The rate of increase also exceeds that of other indictable offences, including those against the person, which, although they have increased somewhat, appear minimal in comparison to those against property.

To summarise, we have shown that the population of Ireland is growing and that there has been a shift from the majority of the population living in rural areas in 1961 to a majority of the population living in urban areas in 1971. The relationship between urbanisation and crime would appear to be as follows—almost three-quarters of indictable crime recorded occurs in urban areas (Dublin, Cork, Limerick, Galway and

Waterford) with the percentage for the Dublin Metropolitan Area being the highest. While the figures for indictable offences have increased, both in real and in absolute terms, this increase is most marked for crimes against property. It would appear therefore that in Ireland the trend towards greater urbanisation has been accompanied by an increase in the number of recorded crimes against property.

A study of the costs, according to Dublin Corporation, of malicious damage to public property appears to reflect the trend we have identified (see Table 1.5) These figures show a substantial increase following the years when the trend towards greater urbanisation became marked.

Table 1.4

Indictable Offences Known to the Police

	1961	1966	1971
Offences Against the Person	701	1,132	1,256
	(2.5)	(3.9)	(4.2)
Offences Against Property with Violence	3,186	4,957	10,654
	(11.3)	(17.2)	(35.8)
Offences Against Property with Violence	10,623	12,631	24,929
	(37.7)	(43.8)	(83.7)
Other Indictable Offences	308	309	942
	(1.1)	(1.1)	(3.2)
All Indictable Offences	14,818	19,029	37,781
	(52.6)	(66.0)	(126.9)

Source: NESC, No. 25, Table 9.1 (partial reproduction). Numbers in parentheses represent the incidence per 10,000 population.

Table 1.5

Criminal Injury Costs—Dublin Corporation 1961–1978

Year Ended	Costs in £'s	Costs in £'s adjusted for inflation
31/3/61	40,209	40,209
31/3/66	47,000	38,330
31/3/71	107,590	66,612
31/12/76	2,363,629	681,093
31/12/78	1,215,000	286,487

Source: Corporation, City Hall figures rounded off to the nearest pound. 'Criminal injuries' cover malicious damage to cars, walls, telephone boxes, etc.

At this point it might seem logical to state that there is a clear correlation between increasing urbanisation and growing criminality. However, again we must beware of oversimplification. The points that were made at the beginning of the chapter about recorded and unrecorded crime are particularly relevant here. For example, it could be suggested that offences against property (the largest category of offences) are more observable and therefore more likely to be recorded than other offences. Burglary, housebreaking and malicious damage (offences against property) seem to be more amenable to detection than membership of an unlawful organisation, possession of drugs or collecting money without a permit. Furthermore, it could be argued that the probability of recording such offences against property is higher in a densely populated urban area than in a sparsely populated rural one.

Despite such reservations about the crime statistics, it nevertheless appears that there is a link between urbanisation and increasing criminality, particularly as regards offences against property. In the light of this knowledge we can look at some of the information available about young offenders in Ireland.

Research carried out in Ireland to date concerning young offenders with convictions shows that most of them tend to come from urban areas. For example, in 1963–64 Hart took a sample of 125 young offenders in an industrial school and a reformatory. He found that 111 of these came from urban areas with a population of more than 20,000 people.[15] In 1967 from a random sample of 32 offenders in St Patrick's Institution, 19 were found to have come from highly populated areas in Dublin.[16] Further research on young Dublin probationers by Hart, in the early 1970s, showed that young offenders on probation who were from central city areas were prone to offend again.[17]

In February 1968 a comprehensive survey was carried out on the origins of young offenders in reformatories. This was undertaken in conjunction with the Reformatory and Industrial Schools Systems Report, hereafter referred to as the Kennedy Report.[18] This survey listed the county or place of origin of all the young offenders in reformatories at the time. It is clear from Table 1.6 that there was a concentration of youngsters from counties with an urban centre such as Dublin, Cork, and Limerick in Irish reformatories in 1968. Overall, it seems reasonable to assume that the common trend

7

in Western societies as regards the relationship between urbanisation and crime is to be found in Ireland also.

Table 1.6

Place of Origin of Young Offenders in Reformatories, February 1968

Reformatories

County or place of Origin	Boys	Girls
Louth	6	—
Longford	2	—
Laois	1	—
Offaly	—	2
Carlow	1	—
Kilkenny	2	1
Wexford	6	—
Dublin	46	11
TOTAL LEINSTER	64	14
Waterford	5	—
Cork	10	4
Kerry	2	2
Limerick	15	1
Clare	1	1
Tipperary	2	1
TOTAL MUNSTER	35	9
Galway	2	—
Mayo	1	—
Sligo	1	—
Roscommon	—	1
TOTAL CONNAUGHT	4	1
Donegal	—	2
Monaghan	1	—
TOTAL ULSTER (part of)	1	2

Great Britain	—	3

TOTAL GREAT BRITAIN	—	3

No Home	—	1
No Fixed Abode	1	3
No reply	—	5

TOTAL NO HOME etc.	1	9

TOTAL IN SCHOOLS	105	38

Source: *Reformatory and Industrial Schools System Report* (Dublin, 1970), p. 103.

Employment and unemployment

> 'I'd go to work, I would, if I was out. Always would if I could have got any other job but shoving a bleeding messenger boy's bicycle about with a hundredweight of stuff on it for ten bob a week.'
> Brendan Behan in *Borstal Boy*.[19]

Finding work at a decent wage for all who sought employment has always been a problem in Ireland. For more than a century emigration eroded the Irish labour force. Nowadays, however, the picture is different. The growth in the population that has taken place in recent years[20] is reflected in Table 1.7 which shows that the labour force (i.e. those at work and those registered as unemployed) increased by 40,000 people between 1961 and 1978. It also shows that by 1976 there were over 108,000 people out of work and that some inroads were made in this huge figure by 1978.

Table 1.7

The Labour Force 1961–1978

(thousands)

	1961	1966	1971	1976	1978
Total at work	1,052	1,065	1,055	1,035	1,048
Out of work	56	52	65	108	100
Total Labour Force	1,108	1,117	1,120	1,143	1,148

9

The National Economic and Social Council, in its analysis of employment in Ireland between 1961 and 1974, identified two distinct phases, one from 1961–1966 and the second from 1966–1974. According to NESC, the first period was one of rapid growth in most sectors, while the second was character-ised by a quickening of the rate of decline in agricultural employment. This decline in agricultural employment put stress on the industrial and service sectors which they were not able to meet. Consequently, there has been a steady increase in the number of unemployed, *and a worsening of the long-term unemployment problem, especially among the younger age groups.* A further cause was the falling off in the number of emigrants. *There is some evidence that emigration for under 21 year olds is no longer an alternative to prolonged periods of unemployment in Ireland.*[21] Therefore it has been extremely difficult for all the young people coming into the labour force each year to find work. In this context a study of youth employment commis-sioned by the Department of Labour and AnCo in 1976 is of particular interest.[22] The study took a sample of the 15 to 18 year olds in North Central Dublin and found that only 22.6% of the sample were still attending school. Of those who had left school 52.2% (108) were found to be employed at the time of the study, while 47.8% (99) were unemployed. The study found that, of those who were employed, few could be 'described as having good pay'.

Table 1.8

Take Home Pay from Present Job of Young People in North Central Dublin

£	Total %	Male %	Female %
Under £10 week	3.7	4.4	3.4
£11–20	62.7	46.9	75.9
£21–£30	27.0	36.7	19.0
£31–£40	5.6	10.2	1.7
£41–£50	1.0	2.0	—
	100	100	100

Source: Murphy and Morrissey, ibid., p. 70.

As can be seen from Table 1.8 over 66% of respondents were taking home less than £20 a week. The study came to some rather depressing conclusions:

10

The problem of unemployment was found to be extremely acute in the study area. Forty eight per cent of the respondents who had left school were unemployed. Fifty per cent of respondents' fathers who were available for work were unemployed and approximately 70% of the households in the survey had at least one person unemployed. ... The problem of unemployment is, of course, more than an inner city problem. It is currently a national one. However, evidence suggests that the inner city has a higher unemployment rate than any other part of the country. . . . .Those who do manage to find employment are restricted in the majority of cases to an unstable, and badly paid working life. Most of those in employment have had previous experience of unemployment: most are presently in unskilled or semi-skilled jobs where they are given little or no training.[23]

Thus it can be seen that, despite the efforts of statutory bodies such as AnCo and the National Manpower Service in the inner city, unemployment presents major problems there.

The question arises as to what relevance unemployment trends have for delinquency. Many criminological studies have associated unemployment and delinquency. For example, West and Farrington have this to say concerning their study of young offenders:

The finding that delinquents, and especially recidivists, tended to have low status jobs and erratic work histories came as no surprise, but the degree of contrast between delinquents and non-delinquents was unexpected. . . .Although delinquents seem to succeed in keeping the job they have, in spite of having been convicted, it may be, as evidence from the United States (Schwartz and Skolnick, 1962), Holland (Buikuisen and Dijksterhuis, 1971) and New Zealand (Boshier and Johnson, 1974) suggests, that convicted delinquents find it more difficult to get jobs in the first place[24]

We consider this suggestion by West and Farrington to be very interesting. Usually it might be expected that a delinquent would have his career interrupted by periods in penal institutions and days in court. However, according to West and Farrington these factors are not as significant as the difficulty a convicted delinquent experiences in getting a job in the first

11

place. Unfortunately there has not yet been any study under-taken in Ireland which is broad enough in scope to test this hypothesis.

However, many of the studies which have been carried out in this country do link unemployment and delinquency. These include those by the Prisoner's Rights Organisation and by Ian Hart. In 1968, Hart's study of young offenders in an Irish industrial school and reformatory showed that the rate of unemployment among the fathers of offenders was higher than would have been expected when compared with the national average. Table 1.9 indicates that this trend was particularly evident where the fathers of delinquents belonged to skilled, semi-skilled and unskilled manual employment category.

Table 1.9

Offenders' Fathers and National Population of Married and Widowed Men by Rate of Unemployment According to Social Group, 1968

Social Group	Rate of Unemployment among Delinquents' Fathers %	Rate of Unemployment among National Population of Married and Widowed Men %
Other agricultural occupations	20 (n = 5)	20
Intermediate non-manual	18 (n = 11)	15
Other non-manual	7 (n = 14)	10
Skilled, semi-skilled and unskilled manual	31 (n = 55)	13
	N = 85	

Source: Ian Hart, 'A Survey of Some Delinquent Boys in an Irish Industrial School and Reformatory', *Economic and Social Review*, Vol. 7 (1968–70), p. 191.

It is interesting to note that ten years later, in 1978, when the Prisoner's Rights Organisation carried out a survey of fifty 12 to 16 year old male offenders from an inner city area of Dublin,[25] they found that only 6 of the 48 fathers alive were employed. Furthermore, of the young offenders themselves, only one was employed while the remaining 49 were neither employed nor attending school.

Another study, carried out by the Prisoner's Rights Organisation in 1979, also links unemployment and delinquency. The study was of 200 ex-prisoners, two-thirds of whom had at least ten convictions each and found that 65% of the respondents described themselves as having been 'seldom or never in employment'.[26]

At this point it seems clear that there is a relationship between unemployment and delinquency, although given the lack of Irish information available it is impossible to spell out the nature of this relationship.

Juvenile crime statistics

Having first examined general crime statistics in Ireland in the context of some of the structural changes that have been taking place in Ireland since 1961, we now turn to an analysis of the statistics that are available on juvenile crime. The main source for this information is the Garda Commissioners' Annual Reports on Crime from 1961–1978.

Participation by juveniles in the growing crime rate?

Earlier in this chapter it was noted that there has been a huge growth in the total number of indictable crimes recorded since 1961, from 14,818, in 1961 to 62,000 in 1978. However, it cannot be shown to what extent young offenders participated in the total number of indictable crimes. Although the official statistics can be broken down into the types of crime, they cannot be examined in terms of *who* committed each crime as not all the crimes recorded will be 'solved' by the police. How then may the extent to which young offenders have shared in the growth of crime be measured? The most useful table for this purpose in the Garda Commissioners' Annual Reports on Crime is that which gives figures referring to the proven charges, whether or not they were followed by a conviction. Table 1.10 reveals some very interesting facts. Firstly, where young offenders are concerned (i.e. offenders under the age of 17), the number of charges proven against them have dropped substantially. Secondly, while the figures for persons under 17 years old have dropped, those for older offenders have risen substantially, they have nearly doubled. A more realistic appraisal of the share of young offenders in the crime statistics can be had by expressing the above figures in terms of percentages. Table 1.11 shows the age groups as a percentage of the proven charges.

Table 1.10

Age Group of Persons Convicted or Against Whom the Charge was Held Proven and Order Made Without Conviction 1961–1978

Year	Under 14 years	14 & under 17	17 & under 21	Over 21	Total
1961	1,319	2,014	1,298	2,449	7,080
1966	1,211	1,957	2,259	3,793	9,220
1971	724	2,027	3,059	5,386	11,196
1976	734	1,888	2,609	5,291	10,522
1977	515	1,784	2,844	5,558	10,701
1978	459	1,479	2,608	4,519	9,065

Source: Compiled from figures given in the *Garda Commissioners' Annual Reports on Crime, 1961–78.*

Table 1.11

Age Group of Persons Convicted as a Percentage of Total Convictions 1961–1978

Year	Under 14 years	14 & under 17	17 & under 21	Over 21	Total Number
1961	18.6	28.4	18.3	34.6	7,080
1966	13.1	21.2	24.5	41.1	9,220
1971	6.5	18.1	27.4	46.9	11,196
1976	6.9	17.9	24.8	50.2	10,522
1977	4.8	16.7	26.6	51.9	10,701
1978	5.1	16.0	28.8	49.8	9,065

Source: Compiled from *Garda Commissioners' Annual Reports on Crime 1961–78.* Percentages are correct to one decimal point.

Again it can be seen that young offenders have had a significantly decreasing share in crime statistics – 47.0% in 1961 and 21% in 1978. **Thus, the statistical evidence is that juvenile crime has not, in fact, increased.**

The figures in Table 1.11 show that there has been a decline in the number of charges proven and convictions of juveniles (i.e. those under 17 years) between 1961 and 1978 and that

14

this decline has taken place despite an increase in our young population and trends of urbanisation and increasing unemployment, trends which are usually related to an increase in juvenile crime. The question must be asked: does the statistical evidence mean that the incidence of deliquent behaviour by juveniles in Ireland has actually decreased?

The Working Party is cautious about making this assertion. As pointed out already at the beginning of this chapter the analysis of official crime statistics is complicated by a number of factors. The unknown incidence of unrecorded crime is one factor. So too is the lack of information on the deployment of gardai throughout the country.[27] It could be argued that the continuing troubles in Northern Ireland, the increase in cross-border security measures, the increase in bank robberies, kidnapping and other serious and sometimes violent crimes, have diverted the attention of the gardai from juvenile to adult offenders in recent years.

Furthermore, the statistics quoted in Tables 1.10 and 1.11 do not include the juveniles coming under the Juvenile Liaison Scheme which has been in operation since 1963.[28] From the time of its inception until 1978 the Juvenile Liaison Scheme had a total of 12,374 cases, i.e. 12,374 juveniles who actually admitted committing an offence. Then there is also the developing role of the School-Attendance Department which has had the effect of keeping many juveniles out of court by working at a more preventive level in recent years. This trend is illustrated in Table 1.12. The changing role of the School-Attendance Department is reflected in this table and the

Table 1.12

Statistics of the School Attendance Department, Dublin 1961–1978

Year	Statutory Notices Served	Legal Proceedings Issued	Sent to Industrial Schools
1961	3,064	1,457	56
1966	1,796	972	40
1971	1,754	978	19
1976	969	447	31
1978	896	390	25

Source: School Attendance Department, Burton Chambers, 19/22 Dame St., Dublin 2.

decreasing use of legal procedure which has occurred, despite the fact that the Department is operating in a geographical area with an increasing population.

Another factor that may help to explain the decrease in juvenile crime statistics is the expansion of the welfare service of the Department of Justice, particularly since the early 1970s, which helps to prevent some young offenders from accumulating charges. Added to this is the growing network of community based social services, both statutory and voluntary, which have probably helped many potential young offenders to find a more constructive direction in their lives.

Despite our reservations about accepting the statistics at face value, the fact remains that the official figures for juvenile crime have declined since 1961 both in absolute numbers and as a percentage of those against whom charges were proven, and this trend is particularly interesting in the context of structural changes over the last 20 years in Ireland, changes which are usually more conducive to a growth rather than a decline in juvenile crime.

A growth in the fear of juvenile crime?
There is another area we believe must be mentioned before concluding this chapter, and it is an area in which hard statistical data is extremely difficult if not impossible to find. This concerns the fear of crime in the community.

Obviously fear is extremely difficult to quantify and one can be afraid of criminal behaviour without having personally experienced it oneself, as the following finding from Vaughan and Whelan's study of the elderly indicates.[29] In this study, which is concerned with the economic and social circumstances of a sample of elderly Irish people, a number of questions were asked related to the respondents' objective and subjective appraisal of crime, including burglary and vandalism (i.e. crimes often attributed to juveniles).[30] Preliminary tables from this study reveal that the percentage of those in the sample who consider such crimes to be a problem is much higher than the percentage of those *who had actually experienced* the offence. For example, it was found that, of 664 men, 21 stated their houses had been burgled (10 within the last three years), while of 727 women, 21 said their houses had been burgled (12 within the last three years). Table 1.13 shows the responses of these elderly people to the question: 'Is Burglary a Problem?'

Table 1.13

Is Burglary a Problem?

Men	Central City	City–Town Other	Village	Open Country	Total %
Very much a problem	10.7	10.6	0	0	3.3
Bit of a problem	17.7	16.0	5.7	4.6	8.3
Not much of a problem	8.8	12.9	9.7	8.9	9.9
No problem	62.8	60.5	84.6	86.5	78.5
	100.0	100.0	100.0	100.0	100.0
Women					
Very much a problem	5.3	8.2	3.1	1.5	4.5
Bit of a problem	11.5	17.2	5.7	4.0	9.9
Not much of a problem	26.9	14.8	8.2	6.6	12.0
No problem	56.3	59.8	83.0	87.9	73.5
	100.0	100.0	100.0	100.0	100.0

Source: Partial reproduction of table in R.N. Vaughan, and B.J. Whelan, op.cit., p.39.

It can be seen from Table 1.13 that many of those who considered burglary to be a problem had never actually experienced it themselves. Likewise a much larger percentage of those living in urban areas saw burglary as 'very much of a problem' and 'a bit of a problem' than those living in a village or open country. A similar pattern was found where vandalism and personal safety were concerned.

Another indicator of the growth in crime and/or the fear of crime in recent years has been the growth in the security industry, i.e. in firms producing or selling burglary alarms and safety devices of various kinds, and in the employment of security guards. The growth in the number of indictable offences which have been described earlier in this chapter may well account for the growth in the security industry.

Members of the Working Party have been told by several politicians and canvassers who worked for the political parties in the general election of 1977 and the subsequent local elections that a problem they regularly encountered in their canvass of urban areas was that of vandalism and a fear of juvenile crime. These canvassers were urged by many citizens 'to do something about the young thugs who roamed the streets'. Certainly the figures quoted for criminal injury costs in Table 1.5 indicate that vandalism in Dublin has increased since 1961. However, as already pointed out, official crime statistics (qualified though these may be) show a drop in juvenile crime. Could it be then that the fear of juvenile crime has increased rather than the actual incidence of such crime?

Conclusions and recommendations

To conclude we wish to draw together some of the important facts, trends, questions and recommendations that have emerged from our analysis of the data presented in this chapter. The first of these is the general trend in Western society charted by criminologists which indicates that, where there is an increase in the population (particularly in males aged between 15 and 24 years), increased unemployment and increased urbanisation, an increase in the crime rate can be expected. Despite such trends in Ireland at different times between 1961 and 1978, and the fact that the official figures for all recorded indictable crimes have risen from 14,818 in 1961 to 62,000 in 1978, the official figures show that there has been a *decrease* in the number of charges proven and convictions against juveniles (i.e. those under 17 years of age) between 1961 and 1978.

However, official crime statistics in Ireland must be interpreted in the light of the following factors: the way in which they are presently compiled does not lend them to detailed statistical analysis because (a) they cannot take account of unrecorded crime, (b) they do not reflect possible changes in the deployment of the gardaí, and (c) they do not show the impact of preventive measures in the community that keep youngsters away from crime. To facilitate more accurate and in-depth analysis of Irish crime statistics and of the measures being taken to combat crime in Ireland, we therefore recommend that:

(1) **As a matter of urgency a Working Party be established under the direction of a trained and experienced researcher to devise a system for the compilation of accurate and comprehensive information on crime in Ireland. The Working Party should consist of people with particular expertise in this area.**

(2) **The Department of Justice publishes a detailed annual report carrying comprehensive statistics of people convicted of various types of crime, details of the ages and convictions of people in prison and other relevant institutions, details of those on probation and supervision orders, details of the numbers and qualifications of staff employed by the Department and the costs of the various aspects of the Department's work.**

Two important questions remain. Is the recorded decrease in juvenile crime in Ireland a real decrease or merely a reflection of changing trends in the criminal justice system? If there is a real decrease in juvenile crime, why has the problem of the young offender attracted so much negative comment and indeed caused the creation of a new closed institution in recent times?

II. Research on the Young Offender in Ireland*

There is a dearth of scientific social research on Irish young offenders. Some information, however, is available in the Annual Prison Reports, the Garda Commissioners' Annual Reports on Crime and the reports of government commissions of inquiry. Since the 1960s a number of small studies and articles specifically concerned with young offenders have been published. The information reviewed in this chapter can be divided into two periods: first, information on young offenders in Ireland from the foundation of the State until the end of the 1950s and secondly, the findings of studies carried out on Irish young offenders from 1960 to the present time.

For the period 1921 to 1959, for which very little published material could be found, the information was examined under the following headings: a) young people in borstal, b) children and young people in reformatory and industrial schools, and c) 'The Supervision of Delinquents in Society'.

For the period from 1960 to the present time the information from the various sources was analysed under the following headings: a) the sex of young offenders, b) urban deprivation and young offenders, c) unemployment and low income, d) types and duration of juvenile crime, e) family size and relationships within the family and f) educational deficiency and low I.Q. among young offenders.

Period I: 1921–1959

a) Young people in borstal

The first Irish borstal was established in Clonmel in 1906.[1] This borstal served the entire country until 1921; however, following the partition of Ireland it was restricted to young offenders from the Republic. At any time there was never more than one borstal institution in the Republic, although on occasions, the institution was temporarily transferred from one location to another.

There are two major sources of information about borstal in Ireland. The first of these is the annual reports of the General

Editor: Dr. Helen Burke, Research Maeve McMahon & The Working Party

Prisons Board in Ireland[2] (until its abolition in the late 1920s), and the second is Nial Osborough's book *Borstal in Ireland*, which looks in some detail at the system in Ireland both north and south[3].

From 1877 until 1927 the General Prisons Board published an annual report. Although they did not undertake any scientific social research, they made many comments and observations which offer a fascinating insight into the borstal system in Ireland. For example, in 1924 the Board gave this description of the youths who were coming to borstal:

> We have within the last few years to deal with an entirely new class of criminal, composed of half educated youths who would appear to have escaped early from parental control. They have grown up in lawless habits and the streets and the cinema have been the main sources of their moral education. Full of new and unsatisfied desires, these youths have been dazzled by sensational reports in newspapers of large sums of money obtained by organised robbery, and they are seduced by the prospect of getting money easily without having to work for it honestly. There is also another fact which we have noticed. Formerly a series of convictions for minor offences preceded offences of a graver nature. Now the first offender starts off with a more serious form of crime, and unlike his forerunners in crime seems after commital more concerned with the comforts or otherwise of his detention than the disgrace which it involves.[4]

The Board did not cite any sources for this information. Indeed some of it is apparently contradicted in tables contained in the report. Thus, although the Board suggest that youths have been 'dazzled' by newspaper reports, literacy tables given by the Board for this and other years clearly show very low standards of literacy among borstal offenders.

There are, however, some issues about which the Board was consistently clear and articulate. These included problems within the borstal institution itself and those facing offenders on release. One of these problems led the Board to question the very existence of the borstal institution. For example, in 1925 the Board stated: 'We have under consideration the question as to whether . . . there is, taking all relevant facts into account, and balancing the gain to society and the individuals themselves with the cost of a separate establishment, a sufficient case to justify the continuance of the Institution to the existing system.'[5]

The central issue in this as in earlier reports was employment. For example, they show that in 1924, of the 21 youths discharged only two were successfully placed in employment. The Board stated that if there were a military establishment nearby (as near the original borstal at Rochester in England), or if there were sufficient industrial life, the case might have been different, but this was not so. In the opinion of the General Prisons Board, given the absence of employment opportunities, the only remaining argument in favour of a separate borstal institution was that it might save an inmate from the *stigma* of an ordinary prison but '. . .we are not impressed by the value of this'.[6] The Board concluded that those detained in borstal at the time should perhaps be accommodated in ordinary prisons.

In the very last report of the General Prisons Board, difficulties associated with employment were mentioned yet again:

> We have observed in a previous communication to the Government as to the drawbacks of Clonmel, both from the point of view of the location and facilities for employment of the boys on outdoor work. No less than 32 of the total number of committals 37, were from Dublin. With the present condition of the labour market, we are not sanguine that such instruction as we are able to impart at Clonmel in trades such as bootmaking and tailoring will be very helpful in enabling the boys to find employment on their return to Dublin on discharge and neither are we satisfied that training for these trades is the best possible method for effecting an improvement in their moral well-being and outlook, seeing that 22 out of the 37 were homelesss strays and will, with no capacity for other occupation, no doubt return to the haunts of their early association. We consider that for this class of friendless and homeless castaway, there is no other proper effective means of influencing them to become useful citizens than by continuing the discipline of the institution with employment on skilful farm work.[7]

These comments from the Board show a basic awareness of some of the problems confronting the youths in their care. The writers realised that not only was the labour market generally in a bad condition but also that the type of training imparted

22

in borstal was not particularly useful. Furthermore, the Board recognised that many of the offenders had no family or stable home life, and suffered from being stigmatised. It is a pity therefore that, given their awareness of some of the relevant issues, the Board made no in-depth investigation into the background of those coming to borstal nor of the prison system as a whole. Some of the issues this Working Party believes to be very important (for example, the selection criteria whereby some youths were sent to borstal while others were sent to prison) appear to have been neglected.

The Annual Reports of the General Prisons Board are very interesting, not only in giving insight into the borstal institution, but indeed into the prison system as a whole. Their general attitude might be summarised as follows. They had a haphazard and scanty knowledge of the origins and experiences of the prisoners. This was balanced, however, by their sense of responsibility towards the youths in borstal and their frustration with the problems of preparing young offenders for reintegration with society. Yet their sense of the need for change never overcame their ambivalence towards the offenders, and, although various problematic issues regularly came to light, the borstal institution continued to function in Ireland without significant change. In 1928 the Board was abolished and responsibility for the entire prison system was given to the Department of Justice. Concerning this development Osborough has made the following comments: 'With the exception of 1934, whatever actually took place, a silence envelopes borstal administration. Indeed as regards physical conditions, on which the official report is not usually slow to provide details, the only recorded development is again for 1934: the installation that year of electric light. The Irish Prisons Board had never been so reticent.'[8]

However, despite the lack of basic factual data provided by the authorities, Osborough has gathered a wealth of information and given a detailed account of 'custodial provision for young adult offenders in Ireland since 1906'. Some of the features associated with the borstal and identified by Osborough include the low number of referrals. Thus, according to Osborough:

Before 1922 the average number of annual committals to Clonmel was 48. Following partition and an end to committals from Northern Ireland, this average fell dramati-

cally. . . .There was a reduction to twenty-six in 1925. . .
.A reduction in the number of committals to eighteen in
1933 and to twelve in 1934, again caused consternation.
. . The annual average declines after 1938 and indeed only
once again, in 1949, does the figure exceed thirty. . . .By
the late nineteen forties not enough borstal sentences were
being passed. . . Numbers of borstal committals continued
to be low and, from 1953, the number of transferred
offenders fell too. For several months in 1953 and 1955,
the population of the institution was so low that all trade
training had to stop and every inmate, borstal detainee
and transferred offender had to be employed on general
maintenance.[9]

It is difficult to understand why there were so few referrals to
borstal. It could, however, be suggested that the courts were
unaware of the potential of the borstal system, or perhaps they
could not see any value in these rehabilitative efforts. It would
appear in fact that the purpose of the borstal was never really
clear either to the public at large or to all those operating
within the system. The relevant documents suggest that con-
ceptions of borstal tended to vary, with the welfare aspects
being stressed at some times and the punitive aspects being
stressed at others.

As a rule there was little public attention directed towards
the borstal system. An exception to this occurred in 1940,
however, when the borstal in Clonmel was commandeered by
the army,[10] and its inmates were moved to Cork. This move
focused some attention on the borstal system in Ireland.
Osborough says: 'Transferring the borstal to Cork had the
unexpected dividend of awakening politicians' interest in the
borstal. At intervals between 1940 and 1946 there was a series
of exchanges in the Dail.'[11]

In 1941, when the borstal was situated in Cork, Edward
Fahy wrote an article strongly criticising the borstal system in
the Republic. Fahy states in this article that, in his opinion,
'. . . .it is a fair and accurate comment that, in essentials, the
Borstal and Prison Systems of Eire are not two distinct Systems. With a few unimportant differences, they are really one
System — the Prison System.'[12]

To support this statement Fahy describes the regime and
general conditions then existing in the borstal. There were
three grades of borstal detention — Ordinary, Special and

24

Penal. Fahy says that, on reception, a boy was placed in the ordinary grade. 'In this he wears brown shorts, and is entitled, once during every six weeks, to write and receive a letter and to receive a visit of twenty minutes duration.'[13]

Fahy goes on to say that, when a youth has completed approximately five months of his sentence and has behaved well, he becomes eligible for the special grade. Those in this grade . . . .'wear blue shorts, and are allowed, once every four weeks to write and receive a letter and to receive a visit of thirty minutes duration. These privileges, together with the privilege of reading books from the Institution library and the entertainment provided at Christmas time, are practically the only reliefs of a monotonous and deadly existence.'[14]

By order of the Governor those believed to be 'exercising a bad influence' could be placed in the penal grade. Those unfortunate enough to be placed in this grade had to do heavy labour in isolation from other inmates. Furthermore, they were denied both letters and visits.

Fahy goes on to describe the daily time-table and how 'just as in the prisons' the day commenced at 6.30 am with lights out at 8.30 pm. According to Fahy the borstal staff were chosen from the prison service, and the 'similarity to prison, already apparent enough', was 'made more real by the way in which the officers are clad', i.e. they wore the same clothes as prison warders, including belt and truncheon. It would seem from this and other evidence given by Fahy that there were very strong similarities between the borstal and the prisons.[15]

In 1947 inmates were transferred back to Clonmel. The institution had been renovated and some of the bars and locks had been removed. In addition there were changes in the regime, including permission to smoke. In 1948, according to Osborough, 'the premises at Clonmel were formally redesignated as St. Patrick's Institution'. Despite all these changes the problem mentioned earlier concerning the low number of referrals continued to exist. To quote Osborough once more:

'Annual committals became insufficient to ensure the survival of an institution ostensibly devoted to borstal training and in 1956 the borstal system as such began to be phased out.
Alternative accommodation somewhere in the Republic had to be found for the detention of young adult male

offenders. This was made available in Dublin in premises which were given the same name that the borstal at Clonmel had held since 1948. The 'new' St. Patrick's Institution still serves this same need'.[16]

b) *Children and young people in reformatory and industrial schools*[17]
The *Report of The Commission into the Reformatory and Industrial School System 1934–1936*[18] is a most useful source of information on this topic. It ranks in importance with its successor *The Report of the Committee on Reformatory and Industrial Schools* of 1970.[19] The Commission, with Mr. G. P. Cussen, Senior Justice of Dublin District Court, as Chairman, was appointed in May 1934. There were nine members of the Commission and their report was submitted to the Minister of Education in August 1936.[20]

At this time there were two reformatories in the Republic, one for boys run by the Oblate Fathers at Glencree, Co. Wicklow (now The Glencree Reconciliation Centre), and one for girls run by the Good Shepherd nuns in Limerick. As for industrial schools, there were 11 catering for the older boys and 5 for the younger boys. For older girls there were 17 industrial schools, 18 for the younger girls and only one mixed school catering for girls and small boys in Killarney.[21] Tables 2.1 and 2.2 show the number of young people and children in reformatory and industrial schools in the early 1930s.[22]

Table 2.1

Reformatory Schools 1929–1934

Table showing the number of young offenders under detention in reformatories, the numbers admitted and discharged from reformatories and the contributions from State funds towards maintenance for each of the five years from 1 April 1929 to 31 March 1934

Year	Number under Detention	Admissions	Discharges	Maintenance Grants paid by State
1/4/29–31/3/30	116	33	43	2,581
1/4/30–31/3/31	106	17	30	2,382
1/4/31–31/3/32	93	36	57	2,151
1/4/32–31/3/33	72	19	14	1,862
1/4/33–31/3/34	77	27	18	1,491

Table 2.2
Industrial Schools 1929–1934

Table showing the number of Children under detention in industrial schools, the numbers admitted and discharged from industrial schools and the contributions from State funds towards maintenance for each of the five years from 1 April 1929 to 31 March 1934

Year	Number under Detention	Number Chargeable to Grant	Admissions	Discharges, etc.	Maintenance Grants paid by State £
1/4/29–31/3/30	6,682	6,006	1,009	990	116,156
1/4/30–31/3/31	6,701	6,044	936	940	117,364
1/4/31–31/3/32	6,697	6,077	901	945	118,330
1/4/32–31/3/33	6,653	6,039	701	873	118,955
1/4/33–31/3/34	6,481	5,982	764	924	117,694

Source: (For Table 2.1 and Table 2.2) *Report of the Commission of Inquiry into the Reformatory and Industrial School System, 1934–1936*, (Dublin), p. 67.

While the 1936 Commission had some reservations about the reformatory and industrial school system and some suggestions as to how it could be improved, their first recommendation was nevertheless that the system be continued and '. . . .that the schools should remain under the management of the Religious Orders who have undertaken the work'.[23] This was a system that went back to the middle of the nineteenth century. The Commission was concerned about the fact that the official inspector of the reformatory and industrial schools (appointed by the Crown in England and by the Lord Lieutenant in Ireland) usually served as an inspector of the prisons service as well. The 1936 Commission stated that 'This connection with the Prisons Service was undoubtedly a further factor in forming the association in the public mind of these institutions with prisons'[24] even after 1924 when the supervision of the system was transferred to the Minister for Education.

The discussion of what the Commission calls the 'Nature of the Problem' is of particular interest:

> The early association in the public mind of Industrial Schools with the Prison system was undoubtedly responsible for a misconception that persists even to the present day regarding these institutions and the children trained in them. The grounds, if any ever existed, for such a misconception have long since disappeared and we draw

attention to this aspect of the matter, not only because the misconception is now altogether unjustifiable, but also because it affects adversely Institutions which have been remarkably successful in carrying out their self-imposed task and, moreover, prejudices very seriously the prospects of the children in after-life.

That in the main the problem is one not of criminal tendencies, but of poverty, will be apparent from the appended figures, showing the percentages of children committed to Industrial Schools during each of the last five years for different causes. (See Table 2.3 for Commissions' figures.) These observations apply also in large measure to Reformatories. Although the young persons committed to the Reformatories have been found guilty of offences it is the case that the percentage of them who subsequently make a further appearance in the Courts is negligible. *It follows, we suggest, that such young persons cannot in any sense fairly be looked upon as criminals.*[25]

Table 2.3

**Reasons for the Committal of Children to Industrial Schools
1930–1934**

Year	Serious Offences	Failure to attend School	Poverty and Neglect	Other Causes
	%	%	%	%
1930	3.8	7.0	89.1	0.1
1931	5.2	5.1	89.4	0.3
1932	3.4	6.2	90.3	0.1
1933	4.5	5.0	89.9	0.6
1934	6.2	6.1	87.7	—

The Commission, while commending the religious orders for their work and recommending that they should continue in this field, note that they are undertaking responsibilities placed by legislation primarily on the local authorities. They go on to add in a rather reprimanding tone:

We think it may be stated that the Local Authorities as a whole would appear not to have sufficiently appreciated their responsibilities under law in regard either to the schools or the children, and the evidence which we have adduced indicates that they still display little interest in the work of the schools beyond the payment of a weekly capitation grant for children committed from their respective districts.[26]

Many of the recommendations in the report centre on the themes of education and training. They suggested that with training, children leaving the reformatory and industrial schools would be better equipped to get work and lead useful lives after they left the schools. The Commission carried out a small piece of research on the jobs obtained by the boys who had left ten of the industrial schools. They found that 19% of the boys were unemployed and that the majority of those who were employed found work with farmers. They point out somewhat acidly that 'the continued efforts of 20 tradesmen teachers of Bootmaking and Tailoring have secured the admission of 38 boys to employment in the trades and some of these have deserted the trades after a year".[27] They recommended that teachers in the schools should be properly qualified and adequately paid; that training in farming should be greatly improved; that many of the trades currently taught were obsolescent; that training should be provided in areas like house-painting, plumbing and electrical work; and where necessary that arrangements should be made to send the children out to vocational schools in the neighbourhood. They also concluded that 'there is room for improvement in the methods of supervision and after-care of children discharged from the schools'.[28]

The Commission was also greatly concerned by the number of handicapped children they encountered. They found that in August 1934 there were '56 mentally defective and 46 physically defective children' in the industrial schools. 'In addition there would appear to be many borderline cases who would receive benefit from specialized treatment.' They regarded it 'as undesirable that mentally defective children. . . .be sent to a certified school'.[29]

The Commission also recommended that the name 'Industrial School' be changed to 'National Boarding School' and that the name 'Reformatory' be changed to 'Approved Schools' and that these titles should be used for legislative or administrative purposes only and that each individual school should have its own individual name which 'should not include the classification title'.[30] They gave no reason for these recommendations. Could it be that they believed there was a certain

29

Table 2.4

Occupations of boys who had left Industrial Schools in 1934

	Total Discharged	Farmers, etc.	Domestic and Personal Service	Home	Bootmaking	Tailoring	Wood-working	Baking	Unemployed and others
Upton	18	10	2	—	2	2	—	—	2
Baltimore	13	6	—	3	—	1	—	—	3
Greenmount	42	12	3	10	1	2	—	2	12
Killybegs	21	5	3	5	—	1	—	—	7
Carriglea	50	13	10	—	3	5	2	—	17
Letterfrack	30	16	3	—	1	2	4	1	3
Salthill	26	15	5	—	2	3	—	1	—
Tralee	23	12	—	—	2	1	2	1	5
Glin	26	15	3	—	2	2	2	—	2
Clonmel	36	19	1	6	4	2	1	—	3
Total	285	123	30	24	17	21	11	5	54

Source: *Report of the commission*, p. 78

stigma associated with the old titles 'Reformatory and Industrial Schools.?

c) *'The Supervision of Delinquents in Society'*
This is the title of a fascinating article written by Justice Henry A. McCarthy in 1945,[31] in which he explains the probation system and 'the extent of supervision of juvenile delinquents in this county'.[32] In 1945 there were ten part-time probation officers in Northern Ireland, while in the Republic there were six full-time probation officers and one Honorary Probation Officer, a Major in the Salvation Army who supervised ten Protestant probationers. The probation services was at that time confined to Dublin.[33]

Four of the probation officers (two men and two women) were attached to the Children's Court in Dublin. Of the male probation officers, one had 124, the other had 108 cases to supervise, while the two women probation officers had 'under their care 70 and 50 cases respectively'. The women officers were also expected to attend the Children's Court three days a week. Justice McCarthy makes the point that their caseloads were far too large and that the probation officers were underpaid and without pensions.

Justice McCarthy refers to the work of the probation officer as 'a vocation which calls for the best qualities of head and heart, immense patience, tact and perseverance and, above all, a deep and abiding faith in human nature'.[34] But he also recognises that 'knowledge of psychology. . . .and a training in general social science should be included in the make-up of every Probation Officer'. He points out that 'this training is now compulsory in England' and that there are now social science courses in the Dublin Universities which should be 'of immense value' to people involved in this type of work.[35]

In this article Justice McCarthy explains the help given to the Dublin probation officers by voluntary workers:

> During the past eighteen months the work of the Probation Officers has been greatly helped by a body of voluntary workers, who, thanks to the efforts of His Grace, the Archbishop of Dublin, are rendering signal service. They number over 40 men and women, and they are drawn from the Legion of Mary. It must be insisted that these workers are in no sense Probation Officers; they are social workers, who, from a sense of vocation, and with consid-

31

erable discretion and assiduity, assist the Probation Officers in many ways.[36]

The Archbishop of Dublin was also involved in the establishment of evening classes for probationers in Dublin. 'The Court makes it a recognisance that the boy must, in suitable cases, attend the evening classes. . . .at present there are some 50 boys attending these evening classes and the transformation caused in some of them has been little short of miraculous.' There were not at that time sufficient girls on probation to warrant an evening class for them. Justice McCarthy concludes: '. . . .it must always be remembered that the problem of juvenile delinquency is, to a very large extent, one of the conduct of boys.'[37]

These three interrelated services, the service given by the full-time probation officers, the help of the voluntary workers from the Legion of Mary and the evening classes for boy probationers, were *the full extent of the supervision of juvenile delinquents in this country* in 1945.[38]

Justice McCarthy goes on to make five final points that are of particular relevance to this report:

(i) He advocates the extension of a full-time trained probation service to the whole State.[39]

(ii) He regrets that a child cannot be placed on probation unless he has committed an offence and states: '. . . .if that supervision had been forthcoming at an earlier stage, there might well have been no offence committed'.[40]

(iii) He is critical of the fact that several government departments are involved with children and young people in Ireland 'with a resulting confusion which is of course, inevitable. The whole law relating to children should be reviewed and brought under one comprehensive statute, which would simplify the procedure concerning delinquent and neglected children.'[41]

(iv) He was also very critical of the position whereby the Manager of an Industrial or Reformatory School could refuse to accept a child and he gives his chapter and verse for this anomalous situation. He continues:

The hands of our Probation Officers should be strengthened — not hampered, as so frequently happens at present. No Industrial or Reformatory School is obliged to accept any child or young person whom the Court, after

32

the most careful and painstaking investigation, may consider suitable only for treatment in such an Institution; and, on frequent occasions the Managers of these Institutions — particularly in the case of the Girls Reformatory School — have refused admittance to a child on the ground that they did not consider him or her a fit subject for treatment in their Institutions. Within the past 12 months the Sisters in charge of the Reformatory School at Limerick have refused to accept girls for no other reason than that they were likely, as they thought, to prove troublesome — and this, although, they had little or no knowledge of the circumstances surrounding the girls' delinquencies, and had not the advantage, shared by the Court and its advisers, of contact with the girls and their relations, sometimes over a period of weeks. One girl was refused admittance because — 'you can understand, I am sure, how hard it is to control a number of these girls who come from the same locality, and have been companions before coming to the Reformatory.' And again: 'I think that this girl, who is almost 17 years, would do much better some place else. . . .We have got a few very difficult children this year from Dublin; that is why, as you can understand, I am not anxious to accept her.' Unfortunately, I must say that the attitude adopted by the School Authorities in both these cases was one that I could *not* understand. No child should be sent to a Reformatory unless he or she is difficult and troublesome, and it surely is a misconception of the functions of a Reformatory when its inmates are, from the very start, expected to conform with its rules and regulations, without some attempt being made to reform them.[42]

And, finally, he closes with this *cri de coeur*:

It is always with the greatest reluctance that I commit any child to an Institution, because I appreciate that, excellent as they are, they can never be more than Institutions, and they cannot, with all the care and affection in the world, supply to a child the loss of its natural home. There are, of course, many children who have never enjoyed the love and affection of their parents in any home, and there are many also whose homes were never fit for them to dwell in. But, day after day, Courts are obliged to remove children from their homes only because their parents, who idolise them, and who are entitled to the joy and solace of their companionship, are unable, through no fault of their own, to keep them from destitution. Surely this should not be tolerated in a State which has enshrined so eloquently its Christian principles in its Constitution. A step forward has been made by the passing of the recent Children's Allowances Act, and we must only hope that we shall soon penetrate beyond the fringe of the problem. When one contemplates the appalling conditions under which so many thousands of our poor children are compelled to live, one can but wonder why it is that so many of them keep out of trouble, attend school so regularly, and escape corruption and immorality. In wondering, let us thank God for the miracle, and bend all our energies to the tasks that lie before us.[43]

These themes, so eloquently expressed by Justice McCarthy, are themes that recur over and over in this report.

Period II: Studies on the Young Offender in Ireland 1960–1979

The major source of information for this period is the *Report of the Committee on Reformatory and Industrial Schools* established by the Government in 1967. This Committee had eleven members and they submitted their report in 1970. Their original terms of reference were 'to survey the Reformatory and Industrial Schools systems and to make a report and recommendations to the Minister for Education'.[44] The Minister subsequently agreed that the report should include all children in residential care. The report examines the history of reformatory and industrial schools, administration of the system at government and service level, the process of coming into care, residential care itself, prevention, aftercare and jurisdiction over children and young persons.

The Committee took a broader approach to their task than their predecessors of the 1934 to 1936 Commission.[45] For example, in the Preface to their report they state:

All children need love, care and security if they are to develop into full and mature persons. For most children this is provided by a warm, intimate and continuous relationship with their parents, brothers and sisters. Children in institutions have for the most part missed this happy relationship. If they are to overcome this depriva-

34

tion they must, therefore, be given love, affection and security by those in whose care they are placed.

The recommendations made by the Committee in this report are based on the assumption that all those engaged in the field of Child and Family Care agree that this must be their fundamental approach to the work they are undertaking.[46]

In their first two major recommendations they indicate how this philosophy should be put into operation:

The whole aim of the Child Care system should be geared towards the prevention of family break-down and the problems consequent on it. The committal or admission of children to Residential Care should be considered only when there is no satisfactory alternative.

The present institutional system of Residential Care should be abolished and be replaced by group homes which would approximate as closely as possible to the normal family unit. Children from the one family, and children of different ages and sex should be placed in such group homes.[47]

A summary of the major recommendations of the Kennedy Report is given in Appendix A. But two other recommendations must be mentioned here. Like Justice McCarthy they recommended that 'all laws relating to child care should be examined, brought up to date and incorporated into a composite Children Act'.[48] The Task Force on Child Care Services, appointed by the Minister for Health in 1974, was also charged to 'to prepare a new Children's Bill, up-dating and modernising the law in relation to children'.[49] At the time of going to press we are still awaiting an up-dated Children's Act in Ireland.

The Kennedy Committee's last major recommendation reads as follows: 'There is a notable lack of research in this field in this country and if work in the area is to develop to meet the needs of Child Care, there should be continuous research.'[50] We thoroughly agree with this recommendation, and in the remainder of this chapter have tried to gather together under the headings outlined at the beginning, the findings contained in the scanty research on young offenders in Ireland. Some of the findings come from research commissioned by the Kennedy Committee.

35

a) *The sex of young offenders*

Irish crime statistics show that the vast majority of those convicted in recent years were male.[51] Some criminologists and social scientists seem to take it for granted that women just do not commit crime. Other arguments suggest that women spend more time in the home and therefore do not have as much opportunity. Finally, some would say that police supervision pays more attention to males than females. Whatever the explanation, it is a universal trend that males are over-represented in crime statistics while females are under-represented. Ireland is no exception. Some believe that with the move towards equality of the sexes women are having an increasing share in crime and crime statistics.

b) *Urban deprivation and young offenders*

In Chapter I it has been shown that in Ireland, as elsewhere, the majority of young offenders came from urban areas. This fact is widely known and often commented on in the literature and in the press. The following editorial from the *Irish Times* — written after a visit by a well-known politician to Dublin's inner city in 1978 — paints the picture well:

> Gardiner St, Sean McDermott St, Sherriff St, Foley St, and Summerhill are areas that dominate any discussion of Dublin's delinquency problems. They are frequently cited as one of the reasons why the Loughan House project must go ahead. Decent law-abiding citizens and their property must be protected from the young criminals who flourish there — the handbag snatcher, the mugger, the car thief and the teenage gangs that terrorise neighbours and local shopkeepers alike. No one disputes that these things happen or that these are areas that few would recommend for a tourist itinerary, particularly after dark. But there is another side to the story, an appalling one of poverty, squalor, overcrowding and a total lack of amenities. . . .
> One can readily understand his (the politician's) sense of shock. And one imagines that most people, whether politicians or not, reading our reporter's account of the. . . .tour. . . .were equally shocked by the grim reality of life — if one can call it that — right in the heart of our capital city. In Summerhill, for instance, one family of 11 live in a two-bedroomed flat at the top of a rat-infested building.

Other families live in buildings that have no front doors and some of which also have their roofs torn off.

In one building in Gardiner St. there are only two toilets for eight families and when the toilets overflow, the water pours through the ceilings. Everywhere there is squalor and an air of hopelessness — sewers with their lids torn off, filth littering the stairways, and rats.

How could any parents, however diligent and dedicated, hope to bring up a family properly in such conditions? How could any child growing up in such an environment be expected to have a sense of civic responsibility or feel an obligation to society? As a Garda spokesman put it: 'How much better would I, or any of us have been, if we had come through the same thing? By and large, these people turn to crime through no fault of their own; they are deprived and condemned through ignorance.'

And yet, despite the handicaps and the hopelessness, the families who live there are desparately anxious for a better way of life. . . .No one suggests that the problems of the inner city can be solved overnight or that, in these times of financial stringency, unlimited funds are available for the massive rebuilding that is really necessary. But more can — and must — be done. Extra social workers might be a better deterrent than additional Gardaí; more facilities and amenities a better solution than more and bigger detention centres.

And is there any reason why private enterprise firms, already lavishing money on sports' sponsorship, should not be encouraged instead to invest it in helping to improve living conditions in deprived centre city areas such as these? Certainly such an initiative would be much more constructive than calls for tougher sentences or a return of the birch.[52]

c) *Unemployment and low income*

The studies reviewed in this report show that unemployment and low income are very real facts of life for the majority of Irish young offenders (see Chapter I). One young offender when asked 'Would you not prefer to be honest all the time?' replied: 'Yes, I would, but I can't be. You see, I don't have money all the time. That's really what I steal for — money. I suppose if my parents were well off I'd be very honest because I'd get money off them.'

This quotation is taken from Fr. Brian Power's study of 50 Dublin boys who had been in trouble with the law.[53] It gives a picture of the scant and irregular work records of these young people. Ten of them had 'hardly ever worked at all'; over half of them had 'regularly given up jobs, shifting from place to place with long spells of unemployment in between'. . . .four worked steadily for a long period and then left or 'were dismissed'; four were steadily employed and 'two who for a long time showed no inclination to get work took up employment on a regular basis and one who had been shifting from job to job eventually gave up working altogether'.[54]

Hart's research on young offenders in an industrial school and a reformatory (1968) showed that young offenders tended to come from low-income groups (see Table 2.5).

The survey of boys in St. Patrick's Institution (1967) had similar results. Of the 17 fathers in the sample of 32 who were

Table 2.5

The Social Group of Young Offenders in an Irish Industrial School and Reformatory, 1968

Social group	Percentage national population	Percentage delinquents
Farmers	28.0	0.0
Other agricultural occupations	9.0	6.0
Higher professional	2.5	0.0
Lower professional	3.0	0.0
Employers and managers	1.5	0.0
Salaried employees	13.5	1.0
Intermediate non-manual	9.5	11.5
Other non-manual	12.0	19.5
Skilled manual	7.0	12.5
Semi-skilled manual	7.0	32.0
Unskilled manual	5.5	16.5
Unknown	1.5	1.0
	100.0	100.0

Source: Ian Hart, 'The Social and Psychological Characteristics of Institutionalized Young Offenders in Ireland', *Administration*, Vol. 16 (1968), p. 17

Source for national data: Vol. III, 1961 Census, p. 171.

working, 15 of these were unskilled or semi-skilled manual labourers.[55] The remaining 15 fathers who were not working were likely to have been in receipt of social welfare benefits which would mean that their families would come within a low-income group.

The Kennedy Report also gives the fathers' occupations of those in reformatory schools in February 1968 (see Table 2.6). Again there is a high proportion of unemployed, unskilled and semi-skilled workers (although the large number of 'no replies' limits the value of this table).

Table 2.6

Fathers' Occupations of Those in Reformatory Schools, February 1968

| Father's occupation | Reformatories | | |
	Boys Schools	Girls Schools	Totals
Clerical worker	3	—	3
Intermediate non-manual worker	4	1	5
Skilled tradesman	6	1	7
Semi-skilled worker	12	5	17
Agricultural labourer	1	1	2
Non-skilled worker	27	3	30
Unemployed	16	—	16
Disabled	5	1	6
Itinerant	4	1	5
'In England'	4	—	4
Occupation unknown	3	1	4
No reply	20	24	44
	105	38	143

Source: Kennedy Report (1970), p. 106 (partial reproduction).

d) *Type and duration of juvenile crime*

The Kennedy Report gives figures which show that most of those committed to reformatories in 1968 had been convicted of offences of house-breaking or larceny (see Table 2.7). The Prisoner's Rights Organisation in a more recent but limited survey gives a breakdown of the types of criminal charges against the 50 offenders interviewed. Their findings are rather similar to those cited in the Kennedy Report (see Table 2.8).

Table 2.7

Offences of Which Those Committed to Reformatories were Convicted, 1968

	Larceny and Receiving	House-Breaking	Miscellaneous (Malicious damages etc.)	Totals
1960/61	56	51	24	131
1961/62	30	49	24	103
1962/63	34	34	16	84
1963/64	35	67	8	110
1964/65	41	25	19	85
1965/66	37	41	11	89
1966/67	39	33	32	104
1967/68	49	45	26	120
1968/69	26	53	24	103

Source: Kennedy Report, op.cit., (1970)', p. 92.

Table 2.8

Types of Criminal Charges Against 50 Young Male Offenders, 1978

	Average per person	Total
a) Number of thefts from vehicles	9	436
b) Number of thefts from shops	8	419
c) Number of thefts from houses	3	149
d) Number of assaults on persons	1	50
e) Number of thefts of vehicles	6	284
f) Any others	Nil	Nil

Source: Prisoner's Rights Organisation, *A Survey of Fifty 12 to 16 Year Old Male Offenders in The Sean McDermott St. — Summerhill Area* (Dublin, 1978), p. 7.

While more up to date and more scientific research is badly needed on this topic, the limited findings cited above suggest that the vast majority of crimes for which young people are charged and convicted are crimes against property and are relatively minor in nature. The recently published *Report of The Children and Young Persons Review Group* in Northern Ireland, in a section entitled 'the nature of juvenile delinquency', stated:

> Most juvenile offences are trivial. . . .Whilst the pattern of detected juvenile crime in Northern Ireland differs from that in the rest of the United Kingdom (Northern Ireland has a greater proportion of robberies and crimes of mali-

cious damage and less theft) the fact remains that the bulk of juvenile crime is still relatively minor. In recent years about 30% of juveniles dealt with by the police in Northern Ireland were cautioned rather than prosecuted and, of those prosecuted, a considerable proportion, over the whole range of offences, were given an absolute or conditional discharge. This would suggest misconduct which was not particularly grave but rather more of a nuisance than a serious source of harm to the community and certainly not sufficient to cause society to feel imperilled.

Fortunately for the community the minor nature of most juvenile crime is matched by its transience. We have already seen that most children and young people contravene the law in some way as they grow up. Many never come into contact with the police or other agencies. Most, however, do not persist in crime. Likewise, as far as we can tell, only a minority among juveniles who are prosecuted persist beyond a first or second offence. The indications are that many juvenile offenders, detected and undetected, mature out of their delinquency.[56]

One of the boys in Fr. Power's study, when asked if he saw an end to his stealing, answered: 'I don't think there is any solution in my case, unless I win the pools or something. Or maybe if I got married my wife might persuade me not to be doing it.'[57]

A basic question raised by this working party is: do our present services for young offenders help them 'to mature out of their delinquency' (as the Black Report puts it) or, alternatively, do some of the strategies of intervention that have been devised to deal with young offenders help to confirm them in their delinquent behaviour?

The limited evidence available also suggests that Irish young offenders, like their peers elsewhere, commmit offences with others. For instance, the survey in St. Patrick's (1967) found that 86% of the crimes committed were with at least one other person.[58] Hart found (1974) that among the 150 young probationers most boys offended in company although not necessarily in a 'tightly organised delinquent' gang.[59]

e) *Family size and relationships within the family*
The studies[60] reviewed in this chapter yield some interesting if limited information on the families of young offenders.

41

Two studies by Hart show that young offenders in Ireland come from large families with the number of children being significantly higher than the national average as shown in the following table. (see Table 2.9)

In his later study (1974) of 150 young Dublin probationers Hart again found that the offenders tended to come from families which were 'generally very large'. In addition to this Hart found that 'about two-thirds of the sample came from inadequate families, as assessed by Glueck's ratings of maternal supervision, maternal discipline and cohesiveness of family. . . .Family inadequacy was linked with a bad relationship between parents and alcoholism on the part of a parent, usually the father.'[61]

Table 2.9

Young Offenders' Families and Families of the National Population by Average Number of Live Children According to Social Group*

Social group	Average number of live children in delinquents' families	Average number of live children in families of national population
Other agricultural occupations, salaried employees, intermediate non-manual and other non-manual	6.31 (n = 39)	4.40
Skilled manual, unskilled manual, unknown	6.74 (n = 31)	4.80
Semi-skilled manual	6.63 (n = 33)	4.74

*National averages are taken from figures for the 25 to 29 year duration of marriage group to improve comparison with the delinquents' families as the modal age of the delinquents was 15. The fact that a certain proportion of couples in that duration of marriage group are childless was allowed for by increasing the average number of children per social group in the population by a fraction based on the proportion of childless married couples in that group. The differences between the three pairs of means were statistically significant.

Source: I. Hart, 'A Survey of Some Delinquent Boys in an Irish Industrial School and Reformatory', *op, cit.*, p. 192.

Hart further states that many of the offenders had experienced periods of separation from either their parents or their parent figures and that 'the majority of boys had little real communication with their parents.'[62]

Likewise Fr Power found that the relationships of the boys with their parents in his sample were poor. Over half of them 'had a bad or completely negative relationship with parents . . . or guardian. About one-third have a bad or negative relationship with one parent only . . . invariably with the father. Of the rest, four boys seem to be on reasonably good terms with their parents but on a superficial plane and having little or no communication with them.' While four others appeared to 'have all-round good home relationships'.[63] A small study of boys in St Patrick's Institution (1967) found that other members of the families of 40% of the sample also had committed crime.[64] Likewise the Prisoner's Rights Organisation survey found that 17 of the 50 boys had fathers who had been in prison and 46 had brothers who had been in prison.[65] The fact that crime tends to be concentrated in certain families and that criminal parents tend to have criminal children has been recognised for years.[66] West and Farrington in their study found that

> The conviction of any one member of a family significantly increased the likelihood of other members being convicted . . . The transmission of vulnerability to criminal convictions could have come about in a number of ways. It is all too easy to see how inadequate housing, parental care, education and social welfare may help to transmit deprivation from one generation to the next . . . Apart from laxity of supervision, little positive evidence was found to support the suspicion that parents with a criminal record brought up their children badly or inculcated antisocial ideas . . . The possibility that some hereditary predisposition is transmitted cannot be ruled out.
>
> Evidence was obtained suggesting that, over and above the consequences of a youth's own misbehaviour, the labelling of his father or another family member with a criminal record contributed to his own chances of being convicted. This was unlikely to have been caused by a deliberate police policy to identify and secure the conviction of youths with criminal relatives. More likely it occurred because these youths tended to come from the poorer, problem-prone families living in delinquent areas, which were liable to be known to the police for a variety of reasons.[67]

f) *Educational deficiency and low I.Q. among young offenders*
The literature on young offenders in Ireland shows that this group is characterised by low I.Q. and educational deficiency. Hart, in his study of the social and psychological characteristics of young offenders in Ireland (1968), found that his sample had a mean I.Q. of 75, which is 'at the mid-point of the borderline mental handicap regions of scores'.[68] Thirty per cent of the group had scores which indicated some degree of mental handicap. These scores are well below those of the general population.

The survey of boys in St Patrick's Institution (1967) had similar findings. The boys interviewed had well below the national average intelligence and well below average reading ability. Over half the sample did not even complete primary school.[69]

Likewise in Fr Power's study (1971) 40% of the boys in his sample were illiterate, 22% had received 'a very low level of formal education' and 38% had received about average education for boys from that area.[70] Figure 2.1 shows the findings of the Kennedy Report from intelligence tests administered to 15 year olds in reformatory schools. This figure shows that the incidence of mental handicap was 38.4% (as compared with approximately 2.5% in the population) and the incidence of borderline mental handicap was 46.2% (as compared with approximately 12.5% in the population in general).Only 15.4% of those tested were of average or above average intelligence, compared to 85% of the general population.

Figure 2.1

Frequency of Mental Handicap[71] and Average and Above Average Intelligence Among Fifteen Year Olds in Reformatory Schools

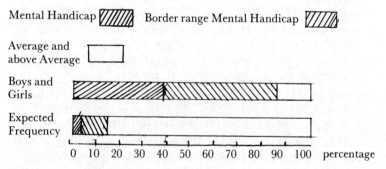

Source: Kennedy Report, *op.cit.,* p. 118.

Hart found that with his sample of 150 probationers (1974) the mean I.Q. was very low —62 points.[72] About one-third of the sample were illiterate. Most of the boys described themselves as having been unhappy at school. Two-thirds had thought that the teachers were too strict and a similar number had truanted at least once. Forty per cent had been referred to the School Attendance Officer and 30% had left school at 14 years and were in dead-end jobs. Hart found that those of low I.Q. tended to fail on probation and that older boys at technical or vocational school had more chance of success.

The survey of 50 young male offenders in an inner city area of Dublin found large gaps in the education of those interviewed.[73] None of the respondents (aged 12 to 16 years) was still attending school and on average they had left at 13 years of age. Only 16 respondents said that they could read and only 17 respondents said that they could write.

In relating educational deficiency and low I.Q. to delinquency it is necessary to be cautious about the conclusions that can be drawn. Studies and reports such as those cited in this chapter should not be interpreted as proving that, for example, mentally handicapped children are more likely than other children to offend. They may however suggest that children of low I.Q. are more likely to get caught than the brighter child. Nor should one consider mental handicap and educational deficiency to be synonomous. These studies also raise further interesting questions. Do children who do not complete primary school and other early school leavers tend to become more frequently involved in delinquent acts than those who remain within the educational system? Why do some children drop out of the educational system? How suited is our educational system to the child from a disadvantaged background?

The Rutland Street Project, an important educational experiment undertaken in Dublin in the 1970s, showed clearly that traditional school systems in Ireland do not meet the educational needs of the child from a disadvantaged background. The research programme of this project was designed and directed by Dr T. Kellaghan, who has published a detailed description of the methodology and an evaluation of the findings.[74] The project was directed by Seamus Holland, a former inspector of the Department of Education, whose comprehensive study of this very interesting experiment was published in 1979.[75]

45

Holland explains that the Rutland Street Project was set up in order '. . . to develop strategies to prevent school failure in disadvantaged areas'.[76] This particular area of central Dublin[77] was selected because its child population in terms of scholastic performance was recognised to be 'several years below what was regarded as normal for children in Dublin as a whole'.[78] The children who participated in the Project were approximately two years' old at the outset. Their first two years in the project were spent in the new Pre-School Centre which had been specially built and specially staffed for the purpose. Their last three years were spent in the normal school system to which they had been transferred at approximately five years of age.

The research design of the project incorporated a psychological testing programme 'designed to yield information, in the first place, on changes taking place in the ability and attainment of the children in the experimental group who were tested at various intervals during the project . . .Secondly, by comparing the performance of the experimental group at the age of 8 with that of two control groups, a measure of the overall effectiveness of the intervention procedures employed in the project' was obtained.[79] Two of the conclusions reached by Holland are of particular interest for this report and for the question raised above about why some children drop out of the Irish educational system:

> One significant inference can be drawn. If the children in the Project who had been taught . . . in educational conditions approaching the ideal, failed to master the task of recognising simple words, then the ability of the school system, in anything like its present form, to serve the needs of disadvantaged children is extremely limited. Indeed the marked superiority of the test scores of the non-disadvantaged control group—which it may be emphasised, was chosen to reflect the average scholastic performance of Dublin children—provides concrete evidence of the failure of existing educational procedures to serve the needs of disadvantaged children. It must be conceded, however, that alternative forms of provision which would guarantee a more favourable outcome have not so far been identified.[80]

But a subsequent follow-up of the children involved in the Project found that they had developed a positive attitude towards school, many actually admit to liking school, the numbers of days lost through absence has shown a significant decline and 'the teachers in the senior schools find that the children are not unwilling to learn, even if the learning process is still a matter of considerable difficulty'.[81] So it would seem that the exceptionally good start these children got in their educational careers has helped them maintain a positive attitude towards schooling. It remains to be seen how far up the educational ladder they will proceed and what sort of jobs they will ultimately attain.[82]

Conclusion

In this chapter we have identified some of the characteristics of the young offender that crop up time and time again in the official reports and research studies. We acknowledge that many of the studies have limitations in sample size and methodology. We want to stress that most of the studies cited here have concentrated on some of the young people *who have been caught* by the law. However, we want to reiterate what countless studies abroad have shown and what the Black Report expresses so well: '. . . most children and young people contravene the law in some way as they grow up. Many never come into contact with the police or other agencies.'[83]

While accepting then that the studies reviewed in this chapter present only a limited picture of juvenile crime, the pictures they paint of the Irish young offender are nevertheless remarkably similar; the conclusion of the St Patrick's study is nowhere contradicted:

> From our investigation a picture of the 16/17 year old delinquent boy in Ireland emerges. He would seem to come from a large family living in the poorer sectors of a town or city. His father's occupation is either an unskilled or semi-skilled job and his mother may work part-time, or may not work at all. His intelligence is below average, and hence his educational attainments are poor. He probably finds it difficult to keep up with an ordinary class and so he is an habitual truant from school. He rarely sits for his Primary Certificate and does not go to technical school afterwards. He commits his crime as a member of a group rather than alone. He seems to be a generally handicapped individual all around.[84]

47

An ex-prisoner puts it like this:

> The average prisoner in St Patrick's or Mountjoy is a product of the slums of Dublin or other cities. His outlook on life will be conditioned by the environment in which he was brought up and lives in, which is one of endemic unemployment, bad housing and poverty generally. As a result of these conditions crimes such as robbery and assault come naturally to him as making money comes to other people.
> He will more likely come from a large family where the father is either unemployed or in very unsteady employment. If he comes from the city centre there will probably be 4 or 5 people of both sexes sleeping in one room.[85]

The evidence presented in these first two chapters therefore tends to support Doleschal and Klapmuts' conclusion:

> It is common knowledge among students of crime and delinquency that the officially designated criminal is the final product of a long process of selection. Studies of this selection process . . . consistently demonstrate that certain groups and certain classes of persons are over represented while others are under represented in the criminal justice system. Those caught up in the system are overwhelmingly poor, lower class, members of minority groups . . . persons of low intelligence and others who are in some way disadvantaged . . . Throughout the world one of the main determinants in the process of selection for punishment is socio-economic status.[86]

Recommendations: The need for research and the danger of labelling

Chapters I and II of this book, while providing much interesting information, have highlighted the dearth of published statistics and scientific social research on young offenders in Ireland. We need to know more about children and young people who do and do not get into trouble with the law, about their families and social circumstances. We need to know more about the results achieved by the various services such as probation, intensive supervision or residential care provided for young people who have committed offences. We will identify specific areas where we believe further research is required as we work through the different sections of this book. However, there is one major priority for social research in Ireland that we want to identify straight away; that is the need for a longitudinal national child development study which would encompass a large cohort of children born in the same period to families in every social class, to study and compare these children and their families at regular intervals from the time of their birth through to adulthood. Such a study, though demanding considerable investment of both financial and human resources, would yield much valuable information about children and young people in Irish society.[87] It could supply information on a variety of topics such as the health, income, education and housing for comparable groups of children and their families, and improve on the limited and piecemeal studies that up to now have dominated the social research scene in Ireland. **The comprehensive data provided by a national child development study would provide hard, scientific information for policy makers, and we recommend that such a study be launched straight away.** Funds would have to be provided by the Exchequer (or by a modern day philantropist!) and the study could be based in an organisation such as the Economic and Social Research Institute.

In the context of young offenders such a project could study the children who get into trouble with the law side by side with those who do not. It could also be designed in such a way as to provide information on unrecorded crime. Only with such a study could the crucial variables associated with juvenile delinquency in our society be established with any degree of certainty.

Before ending this chapter a warning note must be sounded. We need to know more about young offenders if policies based on their needs are to be provided, yet we must if possible avoid labelling them as 'delinquent' or as 'young offenders', thereby stigmatising and setting them apart from society. Sociologists have identified the dangers associated with the very act of labelling a person as a 'delinquent'. Theorists suggest that labelling a person can actually lead to further delinquency. Labelling may set a process of alienation in motion. Those labelled find themselves cut off from the values of society and as a group develop their own values. This then leads to an 'amplification of deviance' as the new values and subsequent behaviour of the deviant group are in conflict with those of the rest of society.[88]

West and Farrington in their study of delinquent youths in London have tested this theory in a practical manner. This was done by comparing the subsequent records of convicted youngsters with equally badly behaved youths of similar age who had not been convicted, using a scale of self-reported delinquency. Their findings support the deviance amplification theory:

> Among boys equally badly behaved at fourteen those who attract an official conviction record become much worse by the time they reach eighteen, whereas those who escape conviction improve to the point where they become indistinguishable from the rest of the population.[89]

From their study West and Farrington make various observations and comments relevant to all those involved in the juvenile justice system and not just to those who may be researching it:

> Court appearances may only aggravate already tense family situations, alienate youths still further from their teachers and employers and discourage their more respectable companions of either sex from continuing to associate with them. The sanctions imposed by the courts in the shape of fines are likely to increase the delinquents' debts, thereby increasing the temptation to dishonesty, while doing nothing to teach him to manage his finances better. Even supervision by a probation officer can be a mixed blessing, if it helps to confirm the youngster's identification with delinquent groups. Detention in a penal institution means forced association with fellow delinquents and isolation from natural learning situations experienced when living in freedom in a normal community. These disadvantages probably outweight any good effects from a contrived training regime.[90]

It is important to question to what extent the present juvenile justice system in Ireland helps to create 'young offenders?' We do not claim to have the answer to this question. The thrust of the recommendations in this book are aimed at avoiding the stigmatisation of young offenders; instead the focus is on the needs of troubled and troublesome young people in Ireland and on considering a series of strategies whereby society may best respond to their needs, and to society's needs, without at the same time rejecting and alienating these young people in the process.

III. Juvenile Justice Systems in England, Scotland and Ireland*

In this chapter the philosophy and procedure of the English and Scottish systems for dealing with the juvenile offender are outlined. It is noted that, in particular, the Scottish system of children's hearings differs markedly from the Irish approach to juvenile justice in that the Scottish system is primarily concerned with the needs of the children and recognises that these needs may change over time. The present court system for juveniles in Ireland, which dates from the 1908 Children Act, is analysed and is found to be primarily formal and legalistic in emphasis. Recommendations are made for fundamental changes in that system. The developments which have taken place in England and Scotland since the 1908 Act are drawn upon where these can be applied in a constructive way in the Irish context.

Historical background

The criminal justice system made no distinction between the legal treatment of adult and juvenile offenders in Britain and Ireland until the case for making separate provision for each group gradually gathered momentum in the nineteenth century. Various institutions willing to accept juvenile offenders were set up by voluntary individuals and groups in the first half of the nineteenth century. In 1851 Mary Carpenter published the first of her books entitled *Reformatory Schools for the Children of the Perishing and Dangerous Classes*, and this publication, in the opinion of Parsloe, 'together with a conference organised in Bristol by Mathew Davenport Hill, seems to have crystallised the many individual supporters of reformatories into a social movement'.[1]

The British government responded to the pressure of this social movement by appointing a committee to enquire into the treatment of criminal and destitute juveniles. After the committee had reported in 1853, a Bill was introduced into Parliament, and the Youthful Offenders Act became law in

Editor: Dr. Claire Carney, Research: Maeve McMahon, Valerie Richardson and members of the Working Party

1854. This Act gave official approval to a system of reformatory and industrial schools; in effect it certified a number of the existing institutions run by religious organisations and charitable persons. Thus young offenders could now be sent to these schools by the courts. The schools were given grants from public funds and became subject to inspection; this was a significant development since the only previous public provision for juveniles had been confined to the workhouses and the only legislation referring to them had been the provisions in the poor laws which related to neglected and orphaned children.

The Youthful Offenders Act, 1854, also took the first tentative steps towards the establishment of separate legal processes for juveniles in that it gave justices the power to try children summarily for simple larceny. However, for the most part juveniles were still subjected to the same legal processes as adults. Thus, even a seven year old child could receive the death penalty.

Throughout the nineteenth century concern for the welfare of the juvenile offender continued to grow, not only among those working in the various institutions, but also among those in the legal field and among social theorists and social reformers. New theories of crime, focused on deterministic forces in society, led to a demand for penal policy to move from punishment to social defence, protection and reformation. Thus, Benjamin Waugh argued for a 'new and distinct tribunal of persons interested in children and possessing special practical knowledge of them'.[2]

Although the Summary Jurisdiction Over Children Act of 1884 did not make the fundamental change suggested by Waugh, it did make it possible for juveniles to avoid the higher courts and to be dealt with in a summary manner. However, they were still appearing in the same courts as adults. Following the 1884 Act, pressure for a reform of the system continued to grow. Throughout the 1890s the General Prisons Board stated many objections to the treatment of juvenile offenders, particularly in relation to their imprisonment. These complaints for the most part fell on deaf ears and large numbers of young people continued to be incarcerated. Thus, at the end of the nineteenth century the situation in Ireland, England and Scotland was that juvenile offenders were still appearing in the courts with adults and usually were dealt with under the same legislation as adults. Perhaps the main achievement of the last century was the establishment and recognition of reformatory and industrial schools as an alternative to the prison system of custodial care.

These trends were not peculiar to Ireland, England and Scotland; they were to be found in other countries also. In 1899 the state of Illinois in the USA enacted the first legislation providing for specifically juvenile courts. This led to the setting up of separate non-criminal procedures for children who had committed offences or who were neglected. Instead of determining the legal culpability of a child, the aim of the court was to ascertain the child's emotional, material and intellectual needs. Hearings were informal and criminal procedures were disregarded.[3] The Illinois model was emulated throughout the United States. The Scandinavian countries too made significant changes. They adopted a welfare approach and appointed a Board consisting of a local judge, a clergyman and a physician, to determine a child's needs. As Morris and McIsaac point out, the American and Scandinavian approaches, while relying on different social institutions, were rooted in what may be described as a social welfare ideology.[4]

In Britain the movement towards the establishment of juvenile courts developed rapidly with the advent of the new Liberal administration in 1906. After piloting the Probation of Offenders Act through Parliament in 1907, Herbert Samuel, a Junior Minister in the Home Office, was visited by a Mrs M. P. Inglis who urged that the government should establish a new ministry to be concerned with all matters relating to children. She pointed out that there were many questions touching on child welfare that were ripe and more than ripe for state action, but that these matters were scattered over a number of government departments so that it was the special business of no-one to press them forward. Samuel also explored the issue and studied various proposals for reform.[5] In due course a comprehensive statute was drafted by the Home Office and when the Home Secretary secured Cabinet approval, the Bill became the Children Act of 1908 with little opposition from either House of Parliament.

Herbert Samuel, in introducing the Children Bill of 1908, declared it to be based on three main principles. First, the child offender should be kept separate from the adult criminal and should receive at the hands of the law a treatment designed to meet his needs. Secondly, the parents should be made to feel more responsibility for the wrongdoings of their children.

Thirdly, the imprisonment of children should be abolished. Samuel envisaged that the new institution of the juvenile court would be an agent of rescue as well as an agent of punishment, with parental responsibility emphasised by making the parents liable to fines for the wrongful acts of their children.

There is no doubt that the 1908 Act was a remarkably innovative piece of legislation in that it made separate legal provision for the care and protection of juveniles who were in trouble with the law. Unfortunately, there also was much ambivalence in this Act. It embodied two contradictory notions of the young offender. On one hand, the child was considered to be a victim of undesirable circumstances who had been denied the benefit of a civilised life, and it was the court's task to promote his care and treatment. On the other hand, the child was considered to be a miniature adult who acted with free will and who required both discipline and control. Subsequent legislative and practical attempts were made in England and Scotland to reconcile these contradictory notions. An ambivalence clearly still persists in Ireland, however, as shown by the fact that there has been so little change in the 1908 legislation.

Juvenile Courts in England

The juvenile justice system in England was similar to that in Ireland until the early 1930s. The turning-point came in 1933 with the Children and Young Persons Act, which for the first time directed attention towards the *welfare* of the juvenile. The Act stated that: 'Every Court, in dealing with a child or young person who is brought before it, either as an offender or otherwise shall have regard to the welfare of the child or young person. . .'[6] It also required that in dealing with the juvenile the court should 'in a proper case take steps for removing him from undesirable surroundings'.[7]

The emphasis on welfare was reflected and developed in subsequent Acts. In 1955 the Ingleby Committee was appointed to examine the hearing and sentencing procedures in juvenile courts. The Committee's report was published in 1960. It examined some of the contradictions within the system, the main one being the contradiction between 'criminal responsibility and welfare'. In the words of the report: 'It is not easy to see how the two principles can be reconciled: criminal responsibility is focused on an allegation about some particular act isolated from the character and needs of the defendant, whereas welfare depends on a complex of personal, family and social considerations.'[8]

The Committee saw two solutions to the problem: firstly, that criminal jurisdiction be abolished with offences by juveniles being interpreted solely as additional grounds for care proceedings; secondly, that local authorities should work at a preventive level with families at risk. Priestley, Fears and Fuller, however, have reservations about the report. They say that the Committee,

> mindful no doubt of public opinion, and the limits it implied for what was politically practicable, appeared to draw back from where its logic had led. Instead of advocating the abolition of criminal courts for children and young persons it proposed the raising of the age of criminal responsibility to twelve years. Below that, only civil proceedings were to be possible, even for children who had committed offences.[9]

The 1963 Children and Young Persons Act which followed, however, raised the age of criminal responsibility to ten years and authorised local authorities to undertake preventive work with families at risk. It also abolished the right of a parent or guardian to bring his or her child before a court as being 'beyond control'.

In December 1963 the Labour Party set up a study group under the chairmanship of Lord Longford, a group which was accused of being committed in advance to the production of a report 'based on a long-term Socialist philosophy' which would 'present an idealistic framework for a constructive policy aimed at the prevention of crime and the enlightened treatment of offenders. Only second would it provide a programme of practical measures'.[10]

The Longford Committee reported in June 1964 with a number of far-reaching proposals.[11] For example, they suggested that the age of criminal responsibility should be raised to school-leaving age, that juvenile courts should be changed to family courts and that youth courts should be set up to deal with offenders under 21 years. The Committee recommended that much more power should be given to social work agencies. Children, therefore, should be referred by the school, police or parents to what was described as a family service wherein the social workers would attempt to work out agreed programmes of intervention, care and protection. In serious cases criminal proceedings could be instituted and these would take place in the juvenile or youth court which would cater mainly for those between 17 and 21 years of age. Thus, the Longford Committee proposed to dissolve juvenile courts as they existed by raising the age of criminal responsibility to 16 years, and all juveniles under this age were to be dealt with under a 'care' rather than a penal scheme.

Within six months of the publication of this report, with the Labour Party now in power many of the proposals outlined became government policy. In 1965 a White Paper was produced, *The Child, the Family and the Young Offender*.[12] The content was generally similar to the content of the report of the Longford Committee, although the proposed model had been elaborated and the powers and roles of the responsible agencies more specifically delineated.

Thus, delinquency was seen as being related to the family. It was envisaged that what were to be called 'family councils' would be set up by local authorities. While these councils would not actually pass sentences they were to be able to direct children into care and to send them for assessment as necessary. Should problems not be solved by the family council, there was to be recourse to family courts (which were to be converted juvenile courts with enlarged jurisdiction in civil matters). All children up to the age of 15 years were to be treated in this way, and for 16 to 21 year olds there was to be a new system of young offenders' courts to deal with criminal charges.

These were radical proposals, and as it turned out, this White Paper met with much opposition from all political quarters. The main objection was based on the principle that people could not be deprived of their freedom except by order of a properly constituted court of law. Of those involved in the existing system, magistrates and probation officers on the whole tended to oppose the proposals, while other social workers tended to receive them favourably.

In 1968 another White Paper, *Children in Trouble*, was produced which in fact formed the basis of the 1969 Children and Young Persons Act.[13] The tone of this White Paper was more traditional than that of its predecessor, with the juvenile court remaining the focal point of the system. However, the juvenile courts were to be used only as a last resort, the aim being that juvenile offenders should be treated as much as possible outside the legal system. Thus criminal proceedings against most young offenders would come under 'care' provisions.

56

Jurisdiction of the juvenile court in England
Under the Children and Young Persons Act, 1969, juveniles between the ages of 10 and 17 come under the civil and criminal jurisdiction of the juvenile court. Care proceedings can be taken for any young person from birth to 17 years. Juvenile offenders may be transferred for trial in the Crown Court if charged with a grave crime or if charged jointly with an adult for an indictable offence.

Under the 1969 Act, as amended by the Children Act of 1975, the requirement for care proceedings is that any of the following conditions be satisfied:

1. His proper development is being avoidably prevented or neglected, or his health is being avoidably impaired or neglected or he is being ill-treated; or

2. It is probable that the above will be satisfied in his case, having regard to the fact that such conditions are or have been satisfied in the case of another child or young person in the same household; or

3. It is probable that such conditions will be satisfied in his case, having regard to the fact that a person who has been convicted of an offence mentioned in Schedule I of the Act of 1933 is, or may become, a member of the same household as the child; or

4. He is exposed to moral danger; or

5. He is beyond the control of his parent or guardian; or

6. He is of compulsory school-age and not receiving sufficient full-time education suitable to his age, ability and aptitude; or

7. He is guilty of an offence, excluding homicide, and that he is in need of care or control which he is unlikely to receive unless the court makes an order in respect of him.[14]

Processes through which juveniles come before the court in England
Only the police can prosecute a juvenile. When an offence comes to their notice they may make a decision not to act at all, to caution the juvenile or to take criminal proceedings. If criminal proceedings are taken the juvenile may be summonsed, arrested and charged. If arrested he usually will be released on bail.

The 1969 Act specifies that a local authority, a constable, or an authorised person (such as a staff member of the Society for the Prevention of Cruelty to Children) can bring a child or young person before a juvenile court for care proceedings. Where a criminal offence is involved it must first be proved that the child or young person is in need of care or control which he is unlikely to receive. This requirement means that the police in all cases must work closely with the local authority and that this liaison takes place *before* a decision to prosecute is made. Since the emphasis is on preventing referrals to the juvenile court, the possibilities of the case being dealt with by a parent or teacher, by a police caution, through local authority powers or by any other means available, must be first exhausted.

In practice an investigation is usually carried out by a local authority social worker, services such as casework are offered and the juvenile court is used only as a last resort.

Court procedure and personnel involved in juvenile courts in England
The juvenile courts are manned by a rota of lay magistrates who are appointed for a three year period following an election from the magistrates of each administrative area.[15] The bench must consist of not less than two, and of not more than three persons, composed of at least one man and one woman. Since 1969 a course of training has been a requirement for juvenile court magistrates. This training includes a period of observation in the juvenile court and a number of visits to institutions. Special instruction is given to magistrates to help them understand the place and procedure of the juvenile courts in the criminal justice system, to understand the social background of juveniles appearing and to know the social services and the dispositional alternatives available.
Besides the magistrates, the child and his parents, the juvenile court will also be attended by the court clerk, by police (when they are prosecuting in a criminal case), by social workers and by ushers. Members of the press may also be admitted although publication of details which might identify a juvenile was forbidden under the 1969 Act.[16] The clerk must have a legal training and is usually a solicitor with at least five years' experience. He or she serves as administrator of the court and as legal advisor to the magistrates.

The way in which those within the courtroom perceive their roles has a significant effect on the atmosphere of the proceedings. In many ways it can be intimidating and difficult, not only for the child and his family but for all of those in the courtroom, to frame what they wish to say in a legally acceptable manner. If a child is treated abruptly by an usher and if the magistrates suddenly leave the court without (apparently) paying him much attention, it is unlikely that he will spontaneously give his side of the story when the time comes. Conventions and legal requirements cause difficulties in communication. Because of this, the welfare of the child is sometimes neglected. Tensions can arise which lead to criticism of the incompetency of those involved in court proceedings.[17]

It has often been suggested that the 1969 Act has not been as welfare-oriented in practice as intended. Priestley et al. commented on juvenile court procedure:

> Despite the simplification of procedures the juvenile court in action still retains the look and the feel of some of the dramatic ritual which dignifies adult justice. The drama . . . is that of making manifest the otherwise disembodied values of justice, social control and welfare. The power of the State is often symbolised in the Royal Crest, set high up and in a central position behind the bench. The bench itself is raised a step or two above the level of the courtroom and the front of it is almost always totally enclosed, in contrast to the tables behind which other servants of the court sit. Defendants and their parents have no such aids to social ease within the courtroom. They sit on straightforward chairs or have to stand whilst being addressed by the court. The dramatic elements in this physical setting are sometimes heightened by the abrupt entries and departures of the magistrates, to the accompaniment of loud commands to rise or 'be seated'. These are uttered in many courts by the ushers who play a considerable part in the proceedings. They are responsible for procuring the appearance in the courtroom of individual children on the list in the same order as they appear on collective charge sheets and with the appropriate parents standing behind them.[18]

In both civil and criminal hearings in England the juvenile has certain rights, including that of legal aid. This takes the form of a legal aid order. The 1969 Act allows for an offence to be the grounds for a civil proceeding, but even so the standards of proof must be the same as would have been required to find the juvenile guilty of an offence, and the juvenile is not a 'compellable witness, and so cannot be required to incriminate himself'.[19] The juvenile is further protected in that, if an offence has served as part of the grounds for a care proceeding, he cannot be charged with this offence later. The juvenile also has the right to appeal to the Crown Court when an offence condition is satisfied, even if the court does not make a care order.

The juvenile in England does not have the right to a jury trial, except in the case of murder. In 1969 this right was abolished in all juvenile courts, a development which has caused concern amongst those who see jury trial as an important protection against arbitrary action.

Children's Hearings in Scotland

The criminal justice system for juveniles in Scotland differs from those of England and Ireland. In Scotland juvenile courts were abolished after 1968 when they were replaced by children's hearings. The emphasis is on the interests of the child and the concept of criminal responsibility appears to be less important even though, as in Ireland, the age of responsibility remains at seven years.

Until the Social Work (Scotland) Act came into force in 1968 the juvenile court system was similar to that of England. Previously, the 1908 Children Act, the Children and Young Persons (Scotland) Acts of 1932 and 1937, the Children Act, 1948 and the Children and Young Persons Act, 1963 formed the basis for juvenile justice. In 1928 the Scottish Departmental Committee on Protection and Training recommended that special Justice of the Peace Courts should hear juvenile cases.[20] This recommendation was embodied in the 1936 Children and Young Persons (Scotland) Act and provided for justices to select a panel from their own colleagues to serve in juvenile courts in any areas for which the Secretary of State issued an order. This provision in fact was availed of only in four areas (Ayr, Fife, Renfrew and the city of Aberdeen).

In May 1961 a departmental committee was set up by the Conservative Secretary of State, Mr John Mackay. This Committee, under the chairmanship of Lord Kilbrandon, reported in April 1964 and provided the basis for subsequent legislation. The purpose of the Committee was 'to consider the provisions of the law of Scotland relating to the treatment of juvenile delinquents and juveniles in need of care or protection or beyond parental control, and in particular the constitution, powers and procedure of the courts dealing with such juveniles.'[21]

The distribution of juveniles within the courts in Scotland in 1962 was estimated by the Kilbrandon Committee as shown in Table 3.1.

Table 3.1

Approximate Distribution of Juveniles in Scottish Courts, 1962

Sheriff courts	—	32%
Burgh courts	—	45%*
Specially constituted Justice of Peace Courts	—	16%
Other Justice of the Peace Courts	—	7%
		100%

Source: Kilbrandon Report, op. cit., para. 45
*The Glasgow Police Courts accounted for about 33% of this figure.

The juvenile court system was complicated not only because there were the several varieties of courts (as listed above), but because some of the courts dealt with criminal and civil juvenile cases while others did not. The sheriff courts retained a jurisdiction concurrent with that of the special Justice of the Peace juvenile courts. Thus, in different parts of Scotland, two juveniles from similar backgrounds and charged with similar offences might be appearing in very different circumstances. For example, one child might appear before the sheriff or his deputy, both lawyers and sitting alone, while the other might appear before local justices who sat as a bench and were lay people.[22]

The Kilbrandon Report closely examined this haphazard structure and concluded that

> . . . the legal distinction between juvenile offenders and children in need of care or protection was, looking to the underlying realities, very often of little practical significance. At one extreme, there were cases in which children committed as being in need of care or protection were by reason of background and upbringing suffering from serious emotional disturbance. This found expression in conduct and behaviour which, while not resulting in criminal charges, clearly demanded sustained measures

61

of education, training and discipline. Equally, there were cases in which, where an offence had been committed by a child, no very drastic steps appeared to be justified on the basis of the offence itself. But these included cases in which, looking to the whole background, it might be that the child's quite minor delinquency was simply a matter of personal or environmental difficulties, so that, for the prevention of more serious offences and for the future protection of society as much as in the child's own interest, more sustained measures of supervision were equally called for.[23]

The Committee, regarding as minimal the distinction between young offenders and those in need of care, developed what they described as a preventive rather than a criminal-responsibility and punishment model. They thus emphasised the needs of juveniles and the importance of educational opportunity and family support. Education, in the broadest sense of the word, was regarded as a preventive measure. For education to be successful, close co-operation with the parents was found to be essential.

The Committee proposed that existing juvenile courts and criminal jurisdiction over children should be abolished. Any juvenile who appeared to need compulsory measures of this social education would be brought before a panel of lay volunteers, who, in conjunction with the juvenile's family, would decide on necessary methods of treatment. In the event of any dispute the case would be referred to the sheriff for an adjudication. It was intended that these measures would be carried out by a social education section in the local authority departments of education.

The Kilbrandon Report was followed by wide publicity and discussion. In 1966 a White Paper was published, titled *Social Work and the Community*.[24] This Paper accepted the proposals to abolish juvenile courts. However, the White Paper took a wider approach and suggested additionally that a new local government department should be established that would provide a service for individuals and families with social problems. The focus thus moved from social education to social work.

These White Paper proposals formed the basis of the Social Work (Scotland) Act, 1968. The Act set up children's hearings in April 1971, responsible for dealing with children who are in trouble and who thus may require compulsory measures of care and supervision. In many ways these hearings have taken over from juvenile courts, although in cases of very serious offences or in certain cases where a child commits an offence with an adult, a child may still appear in court. This discretion is reserved for the Lord Advocate.

The Act set up comprehensive social work departments in local authorities, giving them power and responsibility for providing social services not only for children but also for the aged, the sick and handicapped, for adult criminals and for those with personal, family and other problems. Previously these responsibilities had been split up between several departments. The departments are more comprehensive than the equivalent English ones set up in 1969 in that the probation service is incorporated within them. This is not the case in England.

Jurisdiction of the children's hearings in Scotland
It was the intention of the 1968 Act that juveniles should be dealt with in all possible cases by a voluntary arrangement between the social work department and the juvenile's family. However, Part III of the Act established juvenile hearings to deal with cases where compulsion proved to be necessary. These hearings are not courts within the criminal or civil justice system because they do not have power to make decisions over contested facts. The hearings are mainly concerned with children under 16 years old and there is no lower age limit. Juveniles who are subjected to compulsory measures of care imposed by a hearing may continue to be dealt with by the hearings until their eighteenth birthday.

For a juvenile to be brought before a hearing, at least one of the following conditions must be satisfied:

(a) the child is beyond the control of his parents; or
(b) he is falling into bad associations or is exposed to moral danger; or
(c) lack of parental care is likely to cause him unnecessary suffering or seriously impair his health or development; or
(d) any of the offences mentioned in Schedule 1 to the Criminal Procedure (Scotland) Act 1975 has been committed in respect of a child who is a member of the same household; or
(e) the child is, or is likely to become, a member of the

63

same household as a person who has committed any of the offences mentioned in Schedule 1 of the Criminal Procedure (Scotland) Act 1975; or

(f) the child, being a female, is a member of the same household as a female in respect of whom an offence which constitutes the crime of *incest has been committed by a member of the household*; or

(g) he has failed to attend school regularly without reasonable excuse; or

(h) he has committed an offence; or

(i) he is a child whose case has been referred to a children's hearing in pursuance of Part V of this Act;

In this part of this section 'care' includes protection, control, guidance and treatment.[25]

Processes through which juveniles come before the hearings in Scotland
Juveniles come before a children's hearing through a referral from a person known as a reporter. The reporter is appointed by the local authority from a list of people approved by the Secretary of State. Anyone can notify a reporter if they think that a child is in trouble and may be in need of compulsory measures of care.[26] Thus, referrals may come from not only social workers and police, but also from voluntary organisations, relatives and individuals in the community.

The reporter then investigates the circumstances of the child. He/she gathers information about the child's family background, his schooling and his health. In gathering such information the reporter works closely with the Social Work Department. He/she may decide that the child has no serious problems or that existing problems are already being dealt with satisfactorily. In this case no further action will be taken. He/she may decide that the local authority be asked to work with the child and his family on a voluntary basis. Finally he/she may consider the child to be in need of a compulsory form of care and bring him to a children's hearing.

Procedure and personnel involved in the children's hearings in Scotland
Children's hearings take place in each local authority area in Scotland.[27] These are handled by a panel consisting of a chairperson with two other members. The panels are composed of people from the local community who have volunteered their services. Such volunteers are required to have a knowledge and understanding of children, together with the ability

64

to talk to the children and their parents about the child's problems and to decide on the most appropriate measure of care. The Children's Panel Advisory Committee (made up in some cases of people nominated by the local authority and in others by the Secretary of State) submits names of suitable persons for the panels to the Secretary of State. The Secretary of State then appoints the members and the chairperson from the names submitted. The panel always contains both men and women.

The hearing itself takes the form of a discussion of the child and his problems. Those present include the three panel members, the child, his parents, the reporter and the child's social worker. Parents are obliged to attend and may be prosecuted and fined if they do not. The chairperson has a duty to explain to the child and his parents all the grounds stated by the reporter for referring the case. If the child and parents accept the grounds, the hearing can go ahead.

If the child is incapable of understanding the grounds or is unwilling to accept them, or if the parents are unwilling to accept them, the hearing can either discharge the case or ask the reporter to apply to the sheriff for evidence to be heard. This means a delay of a few weeks and a court appearance for the child and his parents. If the sheriff decides that the grounds are not correct, he discharges the case altogether. If he decides that they are correct, he sends the child back to the hearing.

The hearing, once the grounds have been accepted, discusses the whole circumstances of the child and his social background. This discussion takes place with the family and social worker. The social worker must provide a report for the hearing and there may be other reports from school, psychiatrists and other sources. The chairperson is obliged to inform the family of the content of these reports.

After a discussion the hearing comes to a decision as to whether the child requires compulsory measures of care and, if so, what measures are appropriate. If the hearing decides that a child is to be placed in residential care then the establishment to which the child is to be sent is named. The idea is that the child should be placed in the setting most appropriate for his or her needs.

The child or his parents may wish to appeal to the sheriff against the decision of a hearing. This must be done within three weeks. The sheriff may uphold the appeal or discharge the case or send it back to the hearing for further consideration.

On failure of the appeal the decision of the hearing stands. The hearing may decide that the juvenile be put under supervision. A supervision requirement automatically ends on the juvenile's eighteenth birthday but the social work department may ask the hearing to review the child's case at any earlier time. The child or his parents may ask for a review any time after three months has elapsed since the supervision requirement was made. In every case there must be a review hearing within a year of imposing the requirement. The system of review is valuable because it allows a response to the changing needs and circumstances of the child and his family. Thus, for example, if the child has become less troubled and troublesome because of increased support from his relatives, the review hearing may decide to discontinue supervision.

The whole rationale for the Scottish hearing system has been the separation of decisions regarding legal culpability from decisions regarding children's needs and the avoidance of legalistic, punishment-orientated treatment of children in trouble. The acid test of any juvenile justice system is the quality of care given to young people coming within its purview and the extent to which the care given meets the child's needs. The Scottish hearing system gives ample evidence of the merits of a juvenile justice system, with considerable freedom of manoeuvre by the reporters, the panel themselves and the social work department, firstly, to ascertain the child or young person's needs and secondly, to endeavour to meet those needs humanely and non-punitively. These reforms have been resisted by those who strongly believe in punishment to discourage potential offenders, and by the Diceyists in the legal profession who believe that 'where law ends tyranny begins'. The operation of the Scottish hearing system has not been trouble free as Martin and Murray show in *Children's Hearings*, yet the evidence of a decade of the operation of the panels would indicate that such Diceyite criticism is misconceived.[28]

The Children's Court in Ireland

As has already been noted in this chapter, the Children Act of 1908 is still the relevant legislation in relation to the juvenile offender in Ireland.

The 1908 Act provided for the first time in Britain and Ireland for the actual setting up of special courts for seven to seventeen year old offenders. These courts were to have sittings at a different place or at a different time from the usual sittings for the hearing of adult cases. In Ireland the Courts of Justice Act, 1924, went a step further and made specific provision for the setting up of special children's courts in Dublin, Cork, Limerick and Waterford. However, only one such court has ever come into being. This is the Dublin Metropolitan Children's Court which was established in 1923 and is situated in Dublin Castle. To date there have been no apparent moves to set up corresponding courts elsewhere, with the result that, other than in Dublin, juveniles still appear in the local district court. These appearances usually but not invariably occur on a different day or at a different time to the proceedings for adults.

The children's court or the district court has jurisdiction to deal summarily with a child or young person charged with any indictable offence other than homicide under the provisions of the Summary Jurisdiction Over Children Act, 1884, 4-5.

Processes through which juveniles come before the Children's Court in Ireland
In most cases it is the duty of the garda authorities to take proceedings against juveniles, but such proceedings can also be taken by lay educational authorities (as in school attendance cases), or by some other person in certain special circumstances.[29]

When a juvenile is arrested, unless he is brought immediately to the Children's Court, he will be brought to the garda station for questioning. After he has been charged the juvenile will usually sign a statement. The parents may be notified to come to the garda station and sign a bail bond (only in a very serious case would bail be likely to be refused). Legal aid is not available until the case actually comes to court.

When a juvenile commits a first offence, he may come within the ambit of the Juvenile Liaison Scheme. This scheme was set up in Ireland in 1963 following the recommendations of an interdepartmental committee. It aims at preventing a court appearance for the majority of first offenders and tries to divert them from criminal to legitimate activities.

Juvenile Liaison Officers are selected from the gardaí and receive a specialised training to help them deal with juveniles who are at risk of being involved in deviant or criminal behaviour. According to the 1977 Garda Crime Report, 4 sergeants, 34 gardaí and 2 bean gardaí were working in the scheme in that year, and a total of 11,413 juvenile offenders had been cautioned and supervised over the fourteen years since its inception. The scheme does not operate on a country-wide basis, but the areas it covers have been extending grad-ually. In other areas a less formal type of supervision is operated by the local gardaí.

It is interesting to note that a study of the Juvenile Liaison Scheme was undertaken in 1973 and completed two years later. Unfortunately, the findings were never published, but some of the recommendations were noted at that time in the daily press.[30] The study apparently found that participants in the scheme had a lower than normal rate of recidivism, except in Limerick, and that appearances in the Dublin Metropolitan Children's Court were reduced in the first year after its intro-duction by 22% for boys and by 32% for girls. Once the scheme was introduced there was also a reduction in the number of cases dismissed under the Probation Act. It was found that juveniles sometimes were not included in the scheme because of garda discretion. In some areas very few first offenders were admitted, while in others all first offenders were admitted. A questionnaire about the scheme was said to have been sent to officers and members of the garda but only 31% replied.

The study made various recommendations—the inclusion of re-offenders in the scheme, the establishment of separate juvenile gardaí departments in large centres of the population, the limiting of caseloads to 50 juveniles, the reviewing of each case once every two years and the adoption of a standard form of caution.

A juvenile who comes within the scope of the Juvenile Liaison Scheme in effect is formally cautioned and then released under the care of a Juvenile Liaison Officer. He may not be referred to the scheme because he has previously offended, or because the scheme does not operate in the area in which he is living, or because of a decision by the gardaí not to accept such a referral. Peter Shanley observed some ten years ago that 'The hallmark of the system of formal cautioning in both England and Ireland is the element of police discretion in it.'[31]

Court procedure and the personnel involved in the Children's Court in Ireland

A juvenile offender who does not come within the scope of the Juvenile Liaison Scheme will appear in the Dublin Metropolitan Children's Court. As the Kennedy Report pointed out, the courts '. . . are not bound to take into account the child's or juvenile's welfare',[32] and the procedure is highly formal and legalistic. On the first day in court evidence is given of arrest, charge and caution. If the juvenile's right to legal aid is exercised at this stage, the case normally will be remanded for a period to enable the making of an application. If the accused pleads guilty, evidence of the crime will be given by the garda on which the youngster then may be questioned. A conviction subsequently is recorded against the juvenile. If the accused pleads not guilty the case will be remanded (for the second time if he has previously applied for legal aid) to enable the witnesses to attend. At the end of the prosecution's case the accused is advised that he may say nothing, may give evidence on oath or may make an unsworn statement. Evidence given on oath may be cross-examined, whereas this does not apply to an unsworn statement.

Persons who are present in the Children's Court during proceedings include the juvenile, any other juveniles or adults with whom he may have been charged, the justice, the court clerk, a probation officer, several gardaí, on occasion solicitors, school-attendance officers, parents and witnesses. The justice presides, assesses information relevant to each case and makes the decision as to the outcome. The court clerk keeps records of those appearing and looks after administration, including the paying of fines and the preparation of court lists. The probation officer, if ordered by the justice, may make a report on the background of the accused. The youngster may be placed under the supervision of a probation officer whether or not the case has proceeded to conviction. (More detailed information about the probation service is given in Chapter IV).

At least one garda usually monitors the entrance and exit proceedings at the back of the courtroom. The garda who arrested the juvenile institutes and conducts the proceedings by giving evidence of the arrest and answering questions on relevant circumstances.

In cases where the juvenile has a solicitor of his own, i.e. where his parents can afford to pay the fees or where the service has been granted under the free legal aid scheme, the assigned solicitor defends the accused and has the right to cross-examine evidence produced against the accused. School attendance officers give details of those juveniles under school-leaving age who are not attending school regularly. Some of the juveniles who come in contact with those officers may be found to be in need of care.

The role of parents in the proceedings varies; they may be required to pay a fine, to give evidence, or to take responsibility for the juvenile. Sometimes they may be there primarily to give support to their child. It is the particular parent who is described as having actual control of the child who is required to attend, and, if this is not the father, he may be required to attend also.

Others who might be present in the Children's Court at any given time include witnesses in the case, including their relatives and friends, the relatives and friends of juvenile offenders, and observers with special permission. Newspapers may report on proceedings but in practice do not identify the juveniles by name.

Although the procedure in the Children's Court is formal and legalistic, in actual practice the court often goes beyond the legal requirements in consideration of the welfare and needs of the juvenile. Thus, for example, when a juvenile and adult are charged together, they usually both appear in the Children's Court, although, in law, the juvenile could be required to appear in a district court. Another example of this is the way in which the young offenders are segregated when appearing in court. School non-attenders appear on different days from people charged with criminal offences, and even among criminal offenders there is an attempt to let first offenders be dealt with before regular offenders.

An Analysis of the Dublin Metropolitan Children's Court

Every year 4 to 7,000 juveniles appear in the Children's Court in Dublin. Many of them appear more than once. Thus, for the year ending 31 July 1978, there were 21,157 appearances. These were made up as shown in Table 3.2.

Table 3.2

Appearances by Juveniles in the Dublin Metropolitan Children's Court, 1978

7,384	summary offences
13,650	indictable offences
123	applications for committal to the care of a fit person
Total= 21,157	

Source: Information from Department of Justice

70

At present no more detailed statistical information is available. Thus, it is not possible to give a breakdown of offences by age groups, show from what area these juveniles come or give the average number of appearances for each juvenile. Chapters I and II highlighted the lack of published information about the personal and social characteristics of young offenders. This chapter again shows the need for research, as, although detailed records are kept in the Children's Court, it appears that little analysis of these records has been carried out.

The following analysis of the Children's Court is based on the few publications which refer to that court,[33] on formal interviews with personnel involved in the court and on an observation study carried out by a member of the Working Party in 1979. The analysis is mainly concerned with the procedure in the Children's Court and what this may mean to the child or young person who is appearing there.

Procedure in the Children's Court
On any normal day in the Children's Court the scene is fairly chaotic. The peaceful seclusion of the upper Castle Yard is frequently shattered by the numerous young offenders who make their way to the overcrowded facilities. The bleak waiting-room is often full, and is sparsely furnished with only a few benches. No ashtrays are provided for the many smokers. The boredom of waiting is sometimes relieved by covering the walls and benches with graffiti with the result that the room has to be completely painted several times each year.

The police usually cluster at the foot of the stairs leading to the courtroom and the hall often fills with the overflow from both groups. It is not unusual to see people waiting outside in the Castle Yard itself because of lack of space. Solicitors have no option but to interview their clients under these difficult conditions.

The courtroom itself is markedly different, being a pleasantly painted and carpeted room. There is a dais at one end for the justice, court clerk and probation officer. These are faced by church-style benches for the accused, their families, friends, witnesses and legal representatives (legal representatives alone being provided with cushions).

W. Clarke Hall, a magistrate in the Children's Court in England in 1917 when England was still operating the 1908 Act, commented that '. . . elaborate provision is made for every person who can possibly have any business to be present, but the delinquent child himself seems to have been entirely forgotten'.[34] This statement could still be applied to the Children's Court in Dublin today.

The procedure in the court itself could perhaps be described as formal, legalistic, and bureaucratic though interspersed with informal communication. Outside the door there is a constant flow of people being hustled up and down the stairs. The purpose of this activity is to maintain relative privacy by having only one case heard in the court at any one time, while getting through the caseload as quickly as possible.

The gardaí who institute the proceedings give evidence of the arrest, charge and caution. Much of this evidence is given in terms of reference numbers of charge sheets and named sections of Acts. These can be referred to by the justice who has all the details laid before him or her in writing. However, it is practically impossible for the young person to understand the specific nature of the charge or charges against him. The juvenile's difficulty in understanding is often compounded by the fact that the gardaí tend to address the justice in very low tones. Meanwhile, the court clerk may be shuffling through the mounds of charge sheets before him, looking up, recognising the accused and making various gestures to the garda monitoring the entrance and exit proceedings at the back of the courtroom.

To the outsider it seems that the last person to receive personal attention is the young offender himself. Apart from other considerations, there is simply not enough time at the justice's and solicitor's disposal to explain fully what is going on. Often people working in the court clerk's office try to serve this function.

The procedure in the Children's Court is highly complex. The words of Clarke Hall seem here to be apposite. 'All formalities tend to confuse a child's mind, and every formality that is not absolutely necessary should therefore be abolished.'[35]

Even if the solicitor had enough time with his client before the court appearance, it would be difficult to explain to the young person the different weight attached to each type of statement, and in his confusion the young person will very likely choose the simplest solution, i.e. say nothing at all, which of course has the most disastrous implications for himself. As Barbara Wootton put it:

72

Now imagine explaining to a child of 10 that he may question the policemen and other witnesses who have sworn that he stole the sweets that he denies stealing. Like many adults in similar circumstances, the child fails to understand that he must at this stage confine himself to questioning the witnesses' statements. Instead, he starts to pour out his whole story about how he was with his brother on the way to school, and never in the sweet shop at all at the material time. So at this stage he has to be checked and told that the time for him to tell his own side of the story will come later, which is enough to frighten him into silence altogether.[36]

It is easy to see how the focus of the proceedings may rest completely on the legalities of making statements and questioning those involved. The juvenile who has more to lose than anyone else present, and who is the least familiar with the proceedings, is at a distinct disadvantage. When the time finally comes for him to give his side of the story there are further legal decisions and choices:

. . . the Court has to decide whether he is old enough to understand the meaning of an oath (in the juridicial, not vernacular, sense) and has also to make him appreciate the significance of the choice between giving sworn evidence, or making an unsworn statement or remaining silent. Even if he is thought to be too young to understand the meaning of an oath, he still has the option of giving what will be treated as sworn evidence, if he gives a solemn promise to tell the truth in the witness box. Moreover, on top of all this the court has to see that the rules of evidence are observed throughout, and that an accused child does not make statements based on hearsay. Thus, if he says 'we were late for school and my brother told me to hurry', he must be told not to repeat what his brother said, unless his brother can come to court and say it himself.[37]

At present the juvenile who is not represented by a solicitor is in a worse position than are those who are represented. He will not notice technical flaws in the prosecution case, he is more likely to misunderstand the intricate courtroom procedures, and he may not realise that there is more weight attached to a sworn statement than to an unsworn statement. Sometimes the accused says nothing, not realising that a

73

conviction will probably follow if the prosecution's evidence has not been challenged. As Clarke Hall puts it: 'Could anything better illustrate the hopelessly antiquated attitude of the law towards the child than this amazingly solemn and cumbersome provision for the method of his trial?'[38]

The concepts of criminal responsibility and capacity
Under the 1908 Act the child is held to be criminally responsible at seven years old. Both the Kennedy Report and the CARE memorandum proposed that the age of criminal responsibility be raised, the reason being that children have not reached the cognitive age of reason at seven years, nor have they autonomy of judgement sufficient to make responsible moral decisions.

Linked to the concept of criminal responsibility is that of criminal capacity. Alan Shatter explains:

> A child may be held criminally responsible for his acts from the age of seven. Under common law there is an irrebuttable presumption that a child below that age cannot commit a criminal offence, in that such a child could not distinguish between right and wrong. From the age of 7 to 14 years there is a rebuttable presumption of innocence, i.e. a presumption that a child lacks criminal capacity or is doli incapax. To override this presumption it must be established that at the time of committing the act charged, the child knew it was wrong.[39]

Shatter also says that this obligation to establish knowledge of wrongfulness at the time of the child's act is frequently ignored. This means, in effect, that children are considered as capable as adults of deliberate criminal acts.

In the opinion of this Working Party any arbitrary age of criminal responsibility and capacity has flaws because of wide variations in the rate of children's maturation. The Kennedy Report noted this difficulty and recommended a more flexible approach to a youngster's knowledge of right and wrong: 'We must think in terms of the child in his environment. Different environments may lead to wide variations in the age at which a child comes to this knowledge'.[40] While concepts of criminal responsibility and capacity remain, questions arise which are virtually impossible to answer. What should be the age of criminal responsibility? What is meant by the knowledge of

74

wrongfulness? Is it to be decided by legal, moral or other criteria?

This Working Party would rather see the juvenile justice system focus on the needs of each troubled and troublesome child or young person instead of becoming involved in the questions of the precise age of criminal responsibility and capacity of the individual.

The remanding of cases after conviction

The procedure in the Children's Court can be long and drawn out because of the number of times children are required to appear. Unfortunately, this does not mean that the children receive a great deal of personal attention. It has already been noted that a person on one charge may have to appear a number of times to allow for applying for a solicitor and permitting witnesses to attend. It would appear that a very high proportion of those appearing enter a plea of guilty. This may in part be explained in terms of the choice between pleading not guilty and going through the procedure described above, or of pleading guilty and simply having the garda give evidence and having a conviction recorded.

Procedures in the Children's Court can have a direct effect on the behaviour of the juvenile. The practice of remanding cases after conviction for a long period, with or without supervision, may happen, for example, where a youngster needs residential care when no suitable place is available for him or existing facilities will not accept him. In a situation like this the justice may have no option but to remand the case. Cases may be remanded over a long period while legal and administrative procedures are attended to, and then all of the cases may be disposed of in one day. The age of the juvenile at the time of appearing, however, rather than at the time of the offence, determines the dispositions open to the justice.

A number of unfortunate consequences arise from this system. Firstly, the juvenile offences may be petty, but the sheer volume of offences over a long period of time may make them seem more serious. If they were dealt with individually a relatively small penalty might be imposed for each offence. When the offences are all dealt with on the one day, however, a more severe penalty is likely to be imposed.

Secondly, a long period of time elapsing between the youngster's offence, conviction and disposition is undesirable. If a youngster feels that he has already been convicted on enough charges to be sent to Loughan House or St Patrick's Institution, there is little to deter him from further anti-social behaviour before appearing in court again.

The HOPE Report stated that juveniles know the maximum sentence that can be imposed. They realise that it is only a matter of time before this will be imposed and thus believe they might as well run up another score of charges since these will make no difference to the ultimate judgement. The report stated: 'We have met several young people who see no point in controlling their behaviour because of the system.'[41]

In the opinion of this Working Party, society's response to anti-social behaviour by a child or young person should take place as soon as possible after the offence. This might help to deter the juvenile from offending again, and would narrow the gap between his actions and their consequences thus encouraging him to undertake more responsibility for his own behaviour.

The legal aid entitlements of juveniles
As we have said before, the emphasis in the present juvenile justice system in Ireland is primarily on formal, legal and bureaucratic detail. The structure of the system does not sufficiently take into account the welfare of the child or teenager. This is evident in the administration of legal aid.

When a young person is arrested on a criminal charge and brought to a garda station he is not at this point entitled to legal aid. He will often sign a statement therefore without the benefit of advice from a solicitor. This can have adverse repercussions if a plea of not guilty is later entered after a statement admitting the offence has already been signed. Obviously it is important that the juvenile should have his legal rights protected at this point, whether or not his parents are able to afford the services of a solicitor.

Since the Supreme Court judgment in *The State (Healy)* v. *Donoghue*,[42] the juvenile in a criminal case is likely on his first appearance in court to be informed of his right to claim legal aid. For various reasons, however, he may not always avail of this right even when clearly eligible. If not a previous offender, for example, he may not understand the provisions of the legal aid scheme. If not supported by the presence of family or friends he may be deterred from applying because of the bureaucracy involved, or because he is not literate enough to fill out the application forms. Other difficulties may hamper the satisfactory operation of the state legal aid system as well. Sometimes the solicitor may be delayed at another court, and when he eventually arrives there may only be time for a hurried consultation in the Children's Court waiting-room where there is virtually no privacy. If the solicitor does not make an appearance, the case will have to be put back to a later date. This causes inconvenience and unnecessary expense for all concerned.

A committee was established by the government in 1975 to review the operation of the criminal legal aid scheme; this committee has not yet reported.[43] A Legal Aid Board was set up by the government in January 1980 to establish a statutory system of legal aid and advice in civil cases.

The Working Party would welcome the advertance of these bodies to the specific legal aid requirements of juveniles. It is believed that a unified system of aid and advice both in civil and in criminal cases would best serve these needs and safeguard the interests of society.

Conclusions and recommendations

The Working Party concludes from this examination of the juvenile justice system in Ireland that the existing procedures for dealing with the needs of troubled and troublesome children are outmoded and unnecessarily complex. The impersonal and legalistic structure of the Dublin Metropolitan Children's Court must be as frustrating for the administrators of the system as for the juvenile offender and his parents. The formality of the setting creates a barrier to close communication between all of the parties concerned and diminishes the opportunity for responding appropriately to the juvenile's needs. The cases heard in the Children's Court are often processed within a matter of minutes. The court is not bound to take into account the child's welfare, and for only one charge, he could expect to appear on several occasions to allow for a remand, to claim legal aid, make a plea and obtain necessary witnesses. At present far more attention appears to be given to legal detail than to the circumstances of the juvenile. In the opinion of the Working Party it is vital that the legal procedures for troubled and troublesome young people should ensure the maintaining of a clear focus on the welfare of the juvenile and the greater involvement of the accused, the family, and other significant persons, in decisions which are going to have a deep impact in the lives of all concerned.

Thus, it is recommended that the legal procedures relating to troubled and troublesome children in Ireland be structured in such a manner that the total welfare needs of the juvenile be given primary consideration. In order to achieve this objective it is essential that the juvenile, his family, and other appropriate members of the community, be enabled to participate fully in all such proceedings in which the juvenile is involved.

A new system for Ireland

In considering the establishment of any system of juvenile justice a number of fundamental questions come to mind. How can the welfare of the child, the protection of society and the upholding of law and order simultaneously be reconciled and facilitated? If there is a focus on welfare how can it be ensured that the legal rights of the juvenile are protected and that he is not deprived of freedom for years in the name of welfare when he might only be so deprived for months in the name of the law? How is it ensured that one segment of society is not primarily involved in decision-making while a different segment is primarily affected by such decisions? How can anti-social behaviour leading to the imposition of labels like 'young offender' be reduced? Once so labelled, how should society respond to these young people? The Working Party believes that a recasting of the existing court system for the hearing of juvenile cases in Ireland would best meet these needs of the child and of society. The new structure that is recommended would retain the best features of the existing Dublin Metropolitan Children's Court and combine these with adaptations from the juvenile justice systems abroad. The new system would facilitate a more community-oriented approach to troubled children and their families and would operate nationwide. The avoidance, where possible, of contact between young offenders and the courts would be a major concern.

The flexibility of the Scottish panel system of hearings appears to allow considerable scope for a viable alternative to the traditional court hearing. Morris describes its advantages:

> . . . the Scottish system seems to be more successful than the English at keeping children out of courts or hearings. About 90% of referrals to the reporters come from the police, but only about half of these children are subsequently referred by the reporters to the children's hear-

ings. In 1969, 25,047 children were dealt with in the juvenile courts in Scotland. In 1973, 26,266 children were referred to the reporters, but only 11,534 were referred on by them to hearings. (A further 1,116 were dealt with in the ordinary courts.) This represents a substantial reduction in the number of children being dealt with within the formal system of social control. The reporters in Scotland perform a crucial sifting role and stand as an independent and visible sift between the police (and other referring agents) and the children's hearings.[44]

Parsloe too considers the Scottish system of children's hearings to have distinct advantages because it involves the parents in the planning of the future for their own child:

> . . . courts which have the responsibility of deciding on guilt or innocence are not the place for an unhurried discussion, involving the child and the family, as to the best treatment method. Courts are intimidating places, and the procedures necessary to protect the rights of the accused impose barriers to discussion on a basis of shared concern for the future of a child. One aim of the children's hearing is to involve the parents in planning for their own child. Some would take this further and suggest that courts are forced traditionally and procedurally to see the child as an isolated individual and not as a member of a group, either a family or a community group.[45]

For these reasons the proposed system for Ireland, while drawing upon both the English and Scottish systems of juvenile justice, has been particularly influenced by the Scottish model of children's hearings. It is believed that an informal panel system rather than a formal court system would best ensure an appropriate response to the emotional and material needs of the child.

Under the reconstituted system for Ireland, all juveniles (children and young people under 17 years) who were in trouble or in potential trouble with the law would come before a Juvenile Panel of three persons. The chairman of the panel would be a district justice, while the two non-legal members would be voluntary workers who had been carefully selected and suitably trained. Both sexes would be represented on the panel. The inclusion of volunteers from all walks of life as panel members would help to generate a realistic understanding of the needs of troubled children among the public at large.

Such an understanding would lead to an appreciation of the necessity to allocate more resources for children in trouble and would also serve to informally educate the local community about children's problems. In the words of the Black Report for Northern Ireland:

> The essential quality of lay involvement is in representativeness of the community at large. Within a strategy which seeks to emphasise community responsibility for the containment or control of delinquent behaviour, representation from the widest possible spectrum of society is important. Representatives of the communities from which juvenile offenders come—and therefore people who have a major interest in how such young people are dealt with—should be included. As our overall strategy places responsibility for support on the family, the school and the community, as well as the social and educational agencies, rather than on the court, lay membership should provide the court with a balanced view of society's attitude to juvenile crime and its repercussions on the community at large. To achieve this a broadly-based panel is essential.[46]

Such an involvement would be a logical extension of the long and positive tradition of voluntary effort in the social sphere which already exists in this country.

Members of the panel would receive training based on socio-legal studies rather similar to that which is available to panels in Scotland. This training has been described by Parsloe. It involves 'sitting in on hearings, and also lectures and discussions on the legal aspects of the system, the resources available in the form of supervision, intermediate treatment, residential homes and schools, communications and interviewing and some aspects of child development.'[47] The Black Report also has outlined a formula of training for lay members of the juvenile court panel in Northern Ireland: 'We consider that the lay membership should be given the opportunity to become familiar with legal concepts and the powers available to the court before full membership of the panel is ratified.'[48]

Referrals to the juvenile panel would be made by a person known as a juvenile referral officer. This officer would be required to have a sound knowledge of legal matters and of the range of provision in the child care services. An understanding of the needs of troubled and troublesome children and young persons would be an essential prerequisite to his or her appointment to the post. Any person who believed that a child's personal, family or social needs were not adequately met could inform the juvenile referral officer who would then refer the child to the appropriate service or if necessary to the juvenile panel. Thus the juvenile referral officer would liaise with social workers, both voluntary and statutory, and with many other organisations and individuals, so that the children who came within his sphere of activity would not be categorised as being in trouble with the law. Referrals could be made to a wide variety of services including youth clubs, employment and training organisations, counselling services and social work agencies. Sometimes, as in the case of spurious complaints, it might not be necessary to take any action whatever.

The juvenile referral officer would try to see that the child's needs were met, if possible, by the community through such methods as casework services or membership of a supportive group. A large number of agencies would be involved, ranging from family casework centres, child guidance clinics, and neighbourhood youth projects, to varying forms of residential care. With the advent of these officers, the responsibilities of social work agencies for the acceptance of clients will need to be clearly defined and legally binding, and they will need to be adequately funded by the state. At present, when a number of different agencies and residential homes reject a particularly difficult child, the child may end up receiving no help whatever, a problem discussed at greater length in Chapter IV.

If the juvenile referral officer finds that appropriate help for the juvenile is not available from the local community, or if the juvenile will not voluntarily avail of existing services, then the officer may decide to refer the child to the panel for assessment.

The aim of the juvenile panel would be to resolve the problems of troubled children and their families in a humane manner in which the child and his parents will have fully participated. To achieve this aim it is envisaged that:

- parents *must* attend hearings, which could be held in the evenings or at week-ends if necessary;

- each case is to be heard by appointment and allowed a minimum of 30 minutes;

- focus is to be on the needs of the child in the context of family and community;

81

- sittings should be attended by the child, his parents, panel members, social worker, juvenile referral officer, clerk, and any other persons who may be requested by the juvenile or his parents to attend (e.g. other relative, solicitor, local youth worker, friend or teacher).

The panel members, having thoroughly examined each aspect of the problem in consultation with the appropriate people, would subsequently reach a consensus about the future care of the juvenile. The district justice who was chairman of the panel would then convey his decision to the juvenile and his family. While the panel would deal with the majority of referrals made by the juvenile referral officer, in the event of a dispute or an appeal, or for very serious offences, the juvenile's case could be referred to the circuit court.

The main criticism of the Scottish hearing system has centred on 'the inadequacy of legal protections for children'.[49] As Grant has suggested,

> there is the danger in the hearing setting to the rights of the child. In a system that is informal, whose main actors, the panel members, by and large see themselves as being concerned with helping and treating, and whose personnel generally lack any formal legal training, it is inevitable that at least the potentiality exists that the child's rights will be ignored.[50]

The Working Party recognises this danger, but it is believed that the inclusion in the recommended system of a district justice as chairman of the panel, and of a legal training requirement for the juvenile referral officer, will ensure the adequate protection of the legal rights of the child.

The Working Party concludes that the introduction of a new system of juvenile panel hearings, on the lines which have been outlined, would bring a more humane and more effective system of juvenile justice to Ireland than can be provided within the existing legal structure.

IV. Dispositional Alternatives*

In this chapter the dispositional alternatives presently available in England and Wales for the juvenile offender are briefly outlined. The dispositional alternatives available in Ireland under the Probation of Offenders Act, 1907, and the Children Act, 1908, are examined in some detail. Recommendations are made for a more extensive use of certain existing provisions. It is also recommended that the area health boards be reconstituted to include responsibility for the total care of troubled and troublesome young people.

Dispositions in England
To avoid where possible the bringing of juveniles before a court of law, a wide use is made in England of formal cautioning procedures followed by a short period of police supervision. As noted in the preceding chapter, the police can decide to take criminal proceedings against a juvenile, in which case he will be brought before a juvenile court.[1]

In addition to the powers of the court over juveniles charged with serious crimes[2] the following dispositional alternatives are available to magistrates in the juvenile courts in England:

1. An order which requires the parent or guardian of the juvenile to enter into an undertaking (backed by financial penalty), to exercise proper care and control;

2. A supervision order;

3. A care order;

4. A hospital order (as laid down in the Mental Health Act, 1959, requiring the support of two doctors)

5. A guardianship order[3]

If the court decides that the parents can cope adequately with the care of their child, the juvenile may be sent home on a bond of up to £25 to be of good behaviour for a year. Should some other action be considered necessary, the court may make a *care order*, in which case the local authority becomes

*Editor: Dr. Claire Carney. Research: Maeve McMahon, Valerie Richardson, Máire Stedman and the Working Party.

responsible for the juvenile and decides whether he is to live at home, in a community home or elsewhere. Alternatively, the court may make a *supervision order*, in which case the juvenile will remain at home under the supervision of the local authority or of the probation service.

Where both care and supervision orders are concerned, the local authority, through the social work services, has considerable powers in England to make detailed decisions concerning the kind of treatment the juvenile will receive. These powers include a method of intervention known as *intermediate treatment* aimed at bridging the gap between the retaining of the juvenile in his own home under supervision, or his placement completely away from home in residential care.[4] Intermediate treatment covers a wide and varied range of programmes, many of which have been set up by voluntary organisations with financial backing from the Department of Health and Social Security. The juveniles involved in such treatment programmes may be required to live in a specific setting for a maximum period of 90 days and/or take part in certain specified activities. This form of treatment, which is further discussed in Chapter VI, appears to provide a very useful method of community-based intervention in the lives of troubled and troublesome young people.

Dispositions in Scotland

As noted in Chapter III, in Scotland juveniles are dealt with, where possible, by voluntary arrangements between social work departments and families. If compulsion is considered to be necessary, the juvenile comes before the children's panel hearings which have replaced the juvenile courts.[5]

The hearing, once the grounds stated by the reporter for referral of the case have been accepted, can either discharge the referral or can make what is known as a *supervision requirement*.[6] Under the requirement the juvenile may be required to submit to supervision in accordance with such conditions as panel members may impose, including a period of residence in a named residential establishment. Unless discharged at a subsequent review which must be held at least once per annum,[7] the supervision requirement may remain in force until the young person attains 18 years of age.[8]

As in England, if the juvenile is to be supervised at home, the supervision requirement may include participation in an *intermediate treatment* programme. The juvenile might also be

84

required to report daily to his social worker, live in a hostel or do community service. When the panel has made a supervision requirement the juvenile or his parents have three weeks in which to appeal, if they wish, to the sheriff for a review of the requirement. The sheriff can confirm the requirement, dismiss the referral altogether or require the hearing to arrive at another decision.[9] The sheriff himself cannot specify a new supervision requirement.

Dispositional alternatives in Ireland[10]
In Ireland, the justice alone makes decisions over contested facts and decides what is to be done with a juvenile who is appearing before the court. Certain distinctions and limitations apply in dealing with children and young persons as legally defined.[11] These are as follows:

1. Imprisonment — no *child* may be imprisoned under any circumstances but in certain cases a *young person* may be remanded in, or be sentenced to, a prison.
2. St Patrick's Institution — no child may be sentenced to St Patrick's Institution but *young persons* may be sentenced there.
3. Reformatory and industrial schools — depending on the circumstances, a *child* may be sent to a reformatory or an industrial school. A *young person* may be sent to a reformatory school but not to an industrial school.

The juvenile may also be dealt with by the court in the following manner:

Where a child or young person charged with any offence is tried by any court, and the court is satisfied of his guilt, the court shall take into consideration the manner in which, under the provisions of this or any other Act enabling the court to deal with the case, the case should be dealt with, namely, whether

a) by dismissing the charge; or
b) by discharging the offender on his entering into a recognizance; or
c) by so discharging the offender and placing him under the supervision of a probation officer; or
d) by committing the offender to the care of a relative or other fit person; or
e) by sending the offender to an industrial school; or

85

f) by sending the offender to a reformatory school; or

g) by ordering the offender to be whipped; or

h) by ordering the offender to pay a fine, damages, or costs; or

i) by ordering the parent or guardian of the offender to pay a fine, damages, or costs; or

j) by ordering the parent or guardian of the offender to give security for his good behaviour; or

k) by committing the offender to custody in place of detention provided under this part of this Act; or

l) where the offender is a young person by sentencing him to imprisonment; or

m) by dealing with the case in any other manner in which it may be legally dealt with;
provided that nothing in this section shall be construed as authorising the court to deal with any case in any manner in which it could not deal with the case apart from this section.[12]

These dispositional alternatives available to the courts in Ireland are considered individually in the following section.

a) *Dismissing the charge*
There are two circumstances in which a charge against a juvenile may be dismissed by the justice. The first of these relates to presumptions. As stated in the previous chapter, there are certain presumptions which apply to children. These are the rebuttable presumption of innocence relating to those aged between seven and fourteen years, and the irrebuttable presumption that a child under seven years is incapable of any crime. Added to these is another rebuttable presumption that a boy under fourteen is 'incapable of having sexual intercourse, therefore cannot be convicted as a principle, of rape, or of an assault with intent to commit rape, or of any offence involving sexual intercourse'.[13] A boy of this age may be convicted as a secondary party, however, and be found guilty of indecent or common assault.

Where a charge has been proved, the justice may dismiss the offender on the following grounds:

Where any person is charged before a court of summary jurisdiction with an offence punishable by such court, and the court thinks that the charge is proved, but is of the opinion that, having regard to the character, antecedents,

86

age, health, or mental conditions of the person being charged, or to the trivial nature of the offence, or to the extenuating circumstances under which the offence was committed, it is inexpedient to inflict any punishment, or any other than a nominal punishment, or that it is expedient to release the offender on probation, the court may, without proceeding to conviction, make an order either (1) dismissing the information or charge; or (2) discharging the offender conditionally on his entering into a recognizance, with or without sureties, to be of good behaviour and to appear for conviction and sentence when called on at any time during such period not exceeding three years, as may be specified in the order.[14]

Thus, in a summary case, the charge may be dismissed with or without a condition of good behaviour.

b) *Discharging the offender on his entering into a recognizance*[15]
In the District Court a juvenile may be discharged on entering into a recognizance which may or may not be associated with conditions. Such a discharge is called a Dismissal under the Probation Act (colloquially known as a DPA). Although the juvenile has not been actually convicted, the Garda Síochána keep a criminal record of juveniles who have been dealt with in this manner. If the defendant appears in court on other occasions, and the justice asks for evidence of previous convictions, these DPAs are included by the gardaí. In such circumstances a DPA is, effectively, a conviction.

In the opinion of the Working Party, discharges under this section could be used more constructively within the present juvenile justice system in Ireland. Young offenders could enter into recognizance with requirements similar to those associated with intermediate treatment schemes in England and Scotland. It should be stressed that the youngster is *not* being convicted of an offence when a Dismissal under the Probation Act is given.[16]

c) *Discharging the offender and placing him under the supervision of a probation officer*
Under the Probation of Offenders Act, 1907, a juvenile may be discharged and simultaneously be placed under supervision:

A recognizance order to be entered into under this Act shall, if the court so order, contain a condition that the

87

offender be under the supervision of such person as may be named in the order during the period specified in the order and such other conditions for securing such supervision as may be specified in the order, and an order requiring the insertion of such conditions as aforesaid in the recognizance is in this Act referred to as a probation order.[17]

The Criminal Justice Act of 1914 set out additional conditions that could be imposed:

A recognizance under this Act may contain such additional conditions with respect to residence, abstention from intoxicating liquor, and any other matters, as the court may, having regard to the particular circumstances of the case, consider necessary for preventing repetition of the same offence or the commission of other offences.[18]

It would seem that this legislation also could be regarded in terms of an intermediate treatment approach under which the juvenile might be required to undergo special treatment programmes in residential or nonresidential settings.

A further section of the 1907 probation Act provides for the appointment of Children's Probation Officers:

There shall be appointed, where circumstances permit, special probation officers, to be called children's probation officers, who shall, in the absence of any reasons to the contrary, be named in a probation order made in the case of an offender under the age of sixteen.

The Criminal Justice Administration Act, 1914, provided for the recognition of societies which exist for the care of offenders aged up to 21 years who are on probation:

If a Society is formed or is already in existence having as its object or amongst its objects the care and control of persons under the age of twenty-one whilst on probation under the Probation of Offenders Act, 1907, or of persons while placed out on licence from a reformatory or industrial school or Borstal institution, or under supervision after the determination of the period of their detention in such a school or institution, or under supervision in pursuance of this Act, or some one or more of such objects the society may apply to the Secretary of State for recognition and the Minister, if he approved of the constitution of the society and is satisfied as to the means adopted by the society for securing such objects as aforesaid, may grant his recognition to the Society.

Where a probation order is made by a court of summary jurisdiction in respect of a person who appears to the court to be under the age of twenty-one, the court may appoint any person provided by a recognised society to act as probation officer in the case.

Where a probation officer provided by a recognised society has been appointed to act in any case and it is subsequently found by the society expedient that some other officer provided by the society should be substituted for the officer originally appointed, the society may, subject to the approval of the court, appoint such other officer to act, and thereupon the probation order shall have effect as if such substituted officer had originally been appointed to act as probation officer.[19]

It is only in recent years that probation as a disposition has been used to any great extent in Ireland for both adult and juvenile offenders. Despite the existence of enabling legislation dating back to the Probation of Offenders Act, 1907, a probation officer was first employed by the Department of Justice in 1942. Between 1942 and 1961 not more than six probation officers were employed by the Department at any one time.

In 1945 Justice H. A. McCarthy of the Dublin Children's Court said of the four probation officers working in the Children's Court at that time:

> One man has to supervise 124 cases, his male colleague has 108 cases, and the two women Officers have under their care 70 and 50 cases respectively. . . . It is quite clear from these figures that the two male Officers are greatly over worked, and, in result, the best that can be expected of their efforts is merely a system of surveillance, and not supervision in the proper sense. As I require the presence of one or other of the women Officers on three of the four days on which the Children's Court is sitting, it will be seen that they, too, find it extremely difficult to cope with the numbers of children under their care.[20]

Following the completion of an interdepartmental report on offenders in 1962[21] the service was reorganised and the number of staff was increased to eight, of whom five served the Children's Court, one served the Dublin District Courts, one operated in St Patrick's Institution and one operated in Mountjoy Prison. The service was still confined to Dublin at this stage.

The next major developments occurred in 1969 when an internal enquiry was carried out in the Department of Justice following the Minister's request for an examination of the present and future needs of the Prison Welfare Service.[22] This year marked, in effect, the beginning of the present probation service which rapidly expanded throughout the 1970s. At the end of 1979 the staff included one Principal Welfare Officer, one Assistant Principal Welfare Officer, 15 Senior Welfare Officers, with provision for 116 Welfare Officers (although this number may not necessarily be actually serving). The service is now nationwide.

With the growth in the number of staff there has been a corresponding growth in the number of young people being supervised. The figures for those under 21 years placed on probation by the courts in 1977 and 1978 are shown in Table 4.1.

Table 4.1

Age Categories of Those Under 21 Years Placed on Probation in the Courts during 1977 and 1978

Region	Under 14		14-16		17-21		Total	
	'77	'78	'77	'78	'77	'78	'77	'78
Eastern Region (South)	10	12	44	54	31	23	85	89
Eastern Region (North)	13	10	57	18	39	16	109	44
South/South East Region	13	12	93	49	38	40	144	101
Western Region	4	5	35	47	45	69	84	121
Totals:	40	39	229	168	153	148	422	355

Source: Statistics supplied by the Probation and Welfare Service, Department of Justice. The boundaries of the 'regions' are as follows:

90

Eastern Region (South)	— Dublin South City (and County)
Eastern Region (North)	— Dublin North City (and County)
South/South East Region	— Cork/Waterford/Wexford/ Kilkenny/South Tipperary/ Laois/Carlow
Western Region	— Galway/Mayo/Sligo/Donegal/ Athlone/Longford/Westmeath/ Offaly South/Roscommon

Because of the lack of more detailed information it is not possible to draw hard conclusions from these figures on such questions as the reasons why the figures relating to offenders placed on probation under 21 years of age declined between 1977 and 1978 or the reasons why the decline was more marked in some areas than in others. What exactly is reflected by these figures? Do they represent changes in government policy, or changing patterns in crime and/or sentencing procedures?

A relatively recent development relevant in probation is *adjourned supervision*. This may be used when the case has been proved and the justice adjourns making a decision regarding sentence and puts the offender under the supervision of a probation officer. The usual length of time for cases to be adjourned in this manner is three months. The numbers placed on adjourned supervision can be seen in Table 4.2. This table shows a small increase in the total number of people placed on adjourned supervision between 1977 and 1978, but why the numbers increased in the Eastern Region (North) and the Western Region while declining in the Eastern Region (South) and the South/South East region is not clear.

Another recent development in the Probation and Welfare Service was the initiation of an *intensive supervision scheme* in 1979. Under this scheme the probation officers employed by the Department work closely with a case-load of not more than four young offenders. These offenders may be selected for release from St Patrick's Institution or other place of detention before the end of their sentence, on condition that they take part in the intensive supervision scheme. Once selected they have the right to refuse a place in the scheme. As part of this scheme a 'drop-in' centre has been opened in Marlborough Street for the use of ex-prisoners.

91

Table 4.2

Age Categories of Those Under 21 Years Placed on Adjourned Supervision in the Courts During 1977 and 1978

Region	Under 14 '77-'78		14-16 '77-'78		17-21 '77-'78		Total '77-'78	
Eastern Region (South)	18	25	64	60	44	32	126	117
Eastern Region (North)	13	16	38	66	32	22	83	104
South/South East Region	7	11	31	37	31	14	69	62
Western Region	4	4	8	17	10	23	22	44
Totals:	42	56	141	180	117	91	300	327

Source: Statistics supplied by the Probation and Welfare Service, Department of Justice.

(d) Committing the offender to the care of a relative or other fit person

The term 'fit person' is defined in section 38 (1) of the 1908 Act as follows: 'In this part of this Act, unless the context otherwise requires the expression 'fit person', in relation to the care of any child or young person, includes any society or body corporate established for the reception or protection of poor children or the prevention of cruelty to children.' It appears from the relevant sections of the 1908 Children Act that all young offenders may be committed to the care of a fit person. The Act specifies that offenders under 12 years of age, and first offenders aged 12, 13 or 14, may be so committed. It also specifies that a youthful offender aged 12 to 17 may be committed to the care of a fit person under certain circumstances.[23] These circumstances can occur when the justice makes an order that the offender should be detained in a certified school but that the order is not to take effect immediately. They also can occur if 'at the time specified for the order to take effect the youthful offender or child is unfit to be sent to a certified school',[24] or when there is a delay in finding a suitable school for the juvenile.

Section 63 of the 1908 Act thus opens many interesting possibilities for responding to the needs of young offenders. For example, the justice could make an order for a young offender to go to Scoil Ard Mhuire in Lusk, but could defer the date on which he would actually be detained there and, in the meantime put him under the care of a fit person in his own community. This would encourage the earlier use of community-based resources in the treatment of young offenders in Ireland. It appears, however, that fit person orders are little used in the case of young offenders. The Kennedy Report made the following comment on this point:

> From enquiry this Committee is aware that 'fit person' orders have not been made by the Children's Court for many years and the Committee thinks the failure to make use of the 'fit person' procedure was probably due to the unwillingness of friends or relatives to undertake responsibility especially where there is no financial assistance. If friends or relatives did not come forward there might be no one else available, and it was no one's business to find such people.[25]

This lack of use of the fit person option seems surprising in view of the traditional involvement of volunteers in the social services in Ireland. The difficulty seems to lie in the present structure of the child care services. This structure does not always facilitate an appropriate response to the needs of the individual child because decisions regarding his placement tend to be made according to the availability of care facilities. Thus, a child whose relative is willing to take on responsibility for his care and education but lacks the necessary financial resources might be placed instead in residential care because the second option is easier to implement. It seems to be an anomalous situation that the State is willing to pay a heavy subsidy towards the cost of each child's maintenance in residential care but is unwilling to provide sufficient support and financial incentive for individuals and organisations to provide such care at community level. The Kennedy report considered that this problem in the organisation of community care for juveniles could be overcome without any major legislative change: 'There seems no difficulty in principle in arranging for some authority to accept responsibility for children in need of care and it is suggested that the Health Authority would be a most suitable body to carry out these functions and to be enabled to act as fit persons.'[26]

The Working Party supports the suggestion that the existing Area Health Boards be reconstituted as Health and Social Service Boards to enable them to undertake responsibility for the care of troubled and troublesome young people (see Chapter V for more information on this subject). The Health Boards then could entrust the care of young people to appropriate individuals and organisations which would be named as fit persons and be provided with adequate financial support. This policy should help to reduce the numbers of juveniles requiring care at a residential level, and would avoid the undesirable and unnecessary removal of some children from their local environment. (These ideas are further explored in Chapter VI).

e) *Sending the offender to an industrial school*

Industrial schools are now usually referred to as Residential Homes.[27] Section 58 (1) of the 1908 Act, as amended by section 10 of the 1941 Act, gives details of those children (i.e. aged under 15 years) who may be admitted to such homes. In fact most of the grounds stated do not relate to offenders but rather to conditions such as destitution, inability of parents to have control of the child and residence of the child in a house used for prostitution.[28] The following grounds are particularly relevant to young offenders:

2) Where a child apparently under twelve years is charged before a court of assize or quarter sessions or a petty sessional court with an offence punishable in the case of an adult by penal servitude or a less punishment, the court if satisfied on enquiry that it is expedient so to deal with the child, may order him to be sent to a certified industrial school.

3) Where a child, apparently of the age of twelve or thirteen or fourteen years, who has not previously been convicted is charged before a petty sessional court with an offence punishable in the case of an adult by penal servitude or a less punishment, and the court is satisfied that the child should be sent to a certified school but, having regard to the special circumstances of the case, should not be sent to a certified reformatory school, and is also satisfied that the character and antecedents of the child are such that he will not exercise an evil influence over the other children in a certified industrial school, the

94

court may order the child to be sent to a certified industrial school, having previously ascertained that the managers are willing to receive the child. . . .

6) A petty sessional court may, on the complaint of a local educational authority, made in accordance with the provisions of section twelve of the Elementary Education Act, 1876, for the purpose of enforcing an attendance order, order a child to be sent to a certified industrial school as provided in that section.[29]

To sum up the situation, most of the conditions in the 1908 Act for sending children to residential homes relate to non-offenders. However, offenders under twelve years, first offenders of 12 to 14 years inclusive and school non-attenders may be sent to such homes. Mitchell states that a child:

> may be committed to an Industrial School for such time as the Court may deem proper for the teaching and training of the child. But he cannot be kept there beyond sixteen unless the Minister for Education, with the consent of the child's parents or guardians, directs that he stays on for a further year for the purpose of completing his education or training.[30]

If the child has been committed under section 58 of the 1908 Act the child's parents or guardians can apply to have the child discharged. Application is first made to the Minister for Education who may either refer the application to the court or may refuse the request. In the latter case the parents or guardians may apply to the court. Juveniles committed to industrial schools may be placed on licence by the manager of the school at any time with the consent of the Minister or without this consent after six months have elapsed following the date of committal. The licence permits the juvenile 'to live with any trustworthy and respectable person named in the licence and willing to receive and take charge of him'.[31] The licence can be revoked if any of the conditions on which it was granted are broken by the offenders.

The Kennedy Report pointed out that the system is rarely used, probably for the following reasons: 'This may in some instances be due to the difficulties which managers experience in contacting . . . suitable persons to accept the child, or it may be due to a reluctance to release a child and suffer a reduction in the capitation fee payable to a school.'[32] Once a child has been released from an industrial school he is still legally under the supervision of the managers of the school until he reaches 18 years of age. The Minister for Education, in consultation with the manager, can extend the supervision period by another three years. The implications of this are as follows:

> Where the managers have granted a Supervision Certificate to any person under their supervision, they may recall such person, if of the opinion that recall is necessary for such person's protection, and such person may be detained in the School for a period not exceeding three months and may, at any time, be again placed out on a Supervision Certificate.[33]

The Kennedy Report stressed that school managers should have a duty to release juveniles as soon as possible and to take a deep and personal interest in each child.

On the subject of dispositions open to justices and of the interpretation of the law relating to juveniles, Mitchell makes some interesting points:

> It might be argued that it is unconstitutional for a District Justice to send a child to an Industrial School for a long period. It is already established law that it is unconstitutional for a District Justice to sentence a young person to two years in St Patrick's Institution. Article 38 (5) of the Constitution requires a non-minor criminal offence to be tried by a Jury. It specifies: Article 38 (5) 'Save in the case of the trial of offences under section 2, section 3 or section 4 of this article no person shall be tried on any criminal charge without a jury.' One of the ways in which a minor or major offence is defined is by reference to the length of sentence. Thus, a sentence of two years in St Patrick's Institution is an indication that the offence is a major one. Hence, it was unconstitutional for a District Justice to sentence an eighteen year old to two years in St Patrick's Institution.
> (See: *The State (Sheerin)* v. *Kennedy* (1966) I.R. 379.)
> It could be that this principle, might also be applied to Industrial Schools. Kenny J. is reported in the Irish Times of the 18th September 1974 to have indicated as much when he was dealing with the case of a boy who had been committed to an Industrial School for five years and eight

months. (See *The State* (a ten year old boy) v. *District Justice McKay*, (The Irish Times) 18th September 1974, and see also on Article 38 (5) generally, In *Re Haughey* (1971), I.R. 217 and *de Burca and Anderson* v. *A.G.* (1976) I.R. 38 (Judgement of Walsh J. at page 66).[34]

These points bring into question the constitutionality of a District Justice sending a young offender to an industrial school (residential home), a reformatory school (special school) or to Loughan House for long periods of time. If found to be unconstitutional, it is possible that a change in sentencing procedure will be necessary or perhaps a change in the law or even a change in the Constitution.

f) *Sending the offender to a reformatory school*
No child under the age of 12 years may be sent to a reformatory/special school. Only those aged 12 to 17 years inclusive may be so sentenced. In the relevant legislation the term 'youthful offender' refers to all those in the 12 to 17 age group, while the term 'young person' refers to those in the 15 to 17 age group.

> Where a youthful offender, who in the opinion of the court before which he is charged is twelve years of age or upwards but less than seventeen years of age, is convicted, whether on indictment or by a petty sessional court, of an offence punishable in the case of an adult with penal servitude or imprisonment, the court may, in addition to or in lieu of sentencing him according to law to any other punishment, order that he be sent to a certified reformatory school. Provided that where the offender is ordered to be sent to a certified reformatory school he shall not in addition be sentenced to imprisonment.
>
> Where such an Order has been made in respect of a youthful offender of the age of fifteen years or upwards, and no certified reformatory school can be found the managers of which are willing to receive him, the Minister for Justice may order the offender to be brought before the court which made the order or any court having the like jurisdiction, and that court may in lieu of the detention order make such order or pass such sentence as the court may determine, so however that the order or sentence shall be such as might have been originally made or passed in respect of the offence.[35]

If the managers of a special school are unwilling to accept a young offender, the situation can become very difficult. It is not unknown for a juvenile to be sentenced to a particular institution only to be refused entry, and no special school is obliged to accept any juvenile who has been sentenced there.[36] The question then arises as to where responsibility for the juvenile's care is vested. If, as has been suggested, the Health Boards were assigned responsibility for the overall care of troubled and troublesome children in Ireland, a wide range of responses to their varying needs could be provided and more emphasis could be laid on community rather than on institutional services. It would then be the duty of the new Health and Social Service Boards to find and supervise a suitable placement for each child.

Under the present system, where young persons are not accepted into the special schools, the following options are available. The young person can be (1) sentenced to a 'place of detention' for a duration not exceeding one month, (2) imprisoned, or (3) detained in St Patrick's Institution for a maximum period of 12 months if he is aged 16 years or more. Each of these options will be discussed in the next chapter. As already noted, a situation can also arise in which the case is repeatedly put back even when the offender has been convicted.

Young persons committed to special schools remain under the supervision of the manager from the expiration of the period of their detention up to the age of 19 years, or for up to an additional two years as the Minister for Education may direct. Those who are being supervised may be brought back to the schools for up to three months if they misbehave.

Those who break rules or abscond from a special school may be again convicted and punished as detailed in sections 71 and 72 of the 1908 Act.

g) *Ordering the offender to be whipped*
It appears that whipping may be a lawful option for a male child (s.4 of the Summary Jurisdiction Act, 1884). However, this punishment may well be unconstitutional and is almost certainly in violation of the European Convention on Human Rights. That part of s.5 (1) of the Summary Jurisdiction Act, 1884, which provided for the whipping of young persons was deleted by the Act of 1908. However, O'Connor refers to numerous statutes which authorise the whipping of males under 16 years of age.[37] **The Working Party recommends**

that the disposition of whipping be abolished from the statute books in Ireland as it was abolished in England when the Criminal Justice Act of 1948 became law.

h) *Ordering the offender to pay a fine, damages or costs*
The maximum fine that can be imposed on a child is £2 and on a young person £10.[38] The maximum payment of damages for all juveniles is £2, while the amount of payment for costs is limited to the amount of the fine. In addition, 'all fees payable or paid by the informant in excess of the amount of costs so ordered to be paid shall be remitted or repaid to him, and the court may also order the fine or any part thereof to be paid to the informant in or towards the payment of his costs'.[39] In ordering a child (or a young person) to pay damages or costs the court does not necessarily have to proceed to a conviction if it is believed that,

. . . although the charge is proved, the offence was in the particular case of so trifling a nature that it is inexpedient to inflict any punishment or any other than a nominal punishment.

(1) The court, without proceeding to conviction may dismiss the information, and, if the court thinks fit, may order the person charged to pay such damages, not exceeding forty shillings, and such costs of the proceeding, or either of them, as the court think reasonable; or

(2) The court upon convicting the person charged may discharge him conditionally on his giving security, with or without sureties, to appear for sentence when called upon, or to be of good behaviour, and either without payment of damages and costs, or subject to the payment of such damages and costs, or either of them, as the court think reasonable.[40]

i) *Ordering the parent or guardian[41] of the offender to pay a fine, damages, or costs*
Section 99 of the 1908 Act states:

Where a child or young person is charged before any court with any offence for the commission of which a fine, damages, or costs may be imposed, and the court is of the opinion that the case would be best met by the imposition of a fine, damages, or costs, whether with or without any other punishment, the court may in any case, and shall if the offender is a child, order that the fine, damages or

99

costs awarded be paid by the parent or guardian of the child or young person instead of by the child or young person, unless the court is satisfied that the parent or guardian cannot be found or that he has not *conduced* to the commission of the offence by neglecting to exercise due care of the child or young person.

Thus, in the case of a child, any fine is automatically imposed on the parent or guardian unless it can be shown that the offence was not aided by parental neglect or else that the parent or guardian is missing. In the case of a young person it is decided by the court whether the payment is made by the parent, the guardian or the young person. Again in such cases the amount of payment is limited and the case can be disposed of without conviction. In certain cases the parent or guardian can appeal against such an order of payment.

In the opinion of the Working Party the system of the imposition of fines, costs and damages should be critically examined. If a family has a very low income the imposition of even a £2 fine could be a cause of hardship and only exacerbate the problem. On the other hand, for a well-off family the imposition of a small fine may be totally ineffective. Thus the present structure of the fine system is regressive. There is also a danger in any criminal justice system of merely imposing a fine on juveniles from the higher income groups, while an offender from a low-income group in the same situation might be put into custodial care. The idea of imposing percentage fines related to the family income deserves consideration.

j) *Ordering the parent or guardian of the offender to give security for his good behaviour*
Section 99 of the 1908 Act shows how the court may order the parent or guardian of the child or young person to give security for his good behaviour:

a) Where a child or young person is charged with an offence, the court may order his parent of guardian to give security for his good behaviour.
b) Where a court of summary jurisdiction thinks that a charge against a child or a young person is proved, the court may make an order on the parent or guardian under this section for the payment of damages or costs or requir-

100

ing him to give security for good behaviour, without proceeding to the conviction of the child or young person.

This security may be required even without a conviction.

k) *Committing the offender to custody in a place of detention provided under this part of this Act*
Section 106 of the Act makes the following provisions:

> Where a child or young person is convicted of an offence punishable, in the case of an adult, with penal servitude or imprisonment, or would, if he were an adult, be liable to be imprisoned in default of payment of any fine, damages, or costs, and the court considers that none of the other methods in which the case may legally be dealt with is suitable, the court may, in lieu of sentencing him to imprisonment or committing him to prison, order that he be committed to custody in a place of detention provided under this Part of the Act and named in the order, not exceeding the term for which he might, but for this Part of this Act, be sentenced to imprisonment or committed to prison, nor in any case exceeding one month.

Places of detention are one of the few options available to young offenders who are not accepted in special schools or elsewhere. Hence a young person who has been refused admission into a special school is likely to end up in a detention centre. It is probable that such young offenders are likely to be particularly in need of special care. Therefore, a short term solution such as one month in a detention centre may actually exacerbate their emotional and material problems. As suggested earlier, if the reconstituted Health and Social Service Boards held the responsibility for the welfare of all juveniles in care, and had a range of facilities available to help these juveniles, such an unfortunate situation might be avoided.

l) *Where the offender is a young person by sentencing him to imprisonment*
No child can be sent to prison, but, in certain circumstances a young person may be sentenced. Details of these circumstances are contained in section 102 of the 1908 Act:

> A young person shall not be sentenced to imprisonment for an offence or committed to prison in default of payment of a fine, damages, or costs, unless the court certifies that

101

the young person is of so unruly a character that he cannot be detained in a place of detention provided under this Part of this Act, or that he is of so depraved a character that he is not a fit person to be so detained.

It can be seen that imprisonment is another of the few options left open for those not accepted in other facilities. The Working Party has the same reservations about committing juveniles to prisons as about committing juveniles to places of detention.

m) *Dealing with the case in any other manner in which it may legally be dealt with 'Providing that nothing in this Section shall be construed as authorising the Court to deal with any case in any manner in which it could not deal with the case apart from this section'*

(Section 107 of 1908 Act). This disposition provides a saver against any omissions in the legislation relating to juvenile offenders in Ireland.

Conclusion

In this chapter the dispositional alternatives available in the present juvenile justice system of Ireland, England and Scotland have been described. Detailed information has been given about the dispositions available under the Children Act of 1908 which is still in force, but only general comments and suggestions have been made about these provisions. This is because many specific recommendations are being made elsewhere in this report, in which context section 107 of the 1908 Act will decrease in legal and practical significance. It is clear, however, that even within the provisions of this outdated legislation many more imaginative steps could be taken at present in disposing of young offenders in the Children's Court.

The Working Party recommends that, pending the introduction of new legislation, more extensive use should be made than is at present the custom of the available dispositional alternatives applying to the juvenile offender in Ireland. It is also recommended that the existing Area Health Boards be reconstituted as Health and Social Service Boards with full responsibility for the protection and care of troubled and troublesome young people.

V. Residential Care in Ireland*

As noted in the preceding chapter, the dispositional alternatives presently available in Ireland include the option of committing the juvenile offender to residential care. This chapter focuses primarily on the structure and quality of residential care and its relevance to the formulation of policy in the field of child care as a whole. Throughout the chapter the findings of studies from Ireland and abroad are drawn on and the areas in which further research is required are indicated. Some statistics concerning Irish children in care are presented and analysed. Recommendations are made for improvements in the services, particularly in relation to the numbers of staff in residential child care units and in the working conditions and training opportunities available to the personnel responsible for the care of the young offenders in these institutions.

The discussion is primarily concerned with the residential facilities available to juvenile offenders, because the wider area of children and young persons admitted to care on a voluntary basis, or through the provisions of the Health Acts,[1] was outside the brief of the Working Party.

The objectives of residential care

While the desirability of treating children where possible within the family or local community has been emphasised in earlier chapters, it is clear that residential care services have a legitimate and valuable family-building and family-supportive role to play in the overall structure of the child care services. This form of care will often need to be provided only on a short-term basis because the young people concerned will usually have homes of their own to which they will soon return. The service ideally should be provided as a *service of choice* selected in the best interests of the children and families concerned and not merely as a service of last resort. The units providing such a service should be small in size, with suitably selected and appropriately trained staff, undertaking a clearly defined, socially recognised and adequately remunerated task.

Moss has described the aims and objectives and the essential qualities of residential child care services as follows:

*Editors: Mary Horkan and Valerie Richardson. Research. Maeve McMahon, Mary Harding, Judith Latch and other members of the Working Party.

Residential institutions are means, at least in theory, to meet the objectives that families are judged to be inadequate to attain. Their greatest value is the facility they provide for children ... to be removed from a diverse range of environments (normally family homes), and be placed and contained full-time in an environment which can be organised to exclude certain influences and introduce others so as to hopefully pursue certain goals effectively. The essence then of residential care is its potential for full-time control, and hence for containment and influence.

The essential qualities of residential care, control, containment and influence have been applied to the achievement of numerous ends.[2]

Moss recognises the potential of residential care for the performance of both positive and negative roles in achieving a variety of aims. These aims include: compensation for deprivation, the acquisition of special roles or skills, deterrence or punishment, and protection of the community from 'harmful' influences. The emphasis placed on these aims tends to vary with fashions in child care, with the social and psychological understanding of need and with the values of a particular community.

Current residential provision in the Republic of Ireland
Any discussion of residential child care in Ireland is complicated by the complex administrative arrangements that govern the provision of such care. At present the three government departments of Health, Education and Justice as well as religious orders and voluntary organisations are actively involved in this field. Thus, in one institution the Department of Education may be the body in whom statutory responsibility is vested, while a religious order may have responsibility for the actual day-by-day administration of the establishment. In addition some of the social workers assigned to the institution may be employed by the Department of Health and others by the Department of Justice. Add to this the fact that the young people in the institution may have been committed there by the courts or may have been placed in residential care by the health authorities or may have come voluntarily (i.e. by arrangements with parents or guardians), and the picture becomes even more complicated.

The CARE Memorandum commenting on the overall structure of administration and control of the children's services stated:

> It is a complex picture with no rationale. Three government departments have responsibility in this area and many other authorities, and a great deal of the initiative rests with voluntary bodies including religious orders. There is no means of formulating a coherent comprehensive policy at the top; there is no means of coordinating services at the bottom.[3]

Although there is much overlap between the relevant government departments the role of each can still be defined to some extent. The Department of Health is at present concerned mainly with preventive services and with certain categories of children in care. The Department of Education is concerned with school attendance and reformatory and industrial schools, while the Department of Justice is responsible for probation and for juveniles under detention.

The Department of Health, under the Health Acts and Children Acts, can place children and young people in care

Table 5.1

Type of Care Provided for Children Coming Under Supervision/Care of Health Boards in 1978 as a Percentage of Children Coming into Care/Supervision in Each Health Board

Health Board	Residential Care		Boarded-out		Supervision 'At nurse'*		Total
	No.	%	No.	%	No.	%	No.
Eastern	447	60	100	14	192	26	739
Midland	36	32	74	66	2	2	112
Mid-Western	44	55	31	39	5	6	80
North-Eastern	36	66	17	31	1	3	54
North-Western	52	88	7	12	—	—	59
South-Eastern	41	36	68	61	3	3	112
Southern	80	46	92	53	1	1	173
Western	9	10	83	89	1	1	93
Total	745	52	472	33	205	15	1422

Source: Children Coming into Care, op.cit.. Table 5.

*This term refers to children placed privately for monetary reward but supervised by Health Boards under Boarding Out of Children Regulations, 1952.

(a) by placing them with foster parents, (b) by sending them to children's homes, special schools, and residential homes and (c) by placing them in employment.

The Department of Health has recently carried out a limited analysis of all children admitted to care within their responsibility during 1978. (see Table 5.1).

The reasons for which these children came into care, as set out in the Department of Health Report, are of considerable interest (see Table 5.2)

Table 5.2

Reasons for Supervision/Admission to Care of Children in 1978 by Subsequent Form of Care Provided by the Health Board

Note: 192 returns for children 'at nurse' in the E.H.B. did not give reasons.

Reasons	Reasons for Children subsequently fostered	Reasons for Children subsequently placed in residential care	Reasons for Children subsequently 'at nurse' (see note above)
No parent/guardian	11	—	—
Abandoned/deserted	25	20	—
Short-term illness of parent/guardian	80	136	1
Long-term illness of parent/guardian	21	60	—
Mother deserted, father unable to care	30	56	1
Unmarried mother, unable to care	236	103	2
Mother dead, father unable to care	3	32	—
Parent/guardian in prison/custody	3	17	—
No family home	10	35	—
Travelling family	9	30	—
Non-accidental injury to child	6	9	—
Unsatisfactory home conditions	26	97	—
Other reasons	49	41	—
Total	509	636	4

Total 1,149

Source: Children Coming into Care, op.cit., Table 4 J.

The published Department of Health statistics for children coming into care in 1978 do not refer to the total number of children in care during 1978, nor to those who may have been admitted prior to 1978. Table 5.3, however, gives comparative figures of the total number of children either boarded out or in residential care on 30 September 1978.

Table 5.3

Total Number of Children in Care as a Responsibility of the Department of Health on 30th September 1978 Irrespective of Date of Admission

Health Board	Number of Children in Residential Homes as at 30.9.78	Number of Children Boarded-out as at 30.9.78
Eastern	423	197
Southern	103	88
Midland	46	82
Western	34	156
North-Western	40	80
Mid-Western	46	122
South-Eastern	158*	158*
North-Eastern	58	73
Total	908	956

*estimated

Source: Welfare Section, Dept. of Health (personal communication).

In Ireland little research has been undertaken on residential care.[4] Thus, little information is available on such basic facts as the types of children coming into care, the quality, style and effectiveness of different forms of care, the links with the community while in care and the follow-up services after discharge. In undertaking research on these aspects of the child care services it would be very helpful if standardised statistical data were available on all children in care throughout the country, irrespective of which government department holds responsibility for their welfare. Comprehensive information on a child's background and social circumstances is essential to accurately assess his or her needs. Such information is also necessary for planning a comprehensive scheme of services for all children at risk, since children who get into trouble with the law will often have needs very similar to those of other groups of children in society.

Assessment

A justice may refer a young offender for assessment before deciding to commit him to residential care in a residential home, special school, hostel, or institution run by the Department of Justice. This assessment will be carried out in St Michael's, Finglas, an assessment unit which was opened in 1973 with modern facilities for the care of up to 24 boys. Unfortunately, there is as yet no equivalent facility for the assessment of girls.

The purpose of the assessment carried out in St Michael's has been described as follows:

(a) to endeavour to establish why the child is malfunctioning as an individual, as a member of a family and as a member of society;

(b) to discover his strengths as well as his weaknesses;

(c) to investigate his self-image, his attitude towards self and others, his method of dealing with stress, his fears and hopes, his vocational aptitudes and interests and the compatibility of his personality with his vocational interests;

(d) to suggest the most appropriate programme for his individual needs.[5]

This assessment is carried out over approximately three weeks by the staff which consists of social worker, housefather and housemother, matron, domestic staff, housemasters, probation and welfare officer of the Department of Justice and other specialists including a medical doctor, psychiatrists and psychologists. This team brings attention to bear not only on the boy's personality but also on to his physical state, his social situation and any other relevant factors. The boy's family is encouraged to visit and may also receive counselling help. After assessment, when the boy appears in court again, the District Justice is provided with a report giving the full results of the assessment and outlining the type of care he seems to require.

Unfortunately, assessment and subsequent placement is not a simple procedure because supply and demand are not always in harmony. Frequently a placement in a small group home may not in reality be available. This means that in the case of a boy who has been fully assessed, the origins and present nature of his problems explained, and a detailed programme of residential treatment suitable to his needs set out, there may be no alternative, ultimately, but a return to the original environment or an assignment to a less than optimal placement. Hoghughi has pinpointed this problem of disparity between the ideal and the actual availability of suitable facilities in the United Kingdom:

> . . . assessment of extreme children is not necessarily the most useful, valid and reliable guide to rational social policy making and the allocation of resources for them. . . . Any comparison of the treatment requirements of children and the treatment resources *actually* available would provide a much more rational guide to action than armchair deliberations and political and ideological pressures which usually determine resource allocation.[6]

The Working Party recommends that detailed assessments should be carried out on all children before a decision is made for their future care. The assessment should be based on the child's long term needs and total circumstances and not only confined to his presenting behaviour or immediate needs.

The importance of social assessments in helping the District Justice to reach a decision about disposal was highlighted in July 1979 in the High Court in the case of *The State* (at the Prosecution of Michael Donohue) v. *District Justice Eileen Kennedy,* when Finlay J. stated in his judgment that:

> . . . the reports themselves are intensely valuable to the District Justice in her task of considering the appropriate sentence. They contain a considerable summary of the background and history of the prosecutor and indeed are compassionate and thoughtful recommendations towards the possibility of his future rehabilitation.[7]

In this case the District Justice had made an order for the remand of a 15 year old boy, Michael Donohue, in custody in Mountjoy Prison on the grounds of a report from St Lawrence's School, Finglas, which gave details of persistent absconding from the school and stated that it was not possible to detain the boy there. The order of the District Justice was challenged on the grounds that she 'had reached her decision having considered reports which were not made available to the defendant and which were not deposed to on oath by the persons making them'.[8] The President of the High Court held that the information contained in such reports should be treated in the same way as other evidence and as such should be sworn evidence properly admissible on which the solicitor for the defendant has the opportunity to cross-examine the witnesses. The procedure that should be followed in cases relating to young offenders is that:

> ... a District Justice should be in a position having received an appropriate report from the social workers and other persons concerned at the remand centre to obtain as a matter of practicality the consent of the solicitor representing a young offender to the reading of those reports, making them available to the Solicitor and hearing any submissions or comments he should make upon them.[9]

Special schools

Industrial schools as designated under the 1908 Children Act are now more generally known as residential homes, while reformatory schools are classified as special schools because of the stigma which had become attached to the terms *industrial* and *reformatory*. As far back as 1936 the Cussen Commission[10] had recommended that these names be abandoned. Subsequent publications like the Kennedy Report and the CARE Memorandum had also made this recommendation, although the extent to which the change in terminology affects the degree of stigma is a matter of conjecture.

At present a total of five special schools exist in Ireland, four for boys and one for girls. The Department of Education holds overall responsibility for the administration of four of these schools; Scoil Ard Mhuire, Lusk, Dublin; St Lawrence's, Finglas, Dublin; and St Joseph's, Clonmel for boys and the special school for girls, St Anne's, Kilmacud, Dublin. On 30 June 1979 there were 203 children resident in these special schools.[11] The fifth special school for boys is Loughan House, Co. Cavan, which is administered by The Department of Justice.

Scoil Ard Mhuire, Lusk

Scoil Ard Mhuire is at Lusk in North County Dublin and is

run by the Oblate Order for the Department of Education. The Director is an Oblate Father and the teaching and care staff include both religious and lay persons. Officially the school can cater for up to 65 boys in the 12 to 17 age group who have various delinquency and behavioural problems. However, the school usually aims at the 13 to 15 age group because it is felt that the boys who are past the school-leaving age do not, as a rule, benefit from the school programme. Young offenders sent to the school under the terms of the 1908 Act must stay for at least two years. Most of those in Lusk are committed by the courts, but they may also be admitted under the Health Acts or be transferred by order of the Minister for Education from a junior special school or a residential home.

In Lusk it is considered essential that those admitted have been fully assessed, either in Finglas or at a Child Guidance Clinic attached to the Health Boards. The fact that a youngster is recommended for Lusk does not necessarily mean that he will be accepted, as each case is individually considered and a visit by the boy and his parents to the school is a prerequisite to final acceptance. It is considered very important to have the families involved as much as possible even though it may not have been their original choice to have the youngster go to Lusk. The aim of the school is to rehabilitate boys in a therapeutic situation through the development of good relationships with the staff. The school is divided into four separate units, each with living accommodation, and there is also a dining area, classrooms, workshops, a sports hall and a swimming pool. A residential, recreational and educational programme is provided for each boy. The administrative block has facilities for visiting psychiatrists, psychologists, social workers, medical personnel and other specialists, as well as facilities for visiting families. Little published information is available about Lusk beyond official figures which give the number of boys there and whether they were committed or came in under the Health Acts.

Although the facilities in Lusk are good, a problem of exceptionally high turnover of staff (apart from religious members) was brought to the notice of the Working Party. With new members of staff constantly being appointed, others leaving and others coming and going from full-time courses and placements, there appears to be a constant movement of personnel. Such frequent changes in staff must have an unsettling effect on the boys and on the programme in the school.

St Lawrence's Special School in Finglas, situated beside St Michael's Assessment Centre, has been in operation since 14 January 1972. This school is run by the De la Salle Order for the Department of Education and, as in Lusk, both religious and lay people are involved as teaching and as care staff. The latest official figures available for Finglas are those of 30 June 1978. At that time there were 59 boys in the school, 47 having been committed through the courts and the remainder under the Health Acts.[12] Unlike Lusk, to which a young offender may not sentenced for less than two years, a child is usually not referred to Finglas for more than one year. As in Lusk, there is an emphasis on involving the family in assessment prior to admission and in rehabilitation in a controlled residential setting. Likewise there is a wide range of facilities with well-planned educational, recreational and other programmes developed with the particular needs of the young offenders in mind. Thus, it is considered important to teach not only academic subjects but also those related to everyday needs such as letter-writing and how to apply for a job. Efforts are made to enable each boy to achieve self respect by giving him tasks he is able to carry out — leisure activities such as sports or educational assignments designed for his stage of development. In Finglas there is a housemaster/mistress system with groups of eight boys. Care staff meet the parents and are involved with specialists who work with the children. Housemasters and mistresses are selected if they show themselves to be well-integrated people with previous experience of working with children and an interest in the work. They also follow a specialised course in child care.

It must be stressed that there is a real dearth of empirical research in this area, but, from discussion with members of the staff and various social workers involved in St Lawrence's, the following problems have emerged. The first of these is the fact that many of the boys admitted to St Lawrence's need residential care for more than a year but such facilities are not always available. Therefore at the end of the year's placement these boys must be returned, sometimes prematurely, to their original home environment. This means that their needs are not fully met because of the one year time limit imposed on admissions to St Lawrence's. The boys, both while resident in and on leaving St Lawrence's, have educational problems which could sometimes be avoided. For example, where some boys are leaving St Lawrence's after the commencement of the school year it has been found that the authorities of post-primary schools, although sympathetic, are unwilling to accept new pupils at this late date. Another problem is that certain boys find the transition from remedial teaching to an ordinary classroom difficult. Boys who are older than usual school age may still be studying for the Group Certificate in St Lawrence's, but a boy in this situation might find it awkward and difficult to return to a post-primary school. If St Lawrence's could keep these boys for as long as is considered necessary, either full-time or even only during normal school hours, problems such as these might be avoided.

St Joseph's Clonmel

St Joseph's is run by the Rosminian Order for the Department of Education. As in the other schools the teaching and care staff include both religious and lay persons. A notable feature of the lay staff is that they mainly come from local areas with the result that many informal and friendly links have been built up between the school and those living nearby.

Thus the school receives much support through relationships between local people and the children, through fund raising by groups in Clonmel and surrounding districts and through practical help such as painting and decorating. The Interim Report of the Task Force said of the management and staff of St Joseph's: '. . .we were greatly impressed with their concern, commitment and skill in providing residential care'.[13]

The school provides residential care on a medium or long-term basis. Boys must be under 12 years of age on referral, and there usually is a long waiting list. The Task Force suggested that St Joseph's specifically '. . . should provide residential care for boys who need care or control additional to that provided by their families, and whose deprivation is further characterised by serious emotional retardation'.[14] The Task Force went on to distinguish this group of children from those in need of substitute family care who needed placement in a smaller more personal setting than that provided by St Joseph's.

At the moment the Department of Education is redeveloping Clonmel, and new buildings are being put up because the

113

existing buildings were considered to be inadequate. On 30 June 1978 there were 76 boys in Clonmel, 60 having come through the courts and the remainder having been admitted under the Health Acts. The new complex will consist of smaller units each of which will provide accommodation for approximately 20 boys. As in the other schools the policy is that the families should be involved as much as possible and that the boys should go home for some week-ends and holidays or that family members should visit them in the school. A probation officer from the Department of Justice is based in the school and works with the children and their families, assisted by a social worker in the child's home area. These two workers maintain regular contact with each other for the planning and implementation of a suitable treatment programme for the children. The Task Force stated that those admitted to the school should come from an area near enough to the school so that their parents could visit them and return home on the same day.

As well as identifying problems such as the physical structure of the school and the mixing of boys in need of residential care with those in need of substitute family care, the Task Force also proposed that the new school should accommodate a total of 60 boys as opposed to a total of 100 boys as suggested by the Department of Education. (All members of the Task Force agreed on this proposal, with the exception of the representative from the Department of Education.) The Task Force felt that a residential school providing accommodation for 100 children could lead to detrimental effects of institutionalisation, unlike a school with a smaller number of boys.

St Anne's, Kilmacud
St Anne's Kilmacud, Dublin, is the only special school available for girls committed through the courts for residential care. It is run by the Sisters of Our Lady of Charity and administered by the Department of Education. On 30 June 1978 there were a total of ten children in the school: of whom three were committed by the Court, three were voluntary admissions and four were admitted under the Health Act.

The school is run as an open establishment which also admits girls who are in need of care and protection, slow learners and backward girls referred by the Health Boards. There is no distinction made between the girls according to their mode of referral. The school provides educational and

114

recreational facilities and most of the girls attend the local national schools. Help is given to find employment where appropriate. There is no one social worker assigned to the school. For those girls committed through the courts the social work service is provided on an individual basis by the probation and welfare officer of the Department of Justice who was assigned to the girl when she was placed on supervision.

The Task Force's recommendations on residential facilities for girls included: a hostel for severely disturbed girls in the 14 to 18 age range; a special school for the 12 to 16 age range in the Dublin area to accommodate approximately 25 girls, and a residential assessment centre for 10 girls to be provided in Dublin.[15] Five years later these facilities have not yet been provided.

Hostels for young offenders
The last decade has seen the introduction of hostel facilities for some ex-prisoners, both juvenile and adult, and for those on probation. (See Appendix C for further details on hostels.) The Task Force, in its Interim Report, identified the need for and the role of hostel accommodation, particularly for boys of no fixed abode:

> Most of these boys stay periodically in their family homes, combining this with periods of sleeping in adult hostels, or, as is often the case, sleeping rough. Some of them, however, retain no contact with their families, even on a periodic basis. Many of them have undergone great personal stress and deprivation. Some have been in trouble with the law. Because of their age, the best form of residential provision for them would be of the hostel type, in which the staff would aim to provide guidance, therapeutic relationships, education or employment suited to their age.[16]

The Task Force went on to identify a specific group of severely disturbed boys in need of hostel accommodation and also the need for additional hostel facilities for girls. These hostels would cater for offenders and non-offenders and respond to their needs in general rather than focusing on delinquent behaviour. Some of the existing hostels already have such a policy and, in fact, some of the residents using the facilities may never have been labelled delinquent.[17]

115

Institutions Run by the Department of Justice to which young offenders can be sent

Juvenile offenders may be sent to prison and places of detention run by the Department of Justice. These are:

(1) Mountjoy—for male and female prisoners at North Circular Road, Dublin 7.

(2) Limerick—for male and female prisoners at Mulgrave Street, Limerick.

(3) Cork—for male prisoners at Rathmore Road, Cork.

(4) Shanganagh Castle—an open centre for the detention of male offenders between 16 and 21 years of age, at Shankill, Co. Dublin.

(5) St Patrick's Institution—a place for detention, adjacent to Mountjoy, for male offenders between 16 and 21 years.

(6) Loughan House—a closed institution for 12 to 16 year old offenders at Blacklion, Co. Cavan.

Mountjoy, Limerick and Cork

A young person (i.e. aged between 15 and 17 years) may in certain circumstances be sent to prison in Mountjoy, Limerick or Cork. Table 5.4 gives figures for those young people who have been imprisoned from 1971. The table shows that a considerable number of juveniles have been imprisoned yearly despite the fact that the number detained has been almost halved. These young people experience the same regime as the older prisoners, a situation which has given rise to a number of complaints. For example, the CARE Memorandum commented: 'The heterogeneous population in unspecialised institutions at present makes the objective of individual rehabilitation meaningless.'[18]

116

Table 5.4

The Numbers of Juveniles detained in Irish Prisons 1971-1978

Year	15 and under 17		17 and under 18		Total male & female
	male	female	male	female	
1971	49	12	57	24	142
1972	53	25	76	18	172
1973	16	8	67	20	111
1974	25	8	36	15	84
1975	8	5	43	17	73
1976	15	11	53	12	91
1977	25	4	46	19	94
1978	20	5	47	6	78

Source: Figures taken from the Department of Justice Annual Reports on prisons and places of detention. The statistics exclude those 'committed in default of sureties, contempt of court and debtor cases'.

At the moment no information on the background of juveniles committed to adult prisons or on departmental policy towards them is available. In May 1978 Dr. Noel Browne tabled a Parliamentary Question to the Minister for Justice concerning

the number of boys and girls under 16 who have been certified unruly and depraved and incarcerated in an adult prison for each year since 1966 inclusive: their distribution in each of the State's adult prisons for each year since 1966, and the average period of incarceration of (a) boys, and (b) girls for each year since 1966.

In reply the Minister for Justice stated that:

The information required to enable me to give a full reply to this question is not available and its compilation would involve extensive research which cannot be undertaken at present owing to pressure of work.

In all cases where a boy or girl between 15 and 17 years of age is committed to prison, the warrant from the Court must include a certificate that the boy or girl is of so unruly a character that he/she cannot be detained in a place of detention or a certificate that he/she is so depraved in character that he/she is not a fit person to be so detained. A total of 377 boys and 119 girls in this age group were so committed to prison between 1966 and 1977. Of the total committed it is estimated that approximately half were between 15 and 16 years of age. In the vast majority of cases, the sentence imposed was 1 month.[19]

Because of this depressing lack of information, there is little specific detail the Working Party can give regarding juveniles in adult prisons, but some important issues need to be examined concerning those juveniles. Firstly, it must be asked by what criteria a certificate can be issued which states that 'the boy or girl is of so unruly a character that he/she cannot be detained in a place of detention or is of so depraved a character that he/she is not a fit person to be so detained'. It would appear that juveniles are often imprisoned because of lack of other suitable facilities. Imprisoning a teenager for up to one month is only a very short-term remedy for a young person who may be in need of long-term care and support.

Secondly, the suitability of the prison setting for meeting the needs of a young person must be questioned. The three prisons—Mountjoy, Limerick and Cork—are enclosed institutions with highly structured routines. Young people spending a month or less in these institutions clearly do not have enough time to benefit from any educational or training courses that might be offered and the purpose of their incarceration would appear to be principally for punishment. We would suggest that imprisoning the young offender for a month has none of the advantages of placing him in care, especially where the young person's education is concerned. Indeed, prison routine can be damaging even for adults. Consider, for example, the humiliation of entering Mountjoy, where the prisoner 'is taken to the reception room through which there is a regular flow of prison officers and prisoners. He is searched by an officer and told to turn out his pockets. A list is taken of his personal belongings including his clothes. Personal items are confiscated for the duration of the sentence, the prisoner signing the record book as his only receipt'.[20] Goffman describes the disturbing effects of this kind of relatively simple routine on the individual:

> The process of entrance typically brings other kinds of loss and mortification as well. We generally find staff employing what are called admission procedures such as taking a life history, photographing, weighing, fingerprinting, assigning numbers, searching, listing personal possessions for storage, undressing, bathing, disinfecting, haircutting, issuing institutional clothing, instructing as

118

to rules and assigning to quarters. Admission procedures might be better called 'trimming' or 'programming', because in thus being squared away the new arrival allows himself to be shaped and coded into an object that can be fed into the administrative machinery of the establishment, to be worked on smoothly by routine operations.[21]

If the admission procedure can be described in terms of loss, mortification and ignoring of self-identity, then the effects of even a month in prison may be very damaging indeed. Goffman explains that the requirements of an institutional regime restrict a person's freedom for self-direction and limit and curtail his opportunities for making personally-efficient choices. Vivid subjective examples of the processes described by Goffman are given in Brendan Behan's *Borstal Boy*, Jimmy Boyle's *A Sense of Freedom* and Frank Norman's *Banana Boy*.[22]

The third issue we would like to raise here is that of the fate of the young person on leaving prison. The prisons are staffed by probation officers from the Department of Justice, but there is no responsibility on the Department to assist ex-prisoners with accommodation, employment and other needs. Even when these probation officers have the interest and time to follow-up on cases, it is very difficult to ensure that the basic necessities of life are provided for ex-prisoners. It would appear that the juvenile who has been imprisoned will sometimes suffer the effects of this imprisonment for very much longer than a month.

It is recommended therefore by the Working Party that, when a young offender is discharged from residential care, there should be adequate follow-up services to provide continued support for himself and his family to facilitate reintegration into the community.

St Patrick's Institution

The majority of offenders aged between 16 and 17 years old who are referred to residential or custodial care will be committed to St Patrick's Institution. Only since 1975 have statistics on the ages of those committed to the institution become available. For these years the prisoners under 18 years of age constituted approximately half of the resident population of St. Patrick's (see Table 5.5).

119

Table 5.5
Juveniles Committed to St Patrick's

Year	Under 17 years	17 years and under 18 years	Total Population under 18
1975	179	178	357
1976	153	136	289
1977	170	168	338
1978	144	163	307

Source: Department of Justice; Annual Reports on Prisons, 1975-1978.

St Patrick's is a place of detention and is built to the same design as Mountjoy Prison, although on a smaller scale. Mountjoy itself was modelled on Pentonville Prison with 'four wings converging on a control centre . . . Each wing has three landings, lined on both sides by rows of single cells. The structure of the prison was designed to effect the maximum segregation between prisoners and to prevent them from communicating with each other.'[23] Both institutions were built during the famine years and now are architecturally outdated, and outmoded in organisation and administration. Prison officers still work inder the 1947 prison rules which include the following: (i) An officer shall not allow any familiarity on the part of a prisoner towards himself or any other officer, or servant of the prison . . . (ii) An officer shall not speak to a prisoner unnecessarily . . .[24]

St Patrick's has a capacity of 224 offenders in single cell occupancy. In 1978 the daily average was of 199 offenders. There is a certain amount of segregation in accommodation with long-term prisoners located on a separate landing. Offenders eat their meals alone in their cells. There is less than half an acre of grass in the grounds of St Parrick's and the effect of stone walls, cells, the locking and unlocking of doors and gates and the very limited contact with the outside world makes a depressing situation for young people committed there. The Visiting Committee reported various problems in St Patrick's in 1978.

> *INMATES* . . . It is extremely difficult to achieve a continuously peaceful atmosphere when dealing with a large number of inmates . . . *INDOOR RECREATION* was catered for in the main recreation hall with temporary use

120

of D Block as back up. The standard of comfort and facilities in this latter area left a lot to be desired . . .

BUILDINGS . . . St Patrick's urgently required the use of additional workshops which were awaiting replastering and restoration for an inordinate period of time and if available would have greatly assisted in the further training and useful employment of many more boys . . . Although we referred in last year's report to the Department's approval and consent to cover stone floors with vinyl tiles we must record our disappointment that this work has not yet commenced and the primitive conditions of these floors still prevail . . .

EDUCATION . . . It was a matter of very great concern to the Administration and Visiting Committee that the school was still closed during Summer months. We have repeatedly appealed to the Authorities to resolve the lamentable difficulty in regard to holiday teacher recruitment which denied the essential service of the school to the inmates for almost three months in the year, to the clear detriment of the boys and the institution . . .

EMPLOYMENT . . .The problem of placing a boy in suitable employment was very perplexing and continuously occupied the time of Welfare Staff. Committee members also made every effort to secure employment, but unfortunately success rate was not high. Daily release was invariably sympathetically considered to enable a boy to take up a job. Unquestionably the greatest obstacle to successful rehabilitation is the failure of an inmate to secure early employment. Frequently he can quickly find himself in trouble again.[25]

This report of the St Patrick's Visiting Committee highlights a number of problems besetting the staff and boys in St Patrick's. A full year education programme has since been instituted but there is a need for training in social and practical skills that would increase the boys' chances of employment on release. Particularly for those committed for any length of time, courses such as those provided by AnCO would be very helpful. As in the adult prisons, other less tangible effects of imprisonment must also be considered in St Patrick's — the effect, for example, on a young person's self-image and self-confidence of being incarcerated in prison for several months, the effectiveness of such a policy in preventing further delinquent behaviour and the effects of a prison sentence on relationships with family and friends.

As mentioned in Chapter IV, an intensive supervision scheme, providing boys with early release from St Patrick's under the close supervision of the probation service, was initiated in 1979. Not all boys in St Patrick's are selected for this scheme nor do all those selected accept the offer of intensive supervision in the community.[26] **The Working Party recommends that the Department of Justice should undertake or commission a research project that would compare the boys undergoing the intensive supervision programme with those that do not, and follow up these boys some years later to ascertain which group fared better after discharge.** A comparison of the financial costs of keeping a boy in St Patrick's or keeping him on the intensive supervision programme would also be of considerable interest.

Shanganagh Castle

Shanganagh Castle is an open prison for the detention of male offenders from 16 to 21 years of age. It has a capacity of 50 youths and in 1978 the daily average was 40. The offenders are transferred from St Patrick's and in Shanganagh 'attempts are made to resocialise offenders in a relaxed and relatively homely atmosphere.[27] Unfortunately there is no information available concerning the background of the offenders in Shanganagh nor, as far as the Working Party could ascertain, is there any assessment of the success of Shanganagh in its rehabilitation aims. Even such basic information as the age distribution of the young people resident there is not presently available to the public.

Shanganagh castle is unique in that it is the only institution run by the Department of Justice which attempts to rehabilitate young offenders in an open setting. The property was purchased by the Department in August 1968 following repeated complaints by the St Patrick's Visiting Committee concerning the bleak and overcrowded conditions in that institution, as described by the Kennedy Report: St Patrick's is an old style penitentiary building with rows of cells, iron gates and iron spiral staircases. Offenders, in the main, occupy single cells. These are small and gloomy and each one has a small window almost at ceiling level'.[28] Shanganagh Castle makes a pleasant contrast. The building used to function as a Church of Ireland teacher-training college for girls. It stands on 21 acres, and considerable work has been done by the youths resident there in reclaiming the land and helping with reconstruction. The Department of Justice Annual Report of 1978 described the participation of the young offenders in the running of the institution as follows: 'The work/training programme included assisting trades staff in the maintenance of the Castle and grounds, assisting in the planting and maintenance of the vegetable and flower gardens and assisting in the large greenhouse where tomatoes and flower plants are grown.'[29] The goal of a period of residence for young offenders in Shanganagh Castle is rehabilitation as conceptualised in the regulations governing its administration:

(i) Offenders shall, insofar as the period of their detention permits, be given such training and treatment as will encourage and assist them to lead law-abiding and self-supporting lives.

(ii) Any restriction imposed on the offenders shall be kept to the minimum required for well-ordered community life.

(iii) In controlling offenders, officers shall seek to influence them by example and leadership and to enlist their willing cooperation.

(iv) At all times the training and treatment of offenders shall be such as to encourage in them self-respect and a sense of personal responsibility.[30]

The rehabilitation purpose is reflected in a higher staff/offender ratio than in closed institutions and in a more flexible, more varied and comparatively unrestricted regime:

Restrictions on offenders transferred to Shanganagh are not much more than apply at residential schools. Movement about the house and grounds is almost unlimited . . . sleeping accommodation is in unlocked dormitory cubicles. The boys wear a casual outfit. Incoming and outgoing mail is not examined. There is no unreasonable limitation on visits and they are unsupervised.[31]

The prison officers in Shanganagh do not wear a uniform and they operate a housemaster system. There is a programme whereby the youths are graded and good behaviour is rewarded by additional trips and entertainment. All offenders spend a

123

compulsory half of each day at the education unit and the other half of the day on the work/training programme. Concerning recreation the 1978 Report states:

> Outdoor recreation included monthly educational tours, mountain climbing, pitch and putt and basketball. Regular trips were made to an outdoor swimming pool in the Summer and an indoor pool during the Winter. The indoor activities which included weekly film shows during Winter months, snooker, table tennis, quiz competitions and television were fully availed of in the course of the year. Annual Sports Competitions were held for both outdoor and indoor activities and trophies were awarded to those who were successful.[32]

Week-end release to families is often permitted, and in 1978 a total of 79 full temporary releases were granted, 'generally to employment'.[33] Details are not available on the specific criteria used in deciding which youths should and which should not be transferred to Shanganagh from St Patrick's. However, the 1972 Prisons Report states: 'The open centre at Shanganagh is designed to provide a suitable environment for boys who are not in need of the closer custodial situation which obtains in St Patrick's and who are deemed likely to respond to training in an open setting.[34]

The decision as to which prisoners fall within this category is taken by the Governor, the prison officers and the probation officers of St Patrick's and Shanganagh. All offenders transferred to Shanganagh are interviewed by the Governor and by the Principal Officer (Offenders Division) of the Department of Justice. The Prison Study Group interpreted this system as follows: 'This means that the best behaved inmates in St. Patrick's have the best chance of being transferred. They are judged suitable for an institution "based on trust" by their performance in an institution based on authority.'[35]

Loughan House
Loughan House was built originally by the White Fathers early in the 1950s as a novitiate. It is a large modern institution on 45 acres and is situated two miles from Blacklion in County Cavan. When the building came up for sale in the early 1970s it was purchased by the Minister for Justice and in 1972 was established as an open centre for 16 to 21 year old boys with regulations similar to those at Shanganagh Castle. The Annual

Report of the Visiting Committee[36] to Loughan House for the year ending 31 December 1977 stated that two members of the Committee had

> ... attended a meeting with an official of the Department and were given details of the proposed change-over of Loughan House to a closed centre for offenders in the 12 to 16 year old age group and gave details of the proposed changes to the other members at the December meeting. The members put it on record that whilst recognising the need for a centre to cater for this age group they were most unhappy that Loughan House should have been chosen. They felt that in the five years of its existence as an open centre it had made a big contribution towards the rehabilitation of the boys who had passed through it.[37]

Shortly afterwards Loughan House was closed until 1978 when it reopened as a secure institution. In January 1978 the Minister for Justice issued the following statement containing proposals for the future structure of Loughan House:

> For the next two or three years and purely as a temporary arrangement until the Department of Education has provided adequate accommodation for boys who need residential placement, the Department of Justice will make Loughan House, Blacklion, Co. Cavan available to accommodate boys between the ages of 12 and 16 years, who because of their behavioural problems are not currently acceptable in the existing special schools . . . Loughan House is a particularly fine modern building. Standards of furnishing, equipment, decoration and repair have been maintained at an extremely high level. It is scenically situated on over 40 acres of landscaped grounds. It has 46 furnished and centrally heated and spacious study-bedrooms, with hot and cold water installed in every room. They are designed for single occupancy but the rooms are sufficiently spacious to enable them to be used on a basis of multiple occupancy, if this is considered to be in the best interests of the boys. Apart from a chapel, dining-room, gymnasium and an equipped cinema/theatre, the building has games rooms and a range of classrooms. The grounds provide football pitches, a volley-ball court, a full scale pitch and putt course, and there are facilities for swimming, boating and fishing on the lake.

Because a propensity to abscond is one of the more recurring factors to be expected from the boys concerned and is indeed one of the more important considerations which contributed to their not being acceptable in the existing special schools, provision will need to be made for a closed perimeter. This perimeter will, however, leave extensive grounds readily accessible to the boys in residence and moreover it is being laid out in a way that will not interrupt the open prospect of the surrounding environment. The element of closure envisaged is the minimum necessary to ensure that the residential placement decided by the Courts can be effected and availed of to enable the boys to benefit from a programme of personal development and resocialisation. In circumstances where residential placement is found to be the only course which holds out a prospect of control and re-orientation, the presence of the boys concerned is a preprequisite to any attempt to achieve a desired improvement. It does not follow that because there is perimetering, that a place is 'closed' to an oppressive degree.

It is not possible, for a number of reasons, to forecast accurately the number of boys who will be accommodated at Loughan House. It is envisaged that at the appropriate stage of Court proceedings, each boy will be assessed at the Finglas Children's Centre. That assessment will help the Courts to decide whether any particular boy is to be residentially placed or not. If he is, it will need to be decided whether placement should be to one of the three existing special schools in Finglas, in Clonmel or in Lusk, or whether placement is to be in Loughan House. The extent to which the existing special schools may exercise their option not to accept boys whom they consider to be problematic in terms of control and absconding could also affect the intake in Loughan House. Intake would also be influenced by the availability or otherwise of specialised, primarily health-orientated places under Department of Health auspices. The arrangements will be such as to enable boys who progress to a sufficient extent, to be transferred from Loughan House to the other special schools.

The majority of the staff for Loughan House will be Officers of the Prison Service. They are recruited through open competitive examination conducted by the Civil

126

Service Commission and the recruitment is by Selection Board procedure. The candidates who qualify receive several weeks full-time induction training on their duties. Among those duties, for several years past, has been the staffing of open and specialised places of custody. The Service has had a very rewarding experience in this field and is encouraged by that experience to be confident about its efforts on behalf of the under 16 age group during the next few years.

In addition to the conventional training, the Officers selected to staff Loughan House will receive a full-time course of twelve weeks duration related to the development, problems, needs, care and control of the juveniles for whom they will have responsibility. This training has already commenced. Furthermore, arrangements are under dicussion for ongoing training of staff to extend over the next two or three years.

The plan is that the juveniles in Loughan House will receive full-time education. The programme is being designed to meet general, compensatory and remedial needs as well as practical subjects, social skills and leisure time activities. This Department is liaising with the Department of Education and other educational authorities both in regard to the design of a suitable educational programme and in regard to the educational staff which such a programme will require.

In addition to the staff already mentioned, there will be provision for chaplaincy, medical and nursing care, a social work input by the Welfare Service of the Department of Justice and a psychological and psychiatric service, which is currently being discussed with the appropriate Health Authorities. Every endeavour will also be made to ensure that there is an adequate feminine presence on the staff. There will be a very generous ratio of staff to boys. There will also be financially assisted travelling arrangements for visitors.[38]

Loughan House subsequently was set up and organised along the lines set out by the Minister in these proposals. The government's decision to open a secure unit for young offenders between the ages of 12 and 16 was marked by continuing disagreement, conflict and emotional debate among the various authorities, professionals, politicians and individuals con-

127

cerned. As a result of this controversy the Working Party which has produced this report came into existence. For this reason we focus in particular on an examination of the facilities at Loughan House, but it is possible that many of the points made about Loughan House may equally apply to the other institutions which have been mentioned.

Residential care and the need for secure units

As stated at the beginning of this chapter, it is clear that there will always be a number of children who will require residential care. There are widely varying forms of such care and each deserves close attention. In this section one method of residential care will be examined, i.e. that which is provided in 'security' conditions.

Two questions immediately arise: firstly, what exactly is meant by 'security' and secondly, should any juveniles be subject to such conditions? Dr Masud Hoghughi of Aycliffe Community Home has defined the term 'security' in his study of juveniles in secure accommodation as: 'A condition of feeling or being (kept) safe.'[39] However, as Hoghughi suggests, in reality the meaning of secure for most practitioners is rather different and implies

> a facility for keeping unruly and troublesome youngsters under lock and key. This restricts the freedom of movement of the youngsters, thereby keeping them and others 'safe' from their depredations and presumably readily available for whatever they are deemed to require — trial, assessment, treatment, etc.[40]

Security in fact means many things. Not only is there the physical security of being confined within fixed boundaries under lock and key, but there are also what Hoghughi terms 'human' and 'chemical' types of security. Human security means, for example, that one worker is attached to a young person for most of the day. Chemical security would exist where a youngster is put under medication, one effect of which might be a feeling of drowsiness and dullness. Thus, it can be seen that the concept of security is complex. Some types of security such as heavy tranquillisation or physical bondage would obviously be objectionable to most people in the twentieth century. Other types of security, however, sometimes may be deemed necessary and even at times be recommended.

The need for secure accommodation for some young

offenders in Ireland has been identified on a number of occasions in various reports. For example, the Kennedy Report in 1970 recommended the following closed unit accommodation for certain categories of boys:

> *Special Schools for 12-15 year old boys with a closed unit*
> It was found that there are about 80 boys in the age-group 12-15 at present in Reformatories . . . . It is recommended, therefore, that two Junior Special Schools be set up for boys in this age-group. The schools should be run on 'open' lines with *a small closed wing for difficult cases.*[41]

> *Special Schools for 16-17 year old boys with a closed unit*
> It was similarly established that about 70 boys would fail to be provided for in this group and it is recommended that two Senior Special Schools be established to cater for them . . . . These schools should be run on similar lines to the Junior Schools . . . .[42]

The Task Force in its Interim Report published in 1975 also made various recommendations in the course of its study of child care services. This recognised what was described as 'an urgent need for another specialised residential facility which would be geared to coping with and helping boys who are at present seen as being very difficult and dangerous and we are satisfied that this facility should provide for containment'.[43]

The Task Force found it difficult to estimate the number of juveniles for whom a secure facility was needed. This difficulty was caused by the fact that, if, as recommended, other preventive and residential care services were improved, it was anticipated that the number of those in need of security would diminish. It was also believed that the existence of secure accommodation could in time act as a deterrent to young offenders, a point which also was made by the Minister for Justice in his speech about the opening of Loughan House. The complex nature of secure accommodation was pointed out in the Interim Report of the Task Force which stated that such provision 'should be approached with caution, and that we should guard against over-provision in this area. We would be concerned, also, lest the provision of a facility of this type might encourage people to attempt to solve the problem of the difficult boy simply by putting him away.'[44]

Neither the Kennedy Report nor the Interim Report of the Task Force envisaged that residential facilities with secure units should take in large numbers of juveniles at any one time:

> we recommend that a special school should be established in the Dublin area to cater for boys in the 12 to 16 age group who cannot be coped with in the existing residential institutions . . . . This School should accommodate 25 to 30 boys and should be organised on the basis of three units – secure, intermediate and open, respectively.[45]

In spite of these recommendations, based on lengthy studies of the problem, Loughan House differs from both the Kennedy and Task Force recommendations in that it is situated in a remote area a very long way from the homes of those contained and structurally consists of one large secure unit.

We wish to state clearly our realisation that, when a decision is made to commit a youngster to care, and to secure units in particular, such a decision is made in a situation of diverse and sometimes incompatible needs. Those involved, from the gardai and social workers to the district justice and the Department of Justice, ideally should consider the needs of both the child and the community. The needs of some children are very likely to conflict with those of some sectors of society which require protection from past and potential acts such as arson, violence and assault.

Hoghughi points out in 'Provisions For Extreme Children',[46] that the four general contexts in which children's problems and society's difficulties with them can be alleviated are penal, psychiatric/medical, educational and social services. He also points out that secure accommodation in the social services can be seen as the extreme end of a complex range of facilities, each of which is brought into use as a means of control and alleviation of a child's problem. Finally, he pertinently shows that the definition of an extreme child (i.e. one who ends up in secure accommodation) is a function of (1) the tolerance of the society in which the child lives; (2) the ability of other forms of intervention to make appropriate impact on the life of that particular child.

The Working Party would welcome the making of decisions to deal with the child based on an adequate assessment of the needs of all involved. If a decision is made that the child is in need of a particular form of help, this help should be provided. On no occasion should the situation arise in which a young offender is sent to a particular facility purely in response to the needs of the community and not in response to his own needs. Nor should a youngster be misplaced because of a lack of suitable accommodation or because he is not the right age for the appropriate facility. Personal and social needs should be given first consideration in decision-making rather than legal, political or bureaucratic needs. Ideally, there should be a wide range of facilities available to meet the varying needs of young offenders and their families. However, a growing body of research carried out in the United States and Britain raises serious doubts about the effectiveness of residential care in actually reducing delinquent behaviour, both in adults and juveniles. The following statement, based on research concerning approved schools for juveniles in England, illustrates this point:

> The question of the success of institutional programmes in absolute terms, although of considerable public interest, appears to have been raised comparatively rarely in institutional research, which has been primarily occupied in ascertaining how such programmes, assumed *a priori* to be beneficial – could be improved. The actual success rates of approved schools offer little ground for optimism. While the rates for individual schools differ considerably, such differences have been largely attributed to a difference in intake . . . and overall success rates for a three-year period are only to an order of 30%-35% . . . . Moreover, though even this figure is often put forward as evidence of the schools' effectiveness, such estimations of 'success' rely on the improbable assumption that *all* boys admitted to approved schools would have remained, or become more, delinquent had they been left at home.[47]

This quotation identifies the danger of assuming that residential care *per se* may reduce anti-social behaviour and notes the relative lack of success of approved schools in achieving this aim. At approximately the same time (1975) in the United States the National Assessment of Juvenile Corrections published their report on residential care and deinstitutionalisation. Their report documented the failure of institutions in 'rehabilitating' young offenders.[48] A similar verdict was later reached by Dennis Romig. Romig's scholarly and rigorous *Justice for our Children*[49] examines in detail a wide range of juvenile delinquent rehabilitation programmes. From a total of 825 books and articles (dating from the 1930s to 1970s

131

inclusive) he selected 170 as meeting the primary criterion of having a matched and randomly assigned control group. In common with a number of other methods of intervention, institutional care was judged to be ineffective in the rehabilitation of delinquents. A similar judgement is also reached by Hoghughi: 'There is voluminous depressing research on the ineffectiveness of security as a means of reducing, other than for the duration of the detention, potential for anti social behaviour.'[50]

In addition, in a recent influential paper, Bottoms and McWilliams[51] have pointed out that, 'All those who have responsibly reviewed the relevant literature have reached the same conclusion that dramatic reformative results are hard to discover and are usually absent.'[52] However, Hoghughi identifies children requiring security as 'likely to be the few children who are, in general terms, too great a risk either to themselves or to the community or who, for a variety of reasons, will not stay to receive appropriate treatment unless their movements are curbed'.[53]

Though the evidence suggests that residential care may not be rehabilitative, we wish to examine evidence for its other possible effects. In considering this field it is easy to indulge in stereotyped thinking. Residential provision has been subject to a large volume of negatively critical literature, referred to by Kathleen Jones as 'the literature of dysfunction',[54] which vividly depicts the deleterious effects of residential care. These commentaries, which tended to rely largely on the single case study, have offered relevant insights into residential care and acted as valuable, sensitising influences in calling attention to the dangers in the residential situation. However, as Tizard et al. point out concerning both these psychological and sociological traditions,

> their functioning started not from the obvious fact of institutional variety but from the equally obvious fact that the members of any class of institution tend to resemble each other . . . an uncritical acceptance of this approach can result in a static model which is largely incapable of accounting for differences or change and an assumption that specific characteristics of particular prisons, homes etc. make little difference to the quality of life within them and can be safely ignored.[55]

Tizard's own work, selecting comparative studies on a wide variety of residential settings, refers to a number of variables which can be seen to have great significance in the functioning of institutions. These factors can be grouped under four broad inter-related headings: (i) ideological variations, (ii) organisational variations, (iii) staffing variations and (iv) variations in residents' responses.[56] The dearth of relevant information on such aspects of residential care in Ireland makes it impossible to deliver any final 'verdicts'. However, in a study of research into secure provision, Millham critically considers evidence about the effects, particularly the psychological effects, of security. His discussion concludes: 'At adult level effects of security are still a matter of academic dispute, in spite of careful and contrasting studies, it is impossible for us to be more specific about the consequences of a spell in security for children.'[57] Elsewhere he states: 'Security offers an expensive and very short respite from the age-old problems presented by high-risk boys. It certainly offers no solution.'[58]

It seems that the gaps between research, knowledge, policy and practice are wide, and that a situation exists here similar to that in England where the majority of juveniles in closed units are in fact casualities of the care system. Frequently the demand for security reflects the inadequacy of open institutions and community services rather than the needs of difficult children.[59] It is hoped that this book might bring these four elements research, knowledge, policy and practice closer together and take a constructive step in the path of evolving policy geared to the needs of Irish children and young people and of the Irish community as a whole.

Finally, the Working Party would like to state their belief that most problem children can be dealt with adequately within open provision. Hoghughi points out:

> It is taken for granted that secure provision is only used for extreme children who have either failed to respond to (or been failed by) other facilities or in whose cases intensive coherent assessment (and not just any old collection of reports which may be called assessment) has indicated the need for secure provision.[60]

We would hope that these extreme situations are the only occasions on which secure provision would be resorted to in Ireland.

Some aspects of secure units in Ireland

Although the Working Party believes that juveniles can experience dangerous effects from being held in conditions of security, it is recognised that, in certain circumstances, secure facilities are needed at present and will be needed in future for troubled and troublesome young people. At this point some crucial questions arise. What place should secure units have in the overall child care system? Where should they be located? What type of staffing is needed? Some of these issues are now considered in conjunction with other factors such as decisions about admission to and discharge from a secure unit, policy making, assessment of the effectiveness of the unit and the allocation of finance.

What place should be held by secure units in the overall child care system?
At present young offenders in Ireland may be placed in conditions of security in adult prisons, in St Patrick's Institution and in Loughan House. Each of these are large buildings, totally enclosed, and the impression conveyed is one of a traditional institution surrounded either by high walls or by barbed wire. Each of these institutions is located in isolation from the open centres, a situation which cannot be regarded as satisfactory. The Kennedy Report stated that secure units should be located within special schools. To be specific: 'The schools should be run on "open" lines with a small closed wing for difficult cases.'[61]

Likewise the Henchy Committee Report[62] recommended that any closed facilities for juveniles be located alongside open ones, while the Interim Report of the Task Force gave clear instructions:

> We feel that it is preferable that the secure accommodation provided should be part of, or attached to, open residential facilities. This is to ensure that, when the need for custodial care no longer exists, the child can be prepared gradually for his eventual return to the community, by his being phased through an open facility with increasing degrees of freedom. The facility we envisage could provide for containment in the medium or long term, but for no longer a period than is absolutely necessary and it is imperative, therefore, that the progress of each child should be kept under continuous review.

Other boys already in residential care may require, on occasion, containment for very short periods. We feel that special

134

schools which have to cope with particularly difficult and absconding boys could better cope with them if provision existed for containment for brief periods when occasion demanded.[63]

The Task Force recommended that these facilities should contain 25 to 30 juveniles, while the Kennedy Report suggested approximately 35 contained in three units. i.e. secure, intermediate and open. With secure, intermediate and open units located together, mobility between units can better meet the needs of residents over a period of time. The ultimate aim of this arrangement would be to increase the teenagers opportunity to experience and deal with freedom leading to eventual successful reintegration into society. Conversely, for offenders placed initially in the open unit, the existence of a closed facility within the school may operate as a control.

The Working Party recommends that in the few extreme cases where secure units are necessary they should cater only for a *small* number of children and as part of a facility which also provides intermediate and open units.

Location of secure units

One of the reasons for having secure, intermediate and open facilities situated together is to maintain as far as possible a sense of reality for those contained. It is obviously important, where possible, for the juvenile to maintain contact with his family and community. It is all too easy for both staff and inmates in a residential setting, particularly in a secure one, to experience varying degrees of alienation, isolation, stigmatisation and the effects of institutionalisation.[64] Containment may well involve a considerable degree of physical, emotional and social deprivation. For these reasons it is preferable that secure accommodation, besides being part of an open facility, should be located as close as possible to the homes of those contained. Again, the relevant reports have made recommendations to this effect. To quote the CARE Memorandum: 'Residential establishments should be well distributed geographically so that as far as possible no child is too far from the home or community from which he comes.'[65]

It is easy to underemphasise the importance of the location of residential settings. Even travelling relatively short distances may cause many difficulties for the families of those contained. In Chapter I the background of young offenders, including

135

factors relating to poverty, unemployment and large families, was described and it was pointed out that a second member of a family may also be living in an institution. For a family dependent on social welfare payments, transport fares can impose a heavy expense, and an added difficulty may arise in finding and paying some person to look after the younger children in the absence of the parents. An extraordinary amount of time and effort may be required to visit a member of the family living in a secure unit such as Loughan House.

The difficulties of visiting Loughan House were described at the Commission of Enquiry into the Irish Penal System in April 1979 when several mothers with sons who were confined there submitted a statement.[66] The mothers stated that they receive vouchers for travelling to County Cavan once per month (Loughan House is situated in the north-west corner of County Cavan, close to Northern Ireland). They had to leave home at 8.00 am and did not arrive back until 11.00 pm. They said that normally they did not have a proper meal all day as the food on the train was too expensive and in Loughan House only tea and biscuits were usually provided. Most of the day was spent actually travelling to and from the institution and when the mothers met their sons a prison officer was always present.

It would appear that most problem children can be dealt with adequately in open institutions and that secure accommodation should be considered only at the extreme end of a complete range of facilities and used only where it will be of particular value in meeting the needs of the child.

The Working Party recommends that:

(1) **In a few extreme cases where secure units are necessary, they should cater for small groups as a part of a facility which has intermediate and open units also. Regular reviews and assessments should be an integral part of the provisions in such units. The results of such reviews should determine whether a child should be moved to a more appropriate unit or setting to meet his changing needs.**

(2) **Young offenders should not be placed in a residential or secure unit for a period of more than one year. After that period they should be reviewed and assessed thoroughly following**

which the residential requirement may be terminated or continued, according to the needs of the child.

(3) Those placed in secure units should be as near as possible to their families and communities. Every effort should be made to facilitate visits from the families of those detained.

Staffing
Working with troubled and troublesome young people is a difficult task in any setting, be it in the family, youth club, school or street. Working with young people who have been removed from their natural environment and placed in residential care poses additional problems, particularly when they are living within conditions of security. One possible reason for this, as we have attempted to show, is that these conditions of security can have adverse effects on those contained.

Work in a residential setting has been defined as 'a method of social work in which a team of workers operates together with a group of residents to create a living environment designed to enhance the functioning of individual residents in the context of their total environment.'[67] Creating a 'living environment' can be very difficult when working in a constantly changing situation, as in residential care. The numbers and needs of residents can frequently fluctuate; for example, one disruptive child, within a week of referral, may disturb the response of the group as a whole to a programme largely dependent on trust; the discharge of a youngster may cause insecurity in those left behind; or acting-out behaviour on the part of one juvenile can upset the other residents and the staff.

Residential staff often have to work under tremendous pressure. This in turn leads to stress which, it has been suggested, leads to exhaustion and thus to an increasing rigidity in performing work-tasks and to remoteness from clients.[68] A recent research project in the United States found that symptoms of stress in various human service professionals (including residential social workers) included 'absenteeism, dehumanisation of clients, task avoidance, isolation from colleagues, difficulty in making and explaining decisions, frequent job changes, psychosomatic symptoms, over or under eating and displacement of anger on to a spouse or children'.[69]

It is obvious that, if residential workers are experiencing stress, there are dangers not only to themselves but also to

137

those for and with whom they are working. It is therefore worth taking note of the factors found relevant by Reid in reducing or helping to prevent symptoms of stress. Such factors included the ability of workers to consult with their colleagues, an opportunity for them to participate in decision-making and the development of constructive ways of venting their feelings. It is important that we in Ireland should gain from the experience, knowledge and research from abroad in setting up our residential care institutions, while at the same time recognising our own cultural and social characteristics.

Studies of those working in residential care often identify the difficulty that married workers may have in reconciling the demands of work and of their family commitments. People working in residential care usually have to work irregular hours and, ironically, it may sometimes be their own families that will suffer most from this situation. To quote one worker in a community home in England when questioned about his future:

> ... when we start a family I will have to go into field work, do another course and work in field services. I don't think I'd want to be in residential work with my own family. I've seen too many problems ... the two extremes, one where the boss's kids have been encouraged to mix in with the kids in the establishment and one of these kids burnt down a shed one week and I think he is very disturbed, real peculiar because he is mixing in with these kids and his mum and dad just don't get enough time to see him and care for him because all their time is dissipated among twenty-four other kids. The other extreme I've seen is where the boss's kids are isolated from the community, the parents didn't get enough time with them like in a normal family, they work all hours day and night and the kids would go up to the flat like shadows, you'd never see them walking around the grounds or playing football.[70]

This example is taken from an open institution in England. However, it raises some important issues about staff in residential care and their families. If an institution is located away from the major population centres, the staff may either have to spend a disproportionate amount of time travelling or may have to move into special staff accommodation. Either of these options may be detrimental to their families. When living very

138

close to their work, they may find it difficult to get away from the daily task, and the whole family may become caught up in the relatively narrow world of a residential setting. In rural areas where there are often transport difficulties, the staff member's family may well be isolated from the wider community. It is therefore generally preferable that the homes of staff members also should be reasonably near the staff member's place of work.

The headmaster of a residential school made the following recommendations regarding the working conditions of staff:

> Staff accept the stress of working in a maladjusted school with its intense personal relationships and the possibilities of having one's weaknesses exposed. To make it bearable the pay must be good, the hours sensible and geared to the staff rather than completely child orientated; the off duty time must be honoured and not eroded by moral obligations. Staff need a full and active life outside the school preferably with people who have no contact with the school. The staff need long regenerating holidays. They need to feel that they are doing a vital and unique task for which they are appreciated and probably most important of all they need to be selected really carefully.[71]

We agree with this emphasis on the careful selection of staff and consider it vital that staff should experience personal growth and fulfulment in their role. The various reports concerning child care in Ireland mention this point and also identify the need for adequate training of staff:

> . . . persons looking after children should be attached to the task, should be capable of warmth and affection for children, even children who are troubled or antipathetic. . . But more than the right personality is required. Residential child-care personnel need a certain level of knowledge of human relations: they need to understand such matters as the following: the dynamics of institutional rearing, of separation from natural parents and family of origin, separation anxiety, the significance of acting-out behaviour. In addition they need to have developed skills in dealing with children from a disturbed background, skills in counselling and in disciplining and in providing security for children. These qualities of knowledge and skill have to be acquired. In order to

acquire them residential care staff need training, both training on the job and a more academic foundation.[72]

The Central Council for Education and Training in Social Work in a Discussion Document on *Training for Residential Work* states: 'We believe that caring for people in residential centres involves a concern for their total needs; this includes physical, emotional, social and educational needs as well as an appreciation of the place of work and play in the life of the individual. In our view the emphasis should always be on the needs of the individual.'[73]

Unfortunately the delicate balance between concern and training is not always achieved, and while a lack of training may be made up at a later date a lack of appropriate care cannot be so easily remedied. Young people tend to be very sensitive to the sincerity of those responsible for them. To quote the opinion of a young boy in care:

> The staff say come and tell us when you get fed up, but I can't see they really care much about us. They get paid for the hours they put in and you're just another bunch of papers they lock away when they go home. When some kid bunks it they don't sit up thinking where you are and go out and look for you. I don't see many staff crying when we go.[74]

If residential care staff have large numbers of children to look after, how can they give that depth of caring and security that the troubled and troublesome child so badly needs unless their own needs also receive adequate consideration?

Child care workers and the young offender

While workers in any residential setting are subject to a certain degree of stress, there is no doubt that working entirely with young offenders adds to the normal stress of residential work, owing to the fact that these young people can be severely troubled and troublesome.

It is clear that the administrative and organisational structure of any institution and the quality of staff employed therein can have an enormous impact on the quality of life both in the institution itself and in its relationship with the outside world. Nor is there any doubt that: 'Relations between staff and children in an institutional context seem to be dynamite. . .'[75]

This means that very close consideration must be given to policy and practice within the institution. As Tutt has stated:

> The organisation and decision making processes in an institution are of vital importance since not only do they influence the effectiveness of management, they also influence the therapeutic value of the institution. One of the major objectives of residential treatment is to provide children with acceptable alternative models of human behaviour. It is important that this be done both at the level of individual staff and at the level of the total organisation. . . Polsky has clearly illustrated the importance of institutional organisation in residential establishments. He has shown that where an autocratic, authoritarian regime exists, the residents develop a subculture which mirrors the regime and is itself authoritarian, rigid, based on fear and anti-therapeutic.[76]

It seems that the present trend in Ireland is similar, in that the young offenders are often placed in institutions with autocratic and authoritarian regimes. Once the young offender (who has committed a serious offence) approaches 12 years of age he may be placed in Loughan House where the majority of the care staff are prison officers, both male and female. The rest of the staff are made up of a chaplain, a welfare officer (social worker), teachers from the local Vocational Education Committee, a nurse and domestic staff. Loughan House also draws on the services of a psychologist, a senior probation officer from the Department of Justice, and on the services of a psychiatrist and a general practitioner.

We would suggest that prison officers are not necessarily the most appropriate personnel to meet the needs of the young offender in this age group. At present prison oficers are recruited to the prison service as a whole and not to any particular institution. The qualifications required of prison officers are more concerned with the question of a basic level of general education and with physical requirements than with an interest in, and concern for, any special group of offenders.[77] Many of the prison officers working in Loughan House have, to date, worked in institutions where the emphasis is on punishment and control, although some are new recruits whose first assignment is to Loughan House. The effectiveness of the Juvenile Liaison Scheme within the garda force bears testimony to the fact that agencies primarily concerned with the control of offenders and the protection of the public may have some members who are more suited to preventive and reha- bilitative work. We would suggest, however, that those working in secure units, as well as all those working with children in care, should be recruited because of their ability to work with children and young people. They should also have the basic educational requirements which would make them eligible to apply for training courses in residential care, rather than be appointed through a system unrelated to this area of service.

Working with troubled and troublesome young people in secure units is one of the most demanding forms of child care. It would be considered inadvisable that persons newly trained in child care should work in such a setting. It is, in our opinion, unfair to lay such a responsibility on the shoulders of prison officers who were sent to Loughan House following a prelimi- nary 12 week course in this field, about which course the organisation CARE says, 'it is widely known that a number of social workers, psychologists and psychiatrists have refused to be associated with it because of its total inadequacy.'[78] Since September 1979 some of the prison officers in Loughan House have attended a day-release course in Sligo. This course has not been recognised by the Central Council for Education and Training in Social Work, nor by any other statutory body. (The Central Council for Education and Training in Social Work in the United Kingdom at present provides statutory recognition in Ireland for social work and residential child care training.) It is essential that training courses should be provided for residential workers, not on an *ad hoc* basis to meet the needs of a small group of workers, but as part of a planned development of training facilities for residential workers and other workers in the social services.

Training for residential child care
Training for residential work is vital to enable the child care worker to understand and be effective in his role, to meet the needs of the children in his care and to deal with his own emotional needs and stresses. The demands made on the worker in a residential setting are as many and varied as the needs of the youngsters in care. In recent years the importance of the role of the child care worker has been gaining greater recognition. This work is acknowledged to be important not only to the child care institutions but also to society at large. Children in care must be recognised as having the same basic

needs as children everywhere, while having additional needs because of their lack of home supports or family relationships. Child care workers do not necessarily play the role of substitute parents, because many of these youngsters in care have homes 'and families of their own. Instead, child care workers aim to provide 'warm, supporting and enabling relationships and treatment within the structure of a therapeutic community'.[79] To do otherwise can be meaningless. To quote a youngster who has been in care: 'The little ones call them (staff) "mummy" and "daddy" because they don't know better. But I just can't because they aren't. How'd you think my mum'd feel if she heard me calling – "mum"?'[80]

The broadening horizons of the child care field mean that not only are youngsters in care recognised as being part of a larger community, but child care work itself is considered to be a profession working in conjunction with the other service professions and necessitating training in the relevant disciplines.

A discussion document by the Association of Workers with Children in Care states that the professional child care worker sets out to:

> put the child at ease with himself, his past and his present situation;
> tell him why he is in care and what is being done for him;
> show he is concerned about the child and what happens to him;
> indicate through his personal contact with the child that he respects his uniqueness as a person;
> be available to the child when he wants help;
> 'tune in' on him at regular intervals to sample his personal, psychological world;
> encourage self-reliance, initiative, independence and the exercise of a personal, inward authority;
> provide the child with the opportunity to identify with someone whose life and attitude to life are such that no harm can come from their adoption by the child;
> enable the child to positively and constructively grow through the struggle between loving itself and loving other people, to grow through the struggle between wanting to belong and wanting to be separate, grow through the struggle between the 'real' world as the adult sees it, and the imaginary world of the child;

143

allow the child to be himself, to grow, to go out into the community, and if his place in the community is one which imposes a lot of strain, threat, fear, anxiety, the worker has this out and conveys the information to a social worker, after-care person, or somebody who might be able to help and improve his situation.[81]

Presently the School of Social Education in Kilkenny offers the only one year full-time diploma course in Residential Child Care in Ireland which awards an internationally recognised qualification. This course was set up as a result of the recommendations of the Kennedy Report in 1970 and following a seminar held in Killarney in 1971. As well as training students for child care, the Kilkenny course tries to encourage the human growth and development of those in training:

> At the school we try to explore Psychology, Child Health, Religion, Sociology, Child Care, Art, Literature, Creative Drama, Play Therapy, Psychiatry, Social History, Social Policy and Group Work, in an environment that seeks to enable students to internalise knowledge in such a way as to grow and develop as a person, the individual he is, and to examine how – so that in his own way and with real regard for each individual child – he may create a similar growth environment.[82]

Besides the theoretical aspects of the course, two practical work placements are provided. The first one is for six weeks in a child care setting in Ireland and the second is for eight weeks elsewhere. Students also spend two weeks attached to a social work agency. The course in Kilkenny has received recognition from the Central Council for Education and Traning in Social Work in Britain, where students in the past have obtained the Certificate for the Residential Care of Children and Young People. In 1972, however, the Central Council set up a working party which attempted to formulate a policy on training for residential work. The findings of this body, published in 1974, produced convincing arguments for regarding residential work as a part of social work. These arguments are summarised as follows:

> (1) residential work is part of the profession of social work because it holds values, objectives and clients in common with other social work services; (2) its practice requires the same basic knowledge and skill; (3) while some

aspects of residential practice may require specialised knowledge and skill, the major differences between residential work and other social work specialisations are technical. Differences between residential care and other types of social work practice are assumed to result from the nature of the professional settings in which residential social workers operate and the modes of interaction that are characteristic of practice in these settings.[83]

Consequently the Certificate for the Residential Care of Children and Young People is no longer being offered and in Britain, residential workers in future will obtain either a Certificate of Qualification in Social Work or a Certificate in Social Service, according to the level of training undertaken.

As a result of this change the Residential Child Care Course in Kilkenny has not received professional recognition since October 1980; thus the future of the course is in doubt, leaving Ireland possibly with no full-time professionally recognised course in Residential Care. Up to October 1979 160 child care workers had completed the one-year course in Kilkenny, of whom 52 were members of religious orders (40 women and 12 men), 61 were laywomen and 47 laymen. Table 5.5 shows the type of work undertaken by them after they obtained their qualification in Kilkenny.

Table 5.5
Present Occupations of These 160 Graduates of The Kilkenny Course
(October 1979)

Working in Child Care

Group Homes	40
Hostel/Unit for Girls	3
Hostel/Unit for Boys	3
Special Schools for Boys	28
(Lusk, Finglas, Clonmel, Salthill, Galway)	
Mentally Handicapped	22
Blind Children	2
Adolescent Units	3
Day Care	2
Itinerants	3
Women's Aid	1
Youth Work	2
Working with Families	8
Lecturing	1
Total: =	118

No longer working in Child Care

Married	20
Other Work	11
On Degree Courses	3
Nursing Courses	3
Teaching	1
Studying for Priesthood	1
CQSW Course	1
Rev. Mother of a Convent	1
Counselling Centre	1
Total: =	42
Grand Total: =	160

Source: These statistics were supplied by Mr. P. Brennan, Director of the Child Care Course at the School of Social Education, Kilkenny.

From this table it is clear that many of those who completed the course are actually working with young offenders at various levels.

Other courses are also provided in the Republic but these are less intensive, day-release courses and can only help in meeting the needs of workers in the immediate vicinity.[84] In addition they do not carry a professional recognition in statutory or international terms.

We believe that there is an urgent need for the setting up of a statutory body in Ireland for the recognition of courses in residential work and social work. This body would have responsibility for promoting the provision of training facilities, for recognising, accrediting and equating all training courses, and for ensuring that professional standards achieve international recognition. Since 1974 a group of social work educators[85] along with other groups have been urging successive governments to set up such a statutory body, but there has been no development of such a body despite a statement by Mr Charles Haughey in 1978, when he was Minister for Health, at a conference of the Irish Association of Social Workers, that such a body would be set up within two years.

It is presently estimated that between 50% and 75% of workers in residential care do not as yet have a professional qualification in residential child care.

The Association of Workers for Children in Care has argued

that training for child care workers should be provided at four levels: (i) induction or introductory, (ii) basic qualifying training, (iii) advanced training and (iv) management and senior personnel training. Students completing such training should receive a professional qualification on a par with the qualification existing for other professionals in the social services. The Working Party concludes therefore that the present provision and control of standards of training facilities for residential care workers are totally inadequate and that residential workers should have a recognised career structure and a salary scale commensurate with their work in parity with that of other social service professions.

It is recommended that properly recognised training courses for residential care workers be set up as soon as possible and students completing such courses be awarded an internationally recognised qualification. It is also recommended that a statutory body be set up in Ireland as soon as possible to develop training courses for residential care workers and social workers, to promote training facilities within social work agencies and residential establishments, to recognise and accredit training courses and to ensure that professional standards are such that they are eligible to receive international accreditation.

Conclusion
In this chapter it has been pointed out that various research studies have raised serious doubts as to the value of residential care in reducing juvenile delinquency.[86] When a decision is made about what to do with a young offender, it should not be based on recent behaviour but rather on an overall and objective assessment of his needs. Thus, both offenders and non-offenders could be catered for in the same facility if they were considered to have similar needs, as indeed they are cared for together in some of the residential homes and hostels referred to above. The Working Party has focused attention on the particular problems associated with the provision of secure units for young offenders, and, while recognising that this is a particularly difficult and sensitive area of social provision, the Working Party has identified various deficiencies in the organisation and structure of Loughan House. These include its location, far from the homes of the majority of its residents[87] which can cause problems for the boys and their relatives and

for the staff and their families. The institution is not structurally linked to any intermediate or open child care facilities and is staffed by prison officers rather than by child care workers. It is hard to reconcile the existence of Loughan House with the recommendations of the various reports that have been cited.

There is also the very important question of finance. The Minister for Justice estimated that the cost of converting Loughan House amounted to approximately £600,000,[88] while the organisation CARE estimated that the cost of running the institution would amount to £200,000 annually (1978 figures).[89] To date (May 1980) there have been approximately 20 to 25 boys at any one time in the institution, which means that the running costs amount to approximately £30,000 annually for each resident boy.[90] This Working Party would argue that community-based services would prove to be less expensive, not alone financially, but also in terms of the less tangible personal and social costs involved. There is no evidence to support the contention that the more money spent in 'treating' delinquents, the more effective is that treatment.

Throughout this chapter the Working Party has made specific recommendations about various aspects of residential care in Ireland and about the staffing and training of the personnel in residential units for children and young people. It is important to highlight also some of the broader administrative and structural problems that have a direct bearing not only on residential facilities for children and young people but also on the formulation of policy and the provision of services in the entire field of child care. These problems here are examined under the following headings: lack of provision; lack of co-ordination and lack of research. Recommendations for dealing with at least some of these problems are also made.

Lack of provision
There is a lack in Ireland of certain types of residential care facilities, such as emergency hostel accommodation for girls. In 1974 the Task Force recommended 'that a hostel-type residential service for 12 girls be provided in Dublin as quickly as possible'.[91] In 1979, without the Task Force recommendation having been acted upon, the HOPE Report said of the already existing girls' hostel in Dublin, '. . . it has difficulty in maintaining its policy of always giving a new person the opportunity of staying in the hostel due to the large numbers

of long-term residents. The situation of having to use mattresses on the floor is not unknown.'[92]

The Task Force also identified a lack of accommodation facilities for itinerant children, some of whom 'no longer live with their families and appear to wander through the city sleeping rough. Their ages range from 9 to 15 years and they include both boys and girls. Most of them have already been in conflict with the law.'[93]

The Task Force went on to recommend that three small residential centres be established for these children. Yet it is only very recently that two hostels for itinerant children have been opened in Dublin. The HOPE Report gave details of some young itinerants sleeping in telephone boxes in the middle of winter. It has also been known for itinerant children to be kept in garda stations due to the fact that no residential care facility could or would take them on a particular night.

Another example of a lack of provision is when a child, having been assessed by St Michael's as being suitable for a particular facility, ends up going home for perhaps six to nine months until there is a place ready for him. By this time the facility might not be the most suitable setting for his needs, which might have changed in the meantime. This is indicative not only of a lack of resources but a waste of the resources which do exist. Another need is for modern remand facilities for young offenders, which would prevent their committal to Mountjoy Prison while awaiting trial or sentence.

The Working Party recommends that, where definite needs for child care services are established, the resources be made available for appropriate and speedy action, because an investment in children is the most important long-term investment the country can make.

Lack of co-ordination

As we noted earlier in this chapter, three government departments are involved in the planning and provision of services for deprived children, i.e. the Departments of Health, Education and Justice.[94] Decisions taken in other government departments, notably the Department of Finance, also have an effect. There is lack of overall planning and co-ordination in all the services for children. The Devlin Report of 1970 referred to 'the deficiencies in the social planning area' and described planning in the health and social welfare areas as follows:

Health: There is a Development Unit in the Department of Health which is entirely occupied with prospective legislation . . . . Social Welfare: There is no formal planning section in the Department of Social Welfare but we have been told that it does establish *ad hoc* groups to study problems which arise. In particular, we find that social welfare is thought of in terms of income maintenance or social security; the other concept of welfare, which is the provision of personal social services other than cash benefits, appears to have been neglected.[95]

Obviously at the time of publication of the Devlin Report there was minimal coherent long-term planning. We believe that this situation still exists with the result that services for children are unco-ordinated and often develop in an *ad hoc* manner owing to duplication by government departments and/or lack of responsibility. As we have shown in this report, even with the present legislation, the opportunities for responding to troubled and troublesome youngsters have by no means been fully used, and it appears that a complete overhaul is needed to remedy the dated, cumbersome and unco-ordinated structure that presently exists.

Recommendations
Our recommendations are broad rather than detailed; they tend to concentrate more on the principles and innovative ideas that we believe should guide policies for children. The Task Force is better equipped with both personnel and resources to work out the legislative and other detail than is this Working Party. We believe that there is a clear need for co-ordination at three levels: a) at national planning level, b) at regional level, and c) at the level of the individual child and his family.

a) *Co-ordination at national planning level*
The Devlin Report stressed the need for a separation of the policy-making functions and executive functions. The need for this has come about because

> the greatest single defect that we have found in the present organisation of the Irish public service is that the top levels of the Departments of State are so involved in the pressure of daily business that they have little time to participate in the formulation of overall policy for their

Departments' functional areas or in the management of their Departments.[96]

This statement is as relevant to the provision of services for children as it is in any other area. We believe that this separation of policy-making from day-to-day administration and execution would allow for a more balanced and forward-looking approach to meeting the needs of *all* children and particularly of troubled and troublesome young people.

The Devlin Report also recommended that all functions relating to the welfare of children presently carried out by the Department of Justice should be transferred elsewhere. This Working Party strongly believes that all procedures relating to troubled and troublesome children should be vested in one Department – a new Department of Health and Social Services. This new Department should incorporate the present functions of the Department of Health as well as the relevant functions of the Departments of Justice and Education (i.e. those functions relating to deprived and troublesome children). The new Department would give equal weight to the personal social services and to health services, thus social work, public health nursing, youth services, home help services, child guidance clinics and all other personal services would be seen as being of equal importance to 'the traditional health services' (i.e. hospitals and the general medical services) which in the past have devoured the lion's share of the Department of Health and the Health Boards' budgets.[97]

The creation of this new department would involve an extension and reorganisation of the present Department of Health. The notion of responsibility needs to be stressed and readily identified at every level of care. Under the present system, responsibility is all too often shifted, unacknowledged and, for some groups of youngsters, vested nowhere at all.

Given this co-ordination of functions, there would be less overlapping and fewer gaps in the services. With the separation of the policy-making function from the executive function a more rational approach to long-term planning would be possible, and under the new co-ordinated structure assessment of the effectiveness of services could be undertaken. We envisage that the personnel involved in policy-making should include those with relevant practical, administrative and theoretical backgrounds. We agree with the Devlin Report that such a planning unit 'should be responsible for co-ordination of plans, initiation of overall plans and appraisal of existing policies . . . and that the introduction of outside experts on short-term commissions and part-time service . . . should be encouraged'.[98] There is a need also for a planning unit that would bring together, assess and try to reconcile the needs of *all children* in the country. This planning unit would co-ordinate (a) the plans for deprived, troublesome and sick children as they emerged from the Department of Health and from other interested groups, (b) the plans for 'ordinary children in ordinary schools', (c) the plans for handicapped and backward children as they emerged from the Department of Education, and (d) the plans for income support of children through taxation and/or social welfare. At present no one holds such an overall brief.

To sum up the subject of national co-ordination for troubled and troublesome youngsters, **we recommend that the functions of all Departments in relation to troubled and troublesome children should be brought together under a new Department of Health and Social Services. The relevant Minister would thus have the responsibility for these children. Furthermore, we recommend that the establishment of a planning unit concerned with the needs of family and children, and located in a special section of the Department of the Taoiseach, be seriously considered.**

(b) *Co-ordination at regional level*
The role of a newly created Department of Health and Social Services would need to be defined at regional as well as national level since the needs of young people in a rural area will sometimes differ from those of young people in an urban area. We suggest that, at regional level, there should be one statutory agency with responsibility for troubled and troublesome children, i.e. a Regional Health and Social Services Board. This Board would place a greater emphasis than presently applies to the provision of personal social services and would define clearly the allocation of responsibility for the various categories of troubled and troublesome children. Thus, for example, under the 1908 Act and in any future equivalent Acts, where the terms 'fit person', 'places of safety' and 'certified schools' are mentioned, the Health and Social Services Board would be responsible for the provision of adequate facilities and for the welfare of the young people referred to such services. This would mean that, where a voluntary rather than a statutory

body was providing a service, it would be the responsibility of the Board to support this service as necessary through finance, personnel or administration, and to be ultimately responsible for those availing of the service. We feel that vesting of responsibility is necessary to co-ordinate all services and to ensure the welfare of youngsters. All too often where a voluntary agency has initiative and can provide the appropriate structure to meet a need, the necessary finance may not be available and the child is the loser. Boards similar to those proposed here exist already in Northern Ireland. These Health and Social Services Boards also plan and provide services for groups such as deprived families, the elderly, mentally ill and handicapped people.

We see the role of new Regional Health and Social Service Boards as responding to the needs of vulnerable groups while also seeking to improve the overall quality of life of the region. In the case of young people it would mean encouraging self-responsibility through community development by responding to the needs of troubled and troublesome youngsters in their own environment.

In relation to the need for co-ordination at regional level, **we recommend that there be one statutory agency in the form of a Regional Health and Social Services Board which will have final responsibility for troubled and troublesome youngsters in each region.**

c) *Co-ordination at the level of the individual child and his family*
One of the main purposes of co-ordination of services at national level is the facilitating of co-ordination of services being offered to the young person and his family. Often, in the case of troubled and troublesome youngsters, we must consider more than their anti-social act or their most obvious problems. The Chief School-Attendance Officer, Brian Doolin, has pointed to some of the other problems which must be considered in assessing the needs of these young people:

> Alcoholism, wife beating, child battering, desertion, heavy debt, mental illness, disturbed children in urgent need of residential care and treatment (which is not available), fathers in and out of prison—to mention truancy in this context is nonsense. To offer school as a cure to any child living in a home where one or all of these problems exist as a means of altering or improving

his condition is pure fantasy. His daily social experiences, his family and environment, have doomed him from the day he was born, and unless society makes a positive effort to rescue him, the devastating effect of his living environment will show its effect for as long as he lives. To send in School Attendance Officers, Welfare Officers and Social Workers to talk these people out of their problems is no great help.[99]

Families with problems such as those mentioned here may have numerous welfare workers paying an occasional visit, including social workers from the Health Board, Corporation school-attendance officers, a probation officer from the Department of Justice or a voluntary worker from the Vincent de Paul Society. Often it seems that a multitude of agencies is involved with few positive results. Until there is commitment to the improvement of housing, employment and other basic social needs, only a limited amount can be achieved. However, we believe that with proper co-ordination more effective use can be made of existing resources.

It has been suggested in this report that a Health and Social Services Board be responsible for troubled and troublesome youngsters under the control of the appropriate Minister. We also suggest in the case of the individual young person who has come before a Juvenile Panel that *one named person be assigned responsibility* for his care, control and welfare who will work closely with him. For example, if a juvenile was referred to an Intermediate Treatment Programme by the panel, one youth worker would be given the responsibility not only to see that the juvenile attended the programme but would help him in finding a job and subsequently keep in touch with him and his family. Alternatively, if a juvenile were referred to a hostel, one of the workers there could be given responsibility for his overall welfare. In other words the Health and Social Service Board should be able to make a contract with voluntary bodies to perform certain tasks, and in certain instances the *named person* responsible for a child or group of children in trouble would be attached to a voluntary organisation.

This would be a useful scheme because, rather than having a number of social workers each with heavy caseloads, a lot of bureaucratic detail to cope with and insufficient time or scope to respond to his needs, the young person would have one social worker who could take a deep interest in him and have

154

enough time to help him tackle practical, emotional and social difficulties. We believe that more can be achieved with one social worker regularly working with an individual, his family and peer group for as much time as is required than by a number of workers working with him for intermittent short periods of time. The child may well interpret the inconsistency of intermittent attention as rejection:

> Our group said that one of the most hurtful things about care was this 'chopping' and 'changing' and required moving from home to home. They said that their feelings of impermanence were compounded by the rapid turnover of staff who looked after them. All had had a succession of different social workers. They had lost track of the number with whom they had had contact over the past five years.

In the case of a juvenile being placed in the care of a named person working with a voluntary organisation, that person would be responsible for the child to the voluntary body which in turn would have contracted with the local Health and Social Services Board to carry out this specific task. Thus, when the case of a troubled or troublesome youngster came to the attention of those in the field, the senior social worker of the local Board would automatically be held responsible until this responsibility had been formally delegated to another worker.

The Working Party recommends that, **where a child is referred to a Juvenile Referral Officer (see Chapter III) and is considered to be in need of care or supervision, the JRO should consult with the child, his parents, the senior social worker of the Health and Social Services Board and any other significant person. This group then would decide who should be the 'named person' responsible for the child's supervision. The person might be a youth worker from a voluntary agency, a Health and Social Services Board social worker or a worker from another agency. This named worker would then be responsible for seeing that the child and his family received appropriate help for their particular needs.**

Lack of Research

The lack of research in numerous areas has already been referred to on several occasions in earlier chapters and applies also in the case of residential care. The most serious lack of research is that which monitors the effectiveness of the different programmes. Thousands of children and millions of pounds are involved in these programmes, yet there is no ongoing assessment of residential care as a form of social treatment. This is not to deny great concern by those running the child care facilities, concern which is expressed in many humane policies ranging from the provision of more homely buildings to a deliberate policy of close integration with the local community. If all of those young people who are in care need to receive such care, it is important to assess the effects which residential care can have on these children and to examine the potential of other possible alternatives. These questions are relevant to all of the child care services but are particularly significant where secure units are concerned. We would agree that 'Where research can help is to distinguish those children who are casualties of the system, for whom intervention should have been earlier and more effective, from those disturbed and difficult adolescents for whom the secure institution is the only possibility.'[101] At present there is no way of knowing how many of those young people in Loughan House are casualties of the care system, how many need total physical security and how many could be dealt with otherwise. It would be very helpful to know where the boys presently in Loughan House were living at any point in time over the previous decade, what their needs were then and how they were met.

Although the overall quality of care in the child care system clearly is good, the Working Party believes that deficiencies exist within the system itself. Many of those working in child care and related fields can identify problems but have difficulty in identifying the source of these problems in child care services as a whole or of producing well-substantiated proof of their existence. Often those who are working closest to the problems will not have access to the people who hold decision-making powers and thus the problem may not reach the ears of decision-makers. If a research programme were undertaken to give a clear picture of the child care services as a whole, the problems could be tackled with knowledge and understanding rather than in a haphazard manner as a result of political pressure. We believe that such research would be welcomed by those working in the services, for, in agreement with Millham, we recognise that 'It is extremely easy for anyone looking back over the decision-making process on difficult children to identify the errors and indifferences of the social work services. It is certainly not quite so easy to balance the niceties of care or to work out a prognosis for boys when a screaming adolescent is in the next room.'

Having recognised the need for, and lack of research, **We recommend that funding be made available by a newly constituted Health and Social Services Department for the purpose of carrying out research either by trained employees of the Department or the Area Boards or by other appropriate experts in this field. We recommend that such research should be designed to investigate the needs of troubled and troublesome youngsters in Ireland and believe that it would help to determine the most suitable and effective child care services to meet those needs. All existing child care services should be regularly monitored and evaluated.**

VI. A Community-Based Approach*

The main focus of this chapter is on services and programmes which are or ought to be available to troubled and troublesome children and young people in their local communities. It reviews some new developments in community-based services and mentions the desirability of these being seen in the context of youth services generally. It looks at the problem of young people finding work and goes on to discuss community-based approaches specifically geared to young offenders. The importance of the personal social services and the schools in identifying young people at-risk is outlined. The final section offers a discussion of the wider concept of a community-based approach to prevention.

Recent developments in community-based services relevant to troubled and troublesome young people and children-at-risk
As a result of the recommendations contained in the Interim Report of the Task Force in 1976, community-based projects for young people were set up in Dublin, Cork and Limerick under the overall aegis of the Department of Health. In recommending their establishment, the Task Force stated:

> We believe that society has an obligation to help deprived children but that intervention in their lives should be kept to a minimum. As many deprived children as possible should be supported and provided for in the community. The objective of policy should be to provide a wide range of preventive and day-care services in local areas to meet the needs of deprived children whose total needs are not being met within their own families.[1]

The Task Force went on to describe the problems of the children they had in mind:

(a) children who have lacked stable adult models with whom they could identify and establish relationships of trust;
(b) children whose parents or parent substitutes have been inconsistent, rejecting or disturbed;

Editor: Mary Whelan. Research: Maeve McMahon, Geraldine Cullen, Mary Goode, Aideen O'Connor, Máire Stedman and the Working Party.

(c) children whose parent or parents have become so dependent on their child, emotionally or otherwise, that they are inhibiting the natural growing up process;

(d) children who are having severe personal, family, educational or social problems for which they need outside help;

(e) children who, while not experiencing emotional problems or lacking in stable adult relationships, have established or are likely to establish patterns of persistent and serious delinquency.[2]

Obviously the target group for the pilot projects was to be selected on the basis of need and could include those children who were called delinquent as well as non-offenders. The Task Force went on to give an idea of the wide scope of the pilot projects they had in mind:

A Neighbourhood Youth Project would try to discover the urgent needs of the more deprived young people in the neighbourhood and devise the most useful ways of responding to them. It might provide special services and facilities to meet defined needs or, alternatively, act as a headquarters and back-up service for unattached youth-work with such young people in the neighbourhood, developing links with other facilities and activities when required. It should use and develop the skills of voluntary workers in the neighbourhood. To support the kind of work described, we envisage that some new activities would have to be developed. Attention should be given, not only to providing recreational activities, but also to stimulating learning activities in areas of practical use.[3]

Neighbourhood Youth Projects

Within the broad guide-lines outlined by the Task Force, each project in practice has attempted to respond to the needs of the target group of young people in the community and thus each has developed its own unique character. Tom Ward, Director of the Neighbourhood Youth Project in Limerick, has said:

The NYP system is a response to concern about children who live in densely populated areas and overcrowded families, who lack stable family lives, children who find it

159

difficult to relate to others and who have little chance to grow up as responsible adults. It is also an attempt to create a worthwhile alternative in child care with heavy emphasis on being a preventive strategy. . . . The primary objective of the Projects is to enable the children involved in them to remain in their community while receiving skilled help directed towards resolving or ameliorating severe personal, family and social problems which are endangering their welfare or inhibiting their innate potential for development. A secondary objective would be to act as a catalytic resource to mobilize the potential of the neighbourhood to meet the evolving needs of its younger people. A further objective is to develop strategies which would provide a guide-line to social workers and others throughout the country to help them in their work with groups of children in their own areas.[4]

The Neighbourhood Youth Project in Limerick is based in an area with a population in excess of six thousand people. Eighty per cent of all married couples are between 20–30 years. Children under 14 years make up more than 45% of the population compared with the national average of 25%. The number of teenagers has almost trebled since 1974 when it stood at 301. Fifteen per cent of householders in the area were unemployed at the beginning of 1978.[5]

The NYP in Limerick started in June 1978 and in May 1979 was working with 38 youngsters in the 'high risk' category referred from agencies in the area. The recommended number of youngsters for a NYP is 24 but this would have meant excluding some of those at 'high risk'. The NYP staff have been working intensively with this group and with their families and friends. However, much more than casework is involved, for the staff must assume all of the roles necessary to respond to the needs of those concerned. Nor does the project solely involve those in the high risk category, but rather the community at large. The core group attending the project have considerable influence on the other youngsters in the community and the project aims at fostering a social reconnection, which means 'easing the children back into the lives of their families on a firmer footing and thereafter into the wider community, stage by stage'.[6] This social reconnection involves adjustment not only by the youngsters but also by the com-

160

munity at large, particularly in terms of its thinking on troubled and troublesome children and their families.

To achieve its aims the NYP in Limerick works with the core group of troubled and troublesome youngsters, with their families and with the community through programmes such as discos, summer play schemes and concerts. Members of the community, including parents of those involved, can be on the management committee of the project.

In Dublin a neighbourhood youth project in the north inner-city area consists of three separate but interlinked projects. All three projects are based in the local community and aim to meet the needs of the children in their own environment. Several staff members live in the area themselves and the volunteers are local people.

Project 1 involves about 33 children aged 9 to 16 years with fringe involvement of a larger number of children. It has three staff members. The main activities are in the following areas:

(1) Practical skills – carpentry, painting, cooking and organising a vegetable garden
(2) Creative skills – drama, painting, music
(3) Community service – organising discos, films, a coffee bar for other children in the area; removing furniture, etc. for people in need
(4) Outdoor and other activities – horse-riding, mountain climbing, day trips, and so on

Project 2 involves intensive work with about 13 children ranging in age from 9 to 13 years. They are all very irregular school attenders and the programme has a strong educational element focused on the needs and aptitudes of the individual child. There are three staff members. The main activities are

(1) Literacy and numeracy
(2) Arts and crafts
(3) Recreational activities – games, outings, etc.
(4) Social skills
(5) Work with families of children

(Projects 1 and 2 are run directly by the Eastern Health Board. Project 3 has its own management structure and is grant-aided by the Eastern Health Board.)

Project 3 is a residential hostel for a maximum of six young people ranging in age from 12 to 16 years. There are four staff members. Living accommodation consists of a two-storey four-bedroomed terraced house with front door opening on to the street.

There is major emphasis on the interpersonal relationships between the staff, the children and their families. Many of the children's more serious problems are closely related to inadequate personal relationships. The experience of living together in a small group promotes opportunities for some of these problems to be brought out and every attempt is made to deal with them in a warm, accepting and very informal living situation.

Some of the children in this project avail of the educational opportunities offered by Project 2. There is also a workshop attached to the hostel which presently provides training in carpentry and motor cycle maintenance. Since the focus is on the individual needs of each child, educational and training opportunities have to be carefully matched to the child's abilities and stage of development. Recreational activities include horse-riding, bowling, fishing, squash and night-walking in the country.

Since all three of these interrelated projects are based locally, children can move quite easily from one to the other, depending on their needs and stage of development. While each project has clearly worked out its own focus, it would appear that they all have at least the following major elements in common:

(1) *Emphasis on the relationship between the children, their families and project staff.* Relationships are built and maintained through the wide range of activities and regular contact with families. Because several of the project staff were already working or living in the area, they were known to many of the children before the project began. This 'short-circuited' what might have been a long process of attracting children into the project and building a trusting relationship with them.

(2) *The projects are based in the area where the children themselves are growing up.* Project staff believe that this is a better approach than to remove them to an 'alien' environment for a limited period and then return them to their familiar surroundings perhaps without continuing support. One of the objectives of the locally based projects is to help the

children cope with their own environment in ways other than crime.

To an outsider, two important points seem immediately obvious. First, this project, in common with others, has attracted a staff with a very high degree of commitment. Hours are long and anti-social, success is slow and hard to measure and emotional demands very high. Support from other statutory and voluntary agencies and from the community generally is badly needed in this kind of work. It appears that, at present, this support is not forthcoming and the projects, to a large extent, operate 'in a vacuum'. Secondly, fundamental changes are needed in the community to deal with some of the social and environmental problems which have contributed to making these projects necessary. These changes are outside the scope of neighbourhood youth projects, but some of the knowledge gained about the effects of a particular environment on young children could be used to promote change (a point dealt with more fully at the end of this chapter.)

Youth Encounter Projects

Following the recommendations of the Task Force, further community based initiatives known as 'Youth Encounter Projects' were established under the guidance of the Department of Education. Youth Encounter Projects are officially designated as 'special schools' and emphasise education. However, the emphasis is not on formal education, which has already been rejected by many of the children, but rather on remedial, practical, social and compensatory education. Again the projects are firmly based in the community and involve close co-operation with statutory and voluntary agencies working in the area.

At present, three Youth Encounter Projects are in operation. Two of these are in Dublin and one in Limerick. The aims of these projects are: (i) to improve the ability of the children to cope with their environment, and (ii) to foster positive attitudes towards themselves and their communities on the part of both the children and their parents.[7] The children these projects aim to involve are boys or girls between the ages of about 10 and 15 who (a) have become persistent truants, (b) have become involved in minor delinquency, or (c) are at risk of becoming involved in delinquency.

Each project has full-time, part-time and voluntary staff,

163

has its own work plan which reflects local circumstances and is drawn up within a framework of an overall agreed plan. An evaluation is being carried out on each project as part of its operation.

The need for the 'alternative' types of education such as that offered by the Youth Encounter Projects is particularly obvious in the inner-city areas and in large new housing estates. In January 1979 Brian Doolin, the Chief School-Attendance Officer, stated that there were at least 40 children in an inner-city area of Dublin at that time who were not wanted or were not being admitted to schools for reasons such as anti-social behaviour or being dirty in appearance. Admission to any school will not necessarily provide a solution to this problem. As Doolin has pointed out, many of those who actually are attending school still cannot read or write by the age of 14.[8] An alternative form of education is needed—one which takes account of the family and environmental circumstances of the individual. Some of the children with school-attendance problems may also be suffering from inadequate diets with a consequent retarded state of physical development and little resistance to illness, and often may not go to bed until very late at night.

Intermediate treatment
Intermediate treatment has been mentioned several times in this book, and it is relevant to refer to it in this discussion on community-based services. It would appear that the basic philosophy behind the concept of intermediate treatment has already gained recognition in this country as evidenced by the neighbourhood youth and Youth Encounter Projects. Intermediate treatment was first mentioned in Britain in the White Paper *Children in Trouble* in 1968 as a form of treatment bridging the gap between keeping a child under supervision at home and removing him from home to a residential institution. It has been defined as 'action through a range of community-based programmes planned to meet identified needs of children and young persons who are at risk of appearing or who have appeared before the courts.'[9] It has also been described as a method of social work 'which adds new dimensions to supervision, both statutory and voluntary, seeking to improve the quality of life of young people through community-based opportunities for personal growth and development.'[10]

In practice there are as many types of Intermediate Treatment programmes as there are youngsters availing of them. They may or may not include short residential placements. The concept of intermediate treatment allows tremendous scope for initiative and creativity by those running the programmes. The programmes may include a wide range of activities such as cookery, gymnastics, rock climbing, drama, stock car racing, youth hostelling, archery, self-defence, football, toy-making and gardening. The treatment methods used by those running the programmes also vary according to needs of the youngsters and include individual casework, group work, remedial education, job counselling, work with families and various other methods. Volunteers are often asked to participate and an effort is made to use facilities in the local community. An example of an IT programme in Britain is the *Lodge Farm Teatime Club:*[11]

Dudley Social Services Department runs this intermediate treatment scheme, which is based on a small, very isolated, council estate, where there is a high incidence of social problems. The teatime club is open from 3.45 to 6.00 p.m. five evenings a week and provides a basic preventative service for the children and families on the estate. The club operates in a centre which has been adapted from two council houses joined together. The children attending the club are aged between 5 and 11 years. Some evenings as many as 40 or 50 children attend and there are usually at least 20. There are two members of staff, one a teacher, the other a home help and the demands on them are very high. . . . Mainly creative activities are available, to encourage the children to use a variety of materials and to use their imagination freely. It has been found that many of their homes lack educational toys, even pencils in some cases.

There are paints, clay, knitting and sewing materials, records, cookery utensils, dressing-up clothes, scrap material and paper. The children are encouraged to concentrate on one activity for a period of time each day, rather than darting around too freely. At home they may be subject to inconsistent discipline and control, so a semblance of order is aimed at in the club. . . .To encourage verbal ability and to help the children express themselves better, stories are read to the whole group at the end of each session. . . .During the better weather the group spends time out of doors, going for nature walks and playing outdoor games. . . .Attempts are made to involve parents and other volunteer helpers.[12]

In summary, this Working Party fully supports the philosophy and approach of community-based programmes, particularly because of their emphasis on the needs of troubled and troublesome youngsters and on the needs of their families and communities, and also because of their readiness to experiment with new ways of dealing with old problems. In such an approach the emphasis on the label 'offender' is removed and practical steps are taken to enable individuals to find an acceptable place in society.

We feel that there are several points worth making about these and other recent developments in community-based services geared to young people at risk or already in trouble. In doing so, we are acutely conscious of the problems involved in establishing and maintaining such projects and the extremely high demands on the staff who run them.

a) *Experimental nature of projects*

These are regarded as 'pilot' projects, experimental in nature, established in what were seen as areas of greatest need. Therefore, only a very small proportion of the total number of youngsters at risk are presently being reached. It is very important that the current evaluation of these projects is widely shared and discussed by care personnel and the community at large. Once the most successful aspects of the projects have been established, attention will have to be paid to (1) the establishment of similar projects in other areas and (2) the application of lessons learned from these 'intensive' projects to wider community-based preventive programmes for young people at risk.

b) *Need for overall responsibility*

The projects are presently under the general guidance of two government departments and at least one other statutory body. Some have local management committees. While the unique nature of each local project is vitally important, there is here again, as in other sections of this study, the problem of lack of overall responsibility for comprehensive development of services. We recommend that this responsibility should be vested in the newly constituted Health and Social Services Board as outlined in Chapters IV and V.

c) *Encouragement for groups involved in similar work*
In this section we have mentioned specifically two or three types of recently established community-based programmes backed by statutory funds. There are many other agencies and locally-based voluntary groups which would be prepared to try new and imaginative schemes for working with children at risk and their families. Some, like Barnardo's and the Irish Society for the Prevention of Cruelty to Children, are already doing so.[13] In addition, new groups like HOPE could be involved, but they need financial support and further analysis as to how they fit into the overall framework of services for children in a way that fosters creativity and initiative.

d) *Local co-operation*
At local level, co-operation among programmes aimed at young people is vital. Workers on voluntary and statutory youth projects in one area of north inner Dublin have found fortnightly meetings to be extremely valuable. In Coolock, workers attached to the various statutory and voluntary organisations such as teachers, gardaí, social workers, youth workers, psychologists and home help organisers came together in 1976 to form the Coolock Joint Care Services Group. By working together, they avoid overlapping, pool resources and try to co-ordinate efforts for families and young people in their area.

e) *Referrals by the Courts*
Greater use could be made by the courts of community-based services by referring some young offenders to them. A fairly recent piece of legislation, the Misuse of Drugs Act, 1977, provides that, having considered reports on the medical, social, educational and vocational circumstances of a convicted person, the court may, instead of imposing a penalty,

> permit the person concerned to enter into a recognizance containing such of the following conditions as the court considers appropriate having regard to the circumstances of the case and the welfare of the person, namely:
> (i) a condition that the person concerned be placed under the supervision of such body (including a

Health Board) or person as may be named in the order and during a period specified in the order;

(ii) a condition requiring such person to undergo medical treatment recommended in the report;

(iii) a condition requiring such person for such treatment to attend or remain in a hospital, clinic or other place specified in the order for a period so specified;

(iv) a condition requiring the person to attend a specified course of education, instruction or training, being a course which, if undergone by such person, would, in the opinion of the Court, improve his vocational opportunities or social rehabilitation or reduce the likelihood of his committing a further offence under this Act.[14]

These conditions are alternatives to detention in a designated custodial treatment centre or to imprisonment. Appropriate alternatives to detention also could be used by the courts in the case of young offenders. This implies, of course, that relevant community-based programmes should be much more widely available than at present and should be equipped both with personnel and with facilities to cope with the young people that are sent to them.

f) *Support for existing projects*
The continuing existence, proper evaluation and extension of the community-based projects outlined in this section need a high degree of support from established statutory and voluntary services. This includes, for instance, financial support for further training which may be seen as necessary for full-time staff and for volunteers who run them. The projects should also be seen in a context of existing developments in the communities concerned. A project which seeks to work with young people who are viewed as vandals and generally troublesome can meet with hostility from local residents, unless people fully understand its purpose and, ideally, are involved themselves in running it.

Youth services
It is outside the scope of this study to review the complex area of youth work, except to emphasise that community-based programmes for young people at risk should be closely related to existing youth and community services generally. Maurice

Ahern points out: 'Youth Work can no longer be seen in simplistic terms of giving grants to youth organisations and expecting them to go off and keep young people usefully occupied.[15] Traditionally, youth work in Ireland has been associated with youth clubs, but it is important to remember that these reach only a relatively small proportion of the total population. It should also be remembered that even those children who regularly attend a local youth club may spend most of the remainder of their time hanging around the streets. Overall, only a small proportion of time may be spent in the clubs or other youth services by the children. The HOPE research team found that some of the youngsters they met who were regularly sleeping out were also attending clubs in the locality.

In the opinion of this Working Party it is vital that the youth services have a broad and flexible approach. It is important that the role and functions of 'unattached' youth workers be recognised. Unattached youth workers do not work in a club or formal service; they cover a particular area and concern themselves with the young people they meet 'hanging around' that district. They often act as a link between young people (whose activities are on the street or in coffee bars and other public places) and their families and communities. For youngsters who have received little or no discipline at home, who may not be attending school, who may be alienated from the usual sources of support in the community, such informal contact in their own environment is likely to be more productive than increasing the provision of more formal and highly structured activities. It can also be a source of referral, where appropriate, to such community-based programmes as Neighbourhood Youth and Youth Encounter Projects.

Employment and training of youth workers
Unlike youth work in many other countries, youth work in Ireland has been almost totally voluntary. While statutory grants have aided the development of various youth services, voluntary organisations 'have been the primary influences in the development of a philosophy and approach to youth work'.[16] The work has been mainly done by volunteers and their involvement is something which should be given full encouragement and support. At the same time, the emphasis on voluntary effort in youth work must not obscure the value of the full-time paid youth worker.

Youth services have a broad and important role, for example, in helping to develop communities and to prevent the problems often associated with large housing estates. This is particularly relevant in the new communities which are rapidly growing around Dublin, where provision for the social and recreational needs of large numbers of young people is inadequate or non-existent. In our opinion it is important to employ full-time people to work with local communities for youth and community development. Their geographical area of work should be small and 'manageable' so that they can work closely with community groups to develop programmes which meet local needs. They should also be in a position to work 'face-to-face' with certain groups of young people including 'unattached' youth.

Difficulties such as lack of support, insecurity of employment and the feeling of working in a vacuum must inevitably affect the youth worker in his/her day-to-day tasks. The Hope Report discussed this problem: 'We have come across a situation in which an unattached youth worker had no address to work from, nowhere to stand in out of the rain, nowhere to meet clients, no such 'luxuries' as the use of a telephone, typewriter, chair or desk, not even any regular means of payment.'[17] It is hard to imagine this worker constantly keeping up enthusiasm and maintaining commitment.

However, on the positive side, there has been some recent progress in Ireland in relation to youth work. This has been reflected in practice with the appointment, to date, of 48 development officers to youth organisations, as part of a scheme set up by the Department of Education. Under this scheme grants are given on a sliding scale to voluntary organisations which employ development officers. An in-service training programme has been established to further the expertise of those employed and this programme is financed by the State. The training programme is a joint operation between voluntary youth organisations and the Department of Education and is seen as important to the further development of youth work.

The Catholic Youth Council in Dublin is an example of a youth organisation which has been able to increase its staff because of the Department of Education scheme. It now has both education and development officers whose role is primarily adult education. They work with adult volunteers to develop youth services in specific areas. Even though the new scheme has helped some youth organisations to employ more full-time people, it is obvious that their services are still very thinly spread. There is a need for more commitment to the full development of adequate youth services.

Personal social services
Full-time and voluntary workers in the personal social services have a very important part to play in identifying young people at risk or already in trouble and referring them to an appropriate source of help. While these workers may not live in the communities in which they work, they are frequently locally-based and have opportunities to experience the day-to-day realities of living in the environment and the problems most likely to be encountered.

A professional social worker or a voluntary worker from an organisation like the Society of St. Vincent de Paul may be the first person to make contact with a family where a marital problem exists. He/she may be the first to hear about a young person at risk or of the possibility of a family breakdown. At this stage direct help or advice and referral to the appropriate services has an inportant role to play in preventing the development of further problems. The personal social services can make a valuable contribution in the prevention of family breakdown if they provide a service which may be availed of by families and children who are at risk during a time of crisis. The provision of social work services at this crucial period, together with a range of back-up services such as those of homemaker, income support and day care, can help to prevent the further deterioration of the family.[18] These services may help families to avoid unnecessary separations and may assist them in coping with a crisis by dealing with the underlying problems rather than by attempting to solve these problems through the removal of the child from the family home. Crisis intervention for families at risk requires a 24 hour social work service and the provision of a wider range of possibilities than at present exists for the supervision of the children of these families at times of greatest stress.

At the present time no emergency social work service is provided on a regular basis outside office hours, at night-time or during weekends. If a child is found to be at risk or there is a family crisis, the gardaí are the only personnel available to deal with the problem. If a 24 hour emergency social work service were provided by a statutory body, such as the Health

Board community care teams, there would be greater opportunity for crisis intervention work at a preventive level. The Social Services Departments in Britian and Northern Ireland have provided such a service for many years. Social workers there are available at all times to deal with emergencies which may or may not necessitate the removal of a child into care. The North Dublin Social Work Group carried out a pilot study on such a service in 1976 and their results would seem to indicate some need for a similar type of service in Dublin.

Another issue is the need for a wider range of methods for supervising children at risk in the community without the necessity of removing them from their families. As noted in earlier chapters, the legislation as it stands provides for the removal of children into residential care either voluntarily or through a 'Fit Person Order'. However, there is no legislation which allows for a child at risk who has not been through the courts to be placed on supervision under a social worker and still remain within his own home. To obtain a 'Fit Person Order' under the Children Act, 1908, necessitates a strong element of proof in the court that the child is at risk and should be removed from the home. If there were an opportunity for a child to be placed on supervision while remaining at home, admission to care might sometimes be prevented. This might also prevent the child from getting into greater difficulties and thus perhaps from coming before the courts on criminal charges.

It is also important that the knowledge of social breakdown gained by voluntary and statutory social agencies should be collected and co-ordinated to contribute to an understanding of the causes of the breakdown. This is essential if these agencies are to be genuinely concerned with prevention. Many social service workers are acutely conscious of the 'paltriness' of the changes they are able to achieve in areas of high social and economic deprivation. Their knowledge and ideas must be used for overall social planning for the area, but the fundamental changes necessary are completely outside the scope of any one agency.

Schools

The whole area of education is so vast and so important for young people that it clearly is not possible to discuss the subject in any depth in this book. The school is, in essence, a community-based service. Next to parents and immediate

172

family, teachers are probably in the best position to get to know children and to be aware of actual and potential problems hindering their development. The setting-up of community-based youth encounter projects as mentioned earlier in this chapter is evidence of a recognition by the Department of Education that special provision needs to be made for certain children. Within the schools themselves, however, a great deal also can be done to identify problems associated with troubled and troublesome children and to devise programmes to help them.

The Black Report in Northern Ireland in its chapter called 'A Strategy for Help' states:

> The school is central to the identification of problems facing many children. The teacher is often the first person to become aware that a child is in need of help, although the child's needs may extend beyond those which can be met from within the educational sector. This is particularly so when the difficulties experienced by a child lie primarily within the family, and social work support for the whole family is required. Clearly it is unrealistic to expect teachers to act as social workers, nor would we wish them to. The welfare of the individual child will be served best by a co-operative approach involving not just the education services but the social services and any other agency or service such as the Youth Service which might contribute to the resolution of the problem at hand.[19]

This Working Party endorses the idea of the closest possible co-operation between the schools and the social services on behalf of troubled and troublesome children and their families.

The Irish National Teachers' Organisation, in a report on *The Educational Needs of Disadvantaged Children*[20] has stated that disadvantaged children constitute one of the major social problems in our society. The report suggests a number of criteria for identifying disadvantaged children in primary schools and recommends that special educational provision should be made in schools where a high number of children are disadvantaged. Such special provision should include (1) a programme of home/school liaison, (2) pre-schools, (3) special staffing arrangements, (4) specialised training for the teachers, (5) adaptation of the curriculum and (6) extra facilities and equipment.

Facts and figures have already been given for the growing youth population and the unemployment problem generally in Ireland (see Chapter I). They give rise to serious concern about the problems involved in finding satisfying work for the young people who are our concern.

In 1978 a study of Youth Employment in North Central Dublin, commissioned by AnCO and the Department of Labour, found that 48% of those who had left school were unemployed.[21] It also found that young people in the survey had 'a very low take up of official services such as AnCO and the National Manpower Service. They are therefore not making use of the placement or training facilities available to those seeking employment'.[22] The value of agencies such as AnCO and Manpower is reduced in areas where, for whatever reason, those who could be taking up the services are not even having minimal contact with them. Publicity is thus an important feature of any community-based service, as is the availability of accurate information; otherwise inaccurate ideas and rumours may circulate in the community and dissuade people from availing of the service. For example, young people in one area may believe that AnCO only offers courses in welding and may not be aware that there is, in fact, a wide range of courses available and that one gets paid while attending these courses. Likewise, because they may not know of anybody who has been placed in a job by the Manpower Service, young people in an inner-city area may believe that a policy actually exists of not placing the inhabitants of these areas in employment.

Community-based services need to reach out to people. The Temporary Youth Employment Schemes which have been operating in North Central Dublin have been very successful in this regard because they have initially attracted many young people including some who might not normally choose such activities. One of the main reasons for this success seems to be the fact that local people, who either had been born in or had been living in the area for some time, were involved in organising the projects and recruiting the youngsters. These schemes will only have long-term success, however, when they lead to permanent, satisfying employment for the people concerned. The following ideas for giving permanent status to these temporary schemes involves the co-operation of statutory agencies and local full-time and voluntary workers:[23]

(1) A local group comes up with a proposal, for example, for the establishment of a small upholstery business. They then investigate various possibilities, and find a suitable premises.

(2) A small number of unemployed young people are trained in cooperation with AnCO in a 'protected' environment. Experience has shown that, ideally, a one to two staff-trainee ratio is needed. While training they receive the usual AnCO training allowance.

(3) After 3 to 6 months' training experience they will have developed a skill and will move on to the Temporary Youth Employment Scheme. The funds from this scheme should remain available until the project becomes viable and self-supporting.

Two such projects are already in operation in the north inner-city area and involve young people. Local adults who are also involved believe that an educational input is very important. For instance, if literacy and numeracy present problems, as is often the case, some time should be allocated to these areas of learning. Opportunities should also be provided for the personal development of the young people concerned.

It is important to realise that temporary employment schemes can raise hopes unrealistically and eventually leave young people unemployed again and with bleak prospects for the future. To succeed, these schemes must be linked with continuing employment opportunities provided either by community-based projects or by industry located within the area.

Young Offenders and Community-Based Services

The *needs* of the individual should determine the response of society and the form of services provided rather than one procedure being made available to those labelled delinquent and another to those who have not been so labelled. So far in this chapter we have been concerned primarily with the needs of young people at risk, *some* of whom have been in trouble with the law. However, as this report is mainly concerned with young offenders, we should discuss specifically how community-based services can meet the needs of young people

175

who get into trouble with the law. We will do this in accordance with our earlier recommendations for the development of the Department of Health into a new Department of Health and Social Services, and also in relation to the establishment of a juvenile panel system in Ireland.

The initial contact of the young offender with community-based services will depend on the nature of the offence and the place in which the offence occurs. As stated in Chapter III, any concerned person such as a teacher, parent, clergyman, shopkeeper, doctor, public health nurse. social worker or member of the general public may consider that it is necessary to refer a child to the newly established juvenile referral officer. The officer then will investigate the case and, if a referral is considered necessary, will put the child in contact with the appropriate agency.

The young offender will be dealt with, whenever possible, within his own family with the support of services in the local community, for example, by being referred to the neighbour-hood youth project for help and supervision. If it is considered necessary that he be removed from his family, or if, effectively, he does not have a family, the next option should be that of placement within his own community, i.e. through fostering, or the use of small group homes. Residential care would be used as a short-term placement prior to making arrangements with a suitable fostering family or group home.

Intensive supervision scheme of the Department of Justice Probation and Welfare Service
This scheme. which is at present in its pilot phase and is an alternative to continued detention, is directly relevant to young offenders. Under the scheme, young people in the 16 to 25 year age group in detention centres and prisons are assessed over a four to eight week period for full Temporary Release. They are then assigned to a welfare officer who engages the young person in an intensive social work support programme, which has already been fully discussed with him and his family before his release. To be able to carry out the very intensive work implied by this programme, each welfare officer in the scheme has a small case-load of a maximum of six cases per officer. A 'well-monitored research element' is also planned to observe and analyse the approaches and methods used by welfare officers, the resources they have brought to the task and any other relevant factors that will help in drawing conclusions

176

and in applying what is learned to other areas of work in the Welfare Service.

This is a new scheme and it is to be welcomed. Where intensive social work support is envisaged for a limited period, as in this scheme, follow-up is vitally important. A high degree of commitment by the young person and his family clearly is very important for the success of the scheme, as is the role of local community-based services. If the welfare officer's supportive role is offered within a context of other local programmes, the gradual withdrawal of the welfare officer's support will be less traumatic, it will also allow for continuing liaison between the welfare officer and local workers if the young person shows signs of getting into trouble again. This presupposes that suitable programmes exist in the communities of these young offenders.

The Kent experience

An interesting example of a community-based service for young offenders in England is the Kent Family Placement Scheme. This scheme was set up in January 1975 and states its beliefs as follows

> We believe that lay people working in their own homes can carry out many of the tasks traditionally assigned to experts.
> We believe in the opposite of like-with-like placements, i.e. we think that one delinquent or disturbed adolescent placed in a normal family is more likely to change than one placed in a residential group of other disturbed or delinquent adolescents. We believe that this kind of foster care should be well paid and recognised as equal in esteem and status to social work.
> Those working on the Kent Project believe in the following principles
> (1) Normalisation – the right to live a normal life in the community using the normal services – schools, health care, etc.
> (2) Localisation – the right not to be uprooted from one's home area,
> (3) Voluntariness – the right not to be subjected to coercion,
> (4) Participation – the right to be consulted.[24]

The project was set up in the first place to test the view that many English children were unsuitable for fostering. It also had the aim of finding out whether spending the same amount for a family placement service that would have been spent for residential care would prove to be more effective as a form of treatment for adolescents who had severe problems and could not be managed in their own homes. The plan was to place difficult children in local families. These teenagers had regularly been rejected by various residential institutions and committal to borstal or prison seemed to be the only remaining alternative before the Kent Project began. This approach is known in the Kent Project as 'the methods packages' and contains the following elements:

(1) The concept of foster care as work for which a fee is paid. One placement is estimated as equivalent to a part-time job and two placements constitute a full-time job. We now know that three placements can be possible if built up to. In 1978 the fee (taxable) was £37.50 and in addition the tax-free boarding-out allowance was paid £10-£12 per week.

(2) The group as the focus of work. All Project parents attend the groups which meet every 2-3 weeks and have a number of functions:

(a) Self and group selection. By entering the group applicants learn to understand what is expected of them and either become part of the group *or* are helped to leave it.

(b) Preparation for placement. The group helps applicants to think through their future role and provides appropriate information.

(c) A network for support and transfer. The group offers support both formally and informally. It is also possible for adolescents to transfer from one family to another in case of need, and they appear to accept these moves 'within the tribe'. The mature groups can now manage almost all crises themselves, without asking for a social worker's help.

(d) The development of policy. Issues relating to present and future practice, financial matters, etc., are discussed and decided, or recommendations made in the groups.

(3) Placements are for treatment, i.e. to promote change

rather than to provide a substitute home. The placements are essentially:

(a) Time-limited. A plan is made for the next piece
of time – 'until you leave school' – or any other
convenient period. This can, of course, be recon-
sidered, shortened or extended.

(b) Problem-solving. The objective of the placement
is to deal with problems which the adolescent can
identify. They are usually fairly simple to state,
such as going to school or not running away, but
sometimes more complicated, such as learning to
form better relationships with adults or peers.

The objectives of the placement are written down in
a brief contract for the adolescent and the foster
family. The family of origin may also agree to specific
tasks, but this contract has not so far been written.
The Project and Divisional social workers also have
brief agreements which divide the work between
them. The general principle is that it is the responsibility of the Project worker to recruit and prepare the
families, and to make the match and set the placement
going. Long-term maintenance should, as far as possible, be carried out by the Divisional social worker.
The Project worker has the ongoing task of working
with the foster parents and will act as trouble shooter
when extra help is needed.

(4) Use of publicity. We believe that it is essential for the
general public to understand what we are trying to
do, if we want people to volunteer to help us. The
Project started with a press conference and has suc-
ceeded in retaining the interest of the media. Project
staff, foster parents and adolescents have spoken to
reporters, broadcast and appeared on television. The
parents of origin do not object to this publicity –
indeed why should these boys and girls in placement
feel stigmatized in any way? As a result of this publicity there have been no difficulties in recruitment so
far.[25]

To date the Kent project appears to have been very
successful. Rejection of an adolescent because of unacceptable behaviour is stated to be relatively rare,
absconding to be less than occurs in residential care, and,

significantly, the project claims that success rates have been approximately double the equivalent rates for residential care.

In the opinion of the Working Party there is a need to explore further the aims, methods and results of such community-based schemes as the Kent project in the light of cultural and social factors relevant to Ireland. For example, would some of the adolescents being referred to Ard Mhuire, Lusk or to Loughan House be helped more effectively by being left in their own homes with the necessary community supports? Would fostering, such as that provided in Kent, be the most appropriate option for others? For young offenders leaving care, would a period of residence in a flat attached to the house of a concerned family be a helpful interim measure prior to their becoming totally independent?

The Working Party believes that there is a great need in Ireland for the development of a wide range of community-based services for the care of young people.

Prevention

In this report the problems associated with young offenders in Ireland have been examined in the light of our own and of international experience in this field. It is important to emphasize that these problems cannot be viewed or solved in isolation. The young person in trouble may have a family and a community where he feels he belongs; he has been to school; he has worked or tried to get a job; he has lived, perhaps in over-crowded conditions and played in streets and derelict buildings instead of playgrounds or fields. The relationship between socio-economic deprivation and offences committed by young people has already been outlined in Chapters I and II. This relationship is fundamental to any discussion of prevention. There is clear evidence that a significant proportion of the population in Ireland is socially and economically disadvantaged at the present time.[26] As shown in Chapter II, the research on young offenders demonstrates that the majority of them belong to this group. Confining discussion to the question of how young offenders should be dealt with under the law and within the community-based programmes devised to help them is to ignore large areas where fundamental change is needed, i.e. the disadvantaged circumstances under which the majority of these children and young people have to live.

The Association of Garda Sergeants and Inspectors in its recent discussion paper on proposals to Combat Crime in Ireland calls for 'more active participation of the public and non-law enforcement agencies in helping to eradicate some of the inadequacies in our society which breed and foster criminal activity in the first instance'.[27] It goes on to propose preventive measures which are worth quoting in full:

> Expand and develop the Community Relations Section of the Force so that it can plan and implement a broad ranging policy for the improvement of Garda/Community relations.
>
> Appoint a Community Relations Officer in each Garda District with responsibility for promoting and encouraging good relations between the Gardaí and community and developing and maintaining channels of communication with all sections, not just the cooperative sections, but also the ones with whom we may experience disagreement or conflict.
>
> Increase the members on the Juvenile Liaison Officer Scheme and give them a broader mandate to relate with young people.
>
> Encourage the provision of community facilities and services, especially in deprived urban areas which by their very absence generate a breeding ground for the initiation of anti-social behaviour.
>
> Seek a role for Garda involvement at the planning stages of Housing and Industrial developments, new communities, urban renewal projects, infrastructure development and so on so that possible problem areas in relation to crime can be recognised and provided for well in advance.
>
> Establish in each District Crime Prevention Panels aimed at making the local community aware of the problems that exist, developing effective Garda/Community relations and concrete action programmes for direct community involvement in the prevention of the causes of crime. These panels could be made up of the representatives of local Gardaí, representatives of local authorities,

Health and Social Service Agencies and local community organisations, e.g. Tenants' Association, Junior Chamber, Youth Clubs, the Churches, Educational institutions etc. These panels could be convened and serviced by the Community Relations Office.[28]

Likewise the Inter-Departmental Committee on Dublin Inner City, in its discussion on crime and vandalism, also recognises that crime cannot be considered in isolation. It goes on to say 'remedial action in other fields–such as the provision of better housing and more employment, making the educational process more effective where this is necessary, the provision of recreational facilities for children, the fostering of a strong community spirit–will undoubtedly have a beneficial effect on levels of crime and vandalism'.[29] There is ample evidence (some of which has been mentioned earlier) in Dublin's inner city alone to support the need for remedial action in these areas. However, while attention is rightly being focused on remedial action in one area, problems may be developing or have already developed in others. We welcome therefore the news that a study commissioned by the National Economic and Social Council will be available shortly which will deal with problems of growth and decay in Dublin as a whole.

We see prevention as being closely linked with the concept of development, whereby people are enabled to grow to their full potential as human beings. It is our assumption that people who have the opportunity to develop fully in the society in which they live are much less likely to be engaged in anti-social actions than are people whose growth has been hindered by a deficiency in some area of human need. Thus, instead of starting by examining anti-social acts and how to prevent their occurrence, it is necessary to start at the beginning with the creation of an environment where people can achieve their full human potential. We would see this approach as a form of 'primary prevention'. Caplan's theory of primary prevention is based on the assumption that to be 'healthy' a person needs continual 'supplies' commensurate with his current stage of growth and development. These can be roughly classified in three groups:

(1) physical supplies (i.e. food, shelter, sensory stimulation, opportunities for exercise, etc.);

(2) psychosocial supplies (i.e. stimulation of a person's cognitive and affective development through personal inter-

182

action with family and peers; development of relationships, etc.);

(3) sociocultural supplies (i.e. influences on personality development and functioning which are exerted by the social structure and by the customs and values of the culture).[30] Problems can occur if there are qualitative or quantitative shortages in these supplies. Sociocultural supplies underpin physical and psychosocial supplies because the former are concerned with social structure and the nature of the physical environment.

In areas where delinquency rates are highest, there are shortages of 'supplies' at all three levels outlined by Caplan. These shortages range from inadequate care of the unborn child (because of the poor nutrition and the poverty of many mothers) to the unsuitable nature of the physical environment where housing conditions are often unacceptable and opportunities for exercise and recreation almost non-existent for many young people. There appears to be an assumption about 'new communities' that if people are adequately housed and have more space than previously available to them, they should be able to 'get on with it'. This assumption does not take into account the problems often encountered in obtaining employment, resettlement problems, access to local social and recreational facilities and the general stage of development of the community. Prevention at primary level implies planning for the full development of people before problems have grown to the extent that remedial action is needed.

Policy and planning
The government's Green Paper *Development for Full Employment* states that the emphasis in the paper on economic objectives 'stems from the belief that economic advance carried with it direct social benefits and that substantial social improvements in other areas cannot take place unless there is the necessary economic progress to support and finance them'.[31] The Working Party believes, however, that there are sections of the community which economic progress continually leaves behind and where the theory of 'social spin-off' from economic development just does not work in practice. While economic progress is fundamentally important, it should be accompanied by a full recognition of the need for social planning, particularly for groups in the community that traditionally have been left behind during periods of economic growth. Human progress

183

–as distinct from economic progress–requires action on a wide variety of human needs rather than a focus on only one aspect of development. The Rutland Street Project referred to in Chapter II is an example of an experiment where significant resources and personnel were successfully channelled into an imaginative pre-school education programme. Yet the Chairman of its Steering Committee has pointed out that the most fundamental question raised by the project itself and highlighted by the book, is 'whether special educational intervention for disadvantaged children can achieve its objectives if not accompanied by radical change in the total environment'.[32]

Community education and development

The Working Party believes that community education and development are central to primary prevention in its broadest sense. Thus, integrated economic and social planning must be linked to community development and reflect human needs as they are expressed by people in their local communities and in 'communities of interest' such as trade unions, business associations, women's groups and groups concerned with the interests of children. We would again express grave concern that, while the most vociferous and articulate communities can ensure that they benefit from economic and social planning, the 'marginal groups' can often be left behind. Disadvantaged areas are likely to have a long history of inadequate resources and lack of influence over decision-making which affects them. Intensive community development initiatives are needed so that people can understand their needs and how they can take action on their own behalf:

(1) Knowledge is needed about local development programmes, particularly where these have taken place in disadvantaged areas or with disadvantaged groups of people. An understanding of the methods and approaches used and of the results achieved in one area could provide many relevant insights for further initiatives elsewhere. The work of the Pilot Schemes to Combat Poverty will provide much-needed information about community-based programmes which believe that an element of local participation is central to a successful outcome.

(2) Community development and education alone will not solve the problems of disadvantage in the communities to which we are referring. These are very important in fostering the participation of people in areas which ultimately

184

affect their lives. Community development and education help people to achieve the confidence and self-respect needed to work for change. Yet they must be complemented by widespread recognition of the economic and social needs of these areas and of the need to deploy resources to meet them which no local community has within its own capacity. This requires commitment by central and local government to the needs of deprived areas and full recognition of this commitment in future economic and social planning.

Full-time community development personnel are needed to help communities towards self-development. At present many of the people employed in this work are limited in what they can do because of the wide areas they have to cover. Sometimes their work can be limited to assisting groups in getting grants and to liaising between community groups and statutory bodies. There is a need for more intensive development work with local groups to help them achieve self-reliance. Consideration should be given to the employment of local people in full-time development work, and to provision also for their training. A comprehensive community education programme would also provide opportunities for continuing training in community work for local volunteers. The results of such experiments which have been already carried out should be carefully assessed.

Public education
We believe there is a great need for recognition by the population at large of the relationship between socio-economic deprivation and the problems of young offenders. It has been our experience that knowledge and understanding of these problems is frequently expressed by people who work on a full-time, and sometimes on a voluntary basis, with young offenders and in disadvantages communities. In many cases these people would not themselves have experienced similar deprivation, but their understanding has grown from day-to-day contact with the people concerned. During the period in which this report was written we have heard many of these workers express frustration and sometimes anger at their seeming inability to convince the public that the problems of disadvantage and delinquency are deeper than sometimes recognised. Most people see only what they believe to be the

185

unpleasant personal characteristics of the people involved. Serious consideration should be given to public education initiatives to increase understanding of the causes of social problems often superficially viewed as social irritants and as causing the disruption of 'normal' community life, e.g. vandalism, homelessness, begging, and so on. It is beyond the scope of this report to go into detail about such initiatives, but we strongly believe they are needed. A great deal of attention is being given at present to public health education. Experience is being gained in use of the media and of schools, and an evaluation of the impact of these programmes is also being undertaken. The same methods might be used to educate people about social deprivation and the problems of young offenders.

Conclusion and Recommendations

Many people live in communities. These are the neighbourhoods where they have grown up, the streets they know best, the people they know and who know them. In Dublin, some live in closely-knit inner-city communities where families have known one another for generations. Others are experiencing the anonymity of newly developing areas where there is talk of 'creating community', but its development sometimes appears to be very slow.

In this chapter we have discussed a community-based approach to troubled and troublesome children and young people. In recent years people concerned with their needs have begun to recognise the value of such an approach in responding to these needs and the dangers of removing a person from familiar people and places for 'rehabilitation' purposes. Even if a person is removed for a period of time, he usually returns to his community of origin and perhaps to the sub-group to which he belongs. The behaviour of this group may have very little acceptance locally, but the group belongs there. Services and 'reaching-out' initiatives have most relevance at this level where they take into account the person, family, peer group and wider community.

This chapter reviews some community-based initiatives and suggests further developments. The following is a brief summary of the main recommendations contained in the chapter:

(1) **The community-based pilot projects in existence at present incorporate new and promising approaches**

to young people at risk or already in trouble. It is important that the results of their evaluation be widely shared and that their successful aspects be incorporated in future projects.

(2) Overall responsibility for development of projects should be vested in the newly-constituted Health and Social Services Boards (as outlined in Chapter V). At the same time the local nature of each project must be preserved and voluntary groups prepared to involve themselves in such projects should be encouraged and given financial support.

(3) Greater use should be made by the courts of community-based projects which aim to meet the needs of young offenders. The Misuse of Drugs Act provides a precedent for this approach.

(4) If youth services are to be co-ordinated with community-based services, and if the youth services themselves are to be consistent in responding to ever-changing needs, it is essential that professional youth workers be employed at strategic points throughout the services. These workers are needed both to work directly with young people and also to provide support for the vast amount of voluntary work already in existence.

(5) Attention should be paid to the important preventive role of the schools and the personal social services because of their close contact with children and families.

(6) Temporary employment schemes for unemployed young people should be planned which will lead to permanent satisfying employment wherever possible.

(7) "Needs rather than deeds" should determine society's response to young people who get into trouble with the law.

   (a) There should be easy access to appropriate services for young people at risk and these should be community-based. A child should not have to commit a crime before his/her needs are responded to.

187

(b) **Institutions such as the adult prisons, St Patrick's and Loughan House, should not be used at all for young offenders (i.e. offenders under 17 years of age).**

(c) **The development of a foster-care service and sheltered accommodation for young offenders should be given priority. We recommend that a voluntary organisation prepared to pioneer in this field be identified and funded and that the results of its work be monitored.**

(8) **The problem of young offenders cannot be viewed or solved in isolation. There is a need for clear recognition of the relationship between socio-economic deprivation and the problems of young offenders.**

(9) **While economic progress is fundamentally important, it should be accompanied by full recognition of the need for social planning, particularly in relation to groups in the community which traditionally have been "left behind".**

(10) **Local community development initiatives are needed and full-time community development personnel should be trained and employed to help communities towards self-development.**

The reforms advocated in this chapter and throughout this book will not be easily achieved. They will not come about unless there is commitment in our society and by our government to a redistribution of at least some portion of the nation's assets from those who have to those who have not. They will not come about without a clear-headed approach to social planning, to the formation of specific policies for deprived areas, to the needs of children and their families and to evaluation of the success of these plans and policies in reality. Let our Northern neighbours who expressed it so well have the last word:

> There must be a willingness on the part of the community to accept that children hitherto perceived as disruptive, deviant or difficult, can very often be helped to cope with their problems without recourse to exceptional measures. There is much to be gained from neighbourhood support

188

for families in need and from community-based schemes to interest and support young people. . . .

A caring community must concern itself with the quality of life it offers to *all* its children.[33]

Appendix A

Summary of Major Recommendations of the Kennedy Report

The whole aim of the Child Care system should be geared towards the prevention of family break-down and the problems consequent on it. The committal or admission of children to Residential Care should be considered only when there is no satisfactory alternative.

The present institutional system of Residential Care should be abolished and be replaced by group homes which would approximate as closely as possible to the normal family unit. Children from the one family and children of different ages and sex should be placed in such group homes.

We find the present Reformatory system completely inadequate. St. Conleth's Reformatory, Daingean, should be closed at the earliest possible opportunity and replaced by modern Special Schools conducted by trained staff.

The Remand Home and Place of Detention at present housed at Marlborough House, Glasnevin, Dublin, should be closed forthwith and replaced by a more suitable building with trained child care staff.

The staff engaged in Child Care work, who have responsibility for the care and training of children, their mental and emotional development should be fully trained in the aspects of Child Care in which they are working.

We recognise that education is one of the most important formative influences on the children with whom we are concerned, whether they are deprived or delinquent. All children in Residential Care or otherwise in care, should be educated to the ultimate of their capacities. The purpose of the education they receive should be to help them to develop as adequate persons. To achieve this end, they will need facilities over and above those available to children reared in the normal family.

Aftercare, which is now practically non-existent, should form an integral part of the Child Care system.

Administrative responsibility for all aspects of Child Care should be transferred to the Department of Health. Responsibility for the education of children in care should remain with the Department of Education.

All laws relating to Child Care should be examined, brought up-to-date and incorporated into a composite Children Act.

The age of criminal responsibility should be raised to 12 years.

The present system of payment to the Reformatory and Industrial schools on a capitation basis should be discontinued. Instead the payment should be made to the schools on the basis of a budget submitted by the schools and agreed to by the Central Authority.

An independent advisory body with statutory powers should be established to ensure that the highest standards of Child Care are attained and maintained.

There is a notable lack of research in this field in this country and if work in the area is to develop to meet the needs of Child Care, there should be continuous research.

Appendix B

Diagram of Children's Hearings in Scotland*

PROCEDURE FOR BRINGING COMPLAINT TO HEARING

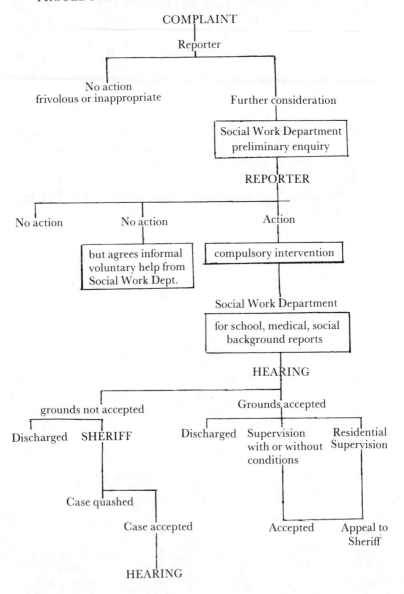

*Taken from F. M. Martin and K. Murray (eds), *Children's Hearings* (Edinburgh, 1976)

Appendix C

Further Information on Hostels for Young Offenders in Ireland

There is a wide variety of hostel accommodation available for young people, although, unfortunately, these hostels often have considerable waiting lists and can provide only limited facilities. All of the hostels for young people in Ireland are managed voluntarily but they may be classified under two headings: (1) those that provide accommodation specifically for discharged prisoners and offenders placed on probation. These hostels work in close liaison with the Probation and Welfare Service of the Department of Justice. (2) Hostels that provide accommodation for both offenders and non-offenders. The extent of liaison with the Probation and Welfare Service varies from hostel to hostel.

Hostels for Offenders

Argus House in Cork is a juvenile probation hostel and is run by a voluntary committee of members of the Society of St Vincent de Paul.

Lions Villa is a hostel in Chapelizod which caters for young offenders on probation and is run by members of the Dublin Lions Club.

Priorswood House is located at Coolock, Co. Dublin. This hostel was set up in 1970 by the chaplain and welfare officer of Mountjoy Prison with support from a group of voluntary workers. The group that runs the hostel is known as PACE — Prisoners Aid Through Community Effort. Priorswood is mainly for adult ex-prisoners but occasionally it caters for juveniles from St Patrick's Institution or from Shanganagh Castle. Those staying in the hostel either have jobs or attend an AnCO workshop for basic industrial training attached to the hostel. The policy of Priorswood emphasises reintegration into normal community life.

Sarsfield House is at Ballyfermot in Dublin and provides accommodation for varying numbers of young offenders who have been placed on probation or discharged from detention centres. The Sons of Divine Providence manage the hostel, and they receive a capitation grant for each boy accommodated.

Waterford Probation Hostel in Ladylane, Waterford, caters for young offenders on probation and its voluntary committee includes members of the local Lions Club.

At present preparations are being made for two more probation hostels in Limerick and Galway. The probation hostels receive a State grant for capital expenditure and part of the running costs, with the remainder of the necessary finance being raised by the voluntary workers involved. All of the hostels in this category have a senior welfare officer of the Department of Justice on the Management Committee. The residents also each have a welfare officer individually assigned

Hostels for Offenders and Non-Offenders
Hostels in the Dublin area include:

Boys Don Bosco
Hope
Los Angeles
Tabor House, Seville Place

Girls An Grianan, High Park Convent, Sisters of Our Lady of Charity of Refuge.
St Mary's Hostel,
Sherrard Street Hostel,
Stanhope Street Hostel.

There are also three hostels specifically for travellers which take travelling children who may or may not have come through the courts. Two of these hostels are in Dublin and one is in Newtownmountkennedy, Co. Wicklow. The latter has a senior welfare officer of the Department of Justice on the Management Committee. They are all run by voluntary organisations.

Appendix D

The Recruitment of Prison Officers*

A newspaper advertisement which appeared in the Irish national papers on Wednesday, 15th February 1978 is given below:

PUBLIC SERVICE

60 Vacancies as

PRISON OFFICER (MALE)
in the (Prisons Service) Department
of Justice

Prison Officers appointed on the results of this competition may be assigned to Mountjoy Prison; Limerick Prison; Portlaoise Prison; St. Patrick's Institution, Dublin; Arbour Hill, Dublin; Shanganagh Castle, Bray; Shelton Abbey, Arklow; Cork Prison; or *Loughan House near Blacklion, Co. Cavan.*

A Prison Officer is concerned with the general custody and welfare of persons confined to prisons or similar institutions. He is also involved in training and education programmes for such persons.

Pay: Starting at £54.90 a week and rising to £75.90 a week. Rent allowance £1.30 per week to single officers and £2.60 per week to married officers is payable to officers not provided with official quarters. Additional allowances for special duties such as working weekends etc.

Age-limits: 19-30 years on 1st March, 1978.

Persons with service in the Permanent Defence Force, Civil Service, Local Authorities or Health Boards may qualify for an extension of the upper age limit.

The following are *extracts* from the Civil Service Commission regulations for the competition for appointment to the position of Prison Officer (Male) (Established) as supplied to intending applicants:

2. The competition shall consist of the following tests:

   (i) a qualifying written examination obligatory for certain candidates only (see Regulation 6 below);

*Taken from CARE, *Who Wants a Children's Prison in Ireland?* (Dublin, 1978).

(ii) an interview (which shall be obligatory and competitive) (see Regulation 7 below);

(iii) an optional language test (see Regulation 10 below).

The optional language test will be held at the interview or at a time as close as possible to the time of the interview.

6. (a) Candidates who have *not* passed, or obtained Grade D at least in either Mathematics or Commercial Arithmetic *and* either Irish or English at the Intermediate Certificate examination of the Department of Education or at the Certificate examination (Day Vocational Courses) of the Department of Education or at an examination of similar standard, must qualify in a written examination; but candidates who have qualified in the written examination at an earlier competition for appointment as Prison Officer will not be required to take the examination again.

(b) The qualifying written examination which will be held on the 15th December 1977 will be on the following syllabus:

Paper I: Arithmetic — the basic elements and in addition percentages, fractions, decimals, ratio and proportion and averages; and their application to practical problems.

Paper II: (i) To write a short passage (about 80 words) on a prescribed topic;

(ii) correction of errors in spelling and grammar;

(iii) questions designed to test intelligence and reasoning powers and ability to do simple clerical work.

8. *Special Physical Requirements:*
At the time of the medical examination referred to in Regulation 3 (Regulations — Part II) candidates must be of good physique, with satisfactory chest development, and be not less than 5 ft. 7 ins. in height (barefooted). Any defect in a candidate's eyesight which would render it necessary for him to wear glasses or contact lenses while on duty will disqualify him for appointment.

Chapter I

[1] D. Rottman, 'The Changing Pattern of Crime in The Republic of Ireland' *Journal of the Statistical and Social Inquiry Society of Ireland*, Vol. XXIII, part v (1977–8), p. 163.

[2] Irish law at present distinguishes between a child, defined by the 1908 Children Act as someone under the age of 15, and a young person, i.e. someone who has attained the age of 15, but is under 17 years of age (Children Act 1908, Sect. 131 as amended by the Children Act 1941, Sect. 21). In this book therefore the term 'juvenile crime' is used to describe a crime committed by someone who has not yet reached his/her seventeenth birthday and the term 'juvenile' is likewise used to describe someone under 17 years of age.

[3] D. West and D.P. Farrington, *The Delinquent Way of Life* (London, 1977), p. 27.

[4] M.L. Erickson and L.T. Empey, 'Court records, undetected delinquency and decision-making' *Journal of Criminal Law, Criminology and Police Science*, No. 54 (1963), pp. 456–69.

[5] K. Elmhorn, 'Study in self-reported delinquency among school children in Stockholm' K.O. Christensen, (ed.), *Scandinavian studies in Criminology*, Vol. 1, (London, 1965).

[6] National Economic and Social Council (hereafter referred to as NESC), *Towards a Social Report*, No. 25 (Dublin, 1977), p. 10.

[7] *Census of Population*, Vol. I (1979).

[8] NESC, *Population and Employment Projections 1986: A Reassessment*, No. 35 (Dublin, 1977), p. 17. We understand that NESC is currently working on revised population projections based on the 1979 census data.

[9] D. Rottman, 'Crime and Law Enforcement' *Towards a Social Report*, NESC, No. 25 (Dublin, 1977), p. 182

[10] Ibid.

[11] Hope Ltd., *Out in The Cold*, (Dublin, 1979), p. 12.

[12] NESC, No. 25, op.cit., p. 16.

[13] See previous reference to NESC, No. 25. Also relevant here is an article by Rottman 'The Changing Pattern of Crime in the Republic of Ireland', op.cit.

[14] D. Rottman, NESC, No. 25, op.cit., p. 183.

[15] I. Hart, 'The Social and Psychological Characteristics of Institutionalised Young Offenders in Ireland', *Administration*, Vol. 16 (1968), p. 169. This research is further reported in 'A Survey of some Delinquent Boys in an Irish Industrial School and Reformatory', *Economic and Social Review*, Vol. 7 (1969–70). The sample, although not random, was a sizeable fraction of the 300 to 400 young offenders in Irish industrial schools or reformatory at the time.

[16] A. Flynn, N. McDonald and E.F. O'Doherty, 'A Survey of Boys in St Patrick's Institution: Project on Juvenile Delinquency', *The Irish Jurist*, Vol. 2 (1967), p. 223. Although the sample is small this is a useful survey.

[17] I. Hart, *Factors Relating to Reconviction among Young Dublin Probationers*, Economic and Social Research Institute, Paper No. 76 (August 1974), p. 9. The approach adopted in this study was to test and follow-up 150 young Dublin probationers to discover factors associated with relapse into crime. A separate group of 57 non-attenders at school was studied for comparative purposes. Fifty eight per cent of the probationers relapsed into crime, 25% being committed to an institution.

[18] Further details on this report are given in Chapter II.

[19] B. Behan, *Borstal Boy* (London, 1958), p. 135.

[20] *Census of Population*, Vol. I (1979).

[21] NESC, No. 25, op.cit., p. 30 (our italics)

[22] B. Murphy and T. Morrissey, *A Study of Youth Employment in North Central Dublin* (Dublin, 1978). The study was broad and included information on educational attainment and housing conditions in the area.

[23] Murphy and Morrissey, op.cit., pp. 121–3.

[24] West and Farrington, op.cit., p. 66. Also R.D. Schwartz and J.H. Skolnick, 'Two Studies of Legal Stigma', *Social Problems*, no. 10 (1962), pp. 133–42; W. Buikhuisen and F.P.M. Dijksterhuis, 'Delinquency and Stigmatization', *British Journal of Criminology*, No. 11 (1971), pp. 185–7; R. Boshier and D. Johnson, 'Does Conviction affect Employment Opportunities?', *British Journal of Criminology*, No. 14 (1974), pp. 264–8.

[25] Prisoner's Rights Organisation, *A Survey of Fifty 12–16 Year Old Male Offenders in The Sean MacDermott St–Summerhill Area* (Dublin, 1978). The selection criterion for the sample was that of 'multiple criminal charges per person'. The number of charges varied between 5 and 80 and the number of court appearances varied between 10 and 200 approximately per person. The average number of criminal charges per person was 27, the average number of court appearances was 52 and the average number of convictions was 6.

[26] This as yet unpublished study was carried out by the Prisoner's Rights Organisation with the assistance of personnel from the Economic and Social Research Institute. The sample of 200 ex-prisoners was not random but was based on an informal communication network through members of the organisation. Two hundred questionnaires were filled in by respondents.

[27] The new garda journal *AGSI News* makes this point very firmly: '. . .official criminal statistics. . .really indicate how the Force and Judicial system operates rather than indicating the true extent of crime. Even in this context the absence of figures showing the numbers of Gardaí in relation to the different sections and geographical division prevent an informed analysis from taking place.' *AGSI News* (March 1980), Vol. I, No. I, p. 11. The analysis of official statistics is therefore hampered by the lack of this information.

[28] Details of the Juvenile Liaison Scheme are given in Chapter III.

[29] R.N. Vaughan and B.J. Whelan, 'The Economic and Social Circumstances of the Elderly in Ireland: A Preliminary Report', ESRI seminar paper, 7 December 1978.

[30] The *Garda Commissioner's Report* of 1978 showed that, of 2,514 burglaries where the charge was held proven, 918 had been committed by offenders under 17 years of age.

Chapter II

[1] The borstal system in Ireland was modelled on that of England. The main purpose of this system was to provide training rather than punishment. In Ireland borstal was for offenders aged 16 to 21 years. Borstal staff were chosen from the prison service and sentences were for a minimum of two years and a maximum of three years. The major power to decide who should go to borstal lay with the courts, although there was also provision to allow for the transfer of an offender from prison to borstal. Sometimes, on conviction, the offender would be sent to prison and when later sentenced, would go to borstal. The borstal system attempted to act as a preventive and reformative measure for those who had not yet become 'hardened criminals'.

[2] The General Prisons Board in Ireland was set up under the General Prisons (Ireland) Act of 1877. The Board was responsible for administering and running the prison system. Throughout the 1890s the General Prisons Board took exception to the imprisonment of children, recommending in 1892 that magistrates make maximum use of the First Offenders Act and in 1896 that juveniles be separated from other prisoners and taught a trade.

[3] N. Osborough, *Borstal in Ireland*, (Dublin, 1975).

[4] *46th Report of the General Prisons Board, Ireland, 1923–1924*, (Dublin), p. VI.

[5] *47th Report of the General Prisons Board, Ireland, 1924–1925*, (Dublin), p. IX.

[6] Ibid.

[7] *49th Report of the General Prisons Board, Ireland, 1926–27*, (Dublin), p. VII.

[8] Osborough, op.cit., p. 61.

[9] Ibid., pp. 77–9.

[10] In the early 1920s inmates were moved several times for the same reason.

[11] Osborough, op.cit., p. 61.

[12] E. Fahy, 'Borstal in Ireland', *Hermathena*, a series of papers on literature, science and philosophy by members of Trinity College, Dublin (1941), p. 80.

[13] Ibid. pp. 80–81

[14] Ibid., p. 81.

[15] Ibid., p. 82.

[16] Osborough, op.cit., p. 56.

[17] The legal criteria by which young offenders are sent to reformatory and industrial schools are discussed in Chapters IV and V. It is important to note that at any given time not all those in reformatory and industrial schools are offenders. Particularly where industrial schools are concerned, very few of the children have been convicted of an offence.

[18] *Report of the Commission of Inquiry into the Reformatory and Industrial School System 1934–1936*, (Dublin, 1936).

[19] Known as the Kennedy Report after its Chairwoman, District Justice Eileen Kennedy.

[20] *Report of The Commission of Inquiry into the Reformatory and Industrial School System 1934–1936*, op.cit., pp. 4–5.

[21] Ibid. p. 61.

[22] Ibid., p. 67.

[23] Ibid. p. 49.

[24] Ibid. p. 9.

[25] Ibid. pp. 10–11 (our italics). The association between poverty and children in trouble recurs over and over in this book.

[26] Ibid. p. 11.

[27] Ibid. pp. 78–9.

[28] Ibid, pp. 50–3.

[29] Ibid. p. 35.

[30] Ibid. pp. 19–20.

[31] H.A. McCarthy, 'The Supervision of Delinquents in Society' in B.G. MacCarthy (ed.) *Some Problems of Child Welfare* (Cork, 1945), pp. 43–51. Justice McCarthy presided over the Dublin Metropolitan Children's Court for many years in the 1940s and 1950s.

[32] Ibid. p. 48.

[33] Ibid. p. 46.

[34] Ibid. p. 45.

[35] Ibid. p. 46.

[36] Ibid., p. 47. Modern social workers will be interested to note the way in which this eminent district justice used the term 'social worker' in 1945.

[37] Ibid., p. 48.

[38] Ibid. (our italics)

[39] Ibid., pp. 48–9.

[40] Ibid., p. 49.

[41] Ibid., p. 50. Almost 30 years later the Task Force on Child Care Services was set up by the Minister for Health with the following terms of reference: (i) to make recommendations on the extension and improvement of services for deprived children and children at risk; (ii) to prepare a new Children's Bill, updating and modernising the law in relation to children; (iii) to make recommendations on the administrative reforms which may be necessary to give effect to proposals at (i) and (ii) above.

[42] Ibid., pp. 50–51.

[43] Ibid., p. 51.

[44] Kennedy Report, p. VIII.

[45] Ibid.

[46] Ibid., p. V.

[47] Ibid., p. 6.

[48] Ibid., p. 7.

[49] *Task Force on Child Care Services: Interim Report* (Dublin, 1975), p. 5.

[50] Ibid., p. 7.

[51] *Garda Commissioner's Report, 1978,* Calculations made from figures in this Report show that for the year ended 31 December 1978, of the 9065 people convicted or against whom the charge was held proven, 7763 were male and 1302 were female; 1938 of the total were under 17 years of age and of these 1772 were male, while only 166 were female.

[52] *Irish Times,* 31 July 1978.

[53] B. Power, 'The Young Lawbreaker', *Social Studies,* Vol. 0, No. 0 (Oct., 1971), pp. 56–79. Power points out that this is not a scientific study but is based on boys he got to know while working as chaplain to a St Vincent de Paul youth conference.

[54] Ibid., p. 58.

[55] Flynn et al., op.cit., p. 226.

[56] *Legislation and Services for Children and Young Persons in Northern Ireland: Report of The Children and Young Persons Review Group* (Belfast, December 1979), p. 37. Known as the Black Report after its Chairman, Sir Harold Black.

[57] Power, op.cit., p. 69.

[58] Flynn, et al, op.cit., p. 228.

[59] Hart, 'Factors relating to Reconviction. . .', op.cit., p. 65.

[60] Hart, 'A Survey of Some Delinquent Boys in an Irish Industrial School and Reformatory', op.cit. and Hart, 'Factors Relating to Reconviction. . .', op.cit.

[61] Hart, 'Factors Relating to Reconviction'. . .*op.cit.,* p. 9.

[62] Ibid., p. 10.

[63] Power, op.cit., p. 59.

[64] Flynn et al, op.cit., p. 229.

[65] P.R.O., 'A Survey of Fifty 12–16 Year Old Male Offenders', op.cit., p. 7

[66] West and Farrington, op.cit., p. 109.

[67] Ibid., p. 125.

[68] Hart, 'A Survey of Some Delinquent Boys. . .' op.cit., p. 188.

[69] Flynn et al, op.cit., p. 224.

[70] Power, op.cit., pp. 58 and 79.

[71] The Kennedy Report used the same definition of mental handicap as that used by the *Commission of Inquiry on Mental Handicap,* 1956. This latter report classified as mentally handicapped those people, including adults, 'who by reason of arrested or incomplete development of mind, have a marked lack of intelligence and either temporarily or permanently, inadequate adaptation to their environment'. In terms of measurement by intelligence testing, those with an I.Q. of less than 70 would be classified as mentally handicapped. Categories of mental handicap used here are: mental handicap (I.Q. of 70 and under) and borderline mental handicap (I.Q. of 70 to 85).

[72] Hart, 'Factors Relating to Reconviction. . .' op.cit., p. 10.

[73] Prisoner's Rights Organisation, 'A Survey of Fifty 12–16 Year Old Male Offenders', op.cit. pp. 2 and 7.

[74] T. Kellaghan, *Evaluation of an Intervention Programme for Disadvantaged Children* (NFER Publications, 1977).

[75] S. Holland, *Rutland Street — The Story of an Educational Experiment of Disadvantaged Children in Dublin* (Oxford, 1979).

[76] Ibid., p. I.

[77] Bounded by Summerhill, Portland Row, Amiens Street, Talbot Street and Gardiner Street.

[78] Holland, op.cit., p. 6.

[79] Ibid. p. 68.

[80] Ibid. p. 75.

[81] Ibid., p. 101.

[82] For a more detailed review of this book see H. Burke, 'An Educational Experiment for Disadvantaged Children in Dublin', *Oideas,* Vol. 21 (1979).

[83] Black Report, op.cit., p. 37.

[84] Flynn et al., op.cit., p. 230.

[85] Quoted by The Prison Study Group, *An Examination of The Irish Penal System* (Dublin, 1973), p. 31.

[86] E. Doleschal and N. Klapmuts, 'Towards a New Criminology' in C.R. Dodge (ed.) *A Nation Without Prisons* (Lexington, 1975), p. 41.

[87] The National Children's Bureau, London, can provide details of the U.K. National Child Development Study which is following the progress from birth to maturity of all the children in England, Scotland and Wales who were born in the week 3–9 March 1958.

[88] For further details of deviance amplification theory see Edwin M. Schur, *Radical Non-Intervention* (Prentice Hall Inc., 1973), and L.T. Wilkins, 'A Behavioral Theory of Drug Taking', *The Howard Journal of Penology and Crime Prevention*, Vol. II (1962–65).

[89] West and Farrington, op.cit., p. 128.

[90] Ibid., pp. 162–3.

Chapter III

[1] P. Parsloe, *Juvenile Justice in Britain and the United States* (London, 1978), p. 119.

[2] B. Waugh, *The Gaol Cradle: Who Rocks it?* (London, 1876), p. 80.

[3] J.W. Mack, 'The Juvenile Court', *Harvard Law Review* (1909), pp. 104–122.

[4] A. Morris and M. McIsacc, *Juvenile Justice* (Heinemann, 1978), p. 9.

[5] Viscount Samuel, *Memoirs* (London, 1945), p. 55.

[6] Children and Young Persons Act, 1933, S. 44.

[7] Ibid.

[8] *Report of the Committee on Children and Young Persons* (London, 1960).

[9] P. Priestley, D. Fears and R. Fuller, *Justice for Juveniles. The 1969 Children and Young Persons Act: A Case for Reform?* (London, 1977), p. 9.

[10] Ibid., p. 10.

[11] *Crime — A Challenge to us all*, Labour Party publication, (London, 1964).

[12] *The Child, the Family and the Young Offender*, (London, 1965).

[13] *Children in Trouble* (London, 1968).

[14] Children and Young Persons Act, 1969, ch. 54, s.1.

[15] Magistrates are appointed for life to each commission of the peace by the Lord Chancellor, on the recommendations of the Lord Lieutenant of the county. Anyone can put forward a name, including his own name to Advisory Committees to the Lord Chancellor. Magistrates are not required to be legally trained.

[16] Unless it is considered to be in the interest of a child or a young person for the press to give such details, for example in a case where the public generally consider an innocent young person to be guilty of a particular act when, in fact, it was committed by somebody else.

[17] As shown in Priestley et al., op.cit., p. 88.

[18] Priestley et al., op.cit., pp. 85–6.

[19] Parslow, op.cit., p. 150.

[20] *Report of the Departmental Committee on Training and Protection* (London, 1928).

[21] *Report of the Committee on Children and Young Persons, Scotland* (London, 1964). Referred to as the Kilbrandon Report after its Chairman, Lord Kilbrandon.

[22] However, all types of courts administered the same statute law as laid down by the Acts which already have been mentioned.

[23] Kilbrandon Report, para., 13.

[24] *Social Work and the Community* (London, 1966).

[25] Social Work (Scotland) Act, 1968, ch. 49, as amended by the Criminal Procedure (Scotland) Act, 1975, and the Children Act, 1975, s. 32(2).

[26] In Scotland care does not necessarily entail the child's removal from his family.

[27] A diagram which details the procedure in children's hearings is contained in Appendix B.

[28] F.M. Martin and K. Murray, *Children's Hearings*, (Edinburgh, 1976), and J. P. Grant, 'The Children's Hearing System in Scotland: Its Strengths and Weaknesses', *The Irish Jurist* (1975), p. 18.

[29] In connection with 'fit persons' orders, e.g. under section 58 of the 1908 Act, parents may bring their child to court on the grounds that he is out of control. Also in connection with 'fit persons' orders a social worker may bring a child to court on behalf of the Health Board.

[30] *Irish Tiimes*, 9 May 1975.

[31] P. Shanley, 'The Formal Cautioning of Juvenile Offenders', *The Irish Jurist*, Part 2 (Winter 1970), p. 278.

[32] Kennedy Report, p. 70.

[33] Including those by Justice H.A. McCarthy, 'The Children's Court' *Christus Rex*, vol. 1–2 (1948), J. O'Connor, 'The Young Offender', *Studies* (Spring 1963), the Kennedy Report, and the HOPE Report.

[34] W. Clarke Hall, *The State and the Child* (London, 1917), p. 45.

[35] Ibid., pp. 49–50.

[36] B. Wooton, *Crime and Penal Policy* (London, 1978), p. 160.

[37] Ibid.

[38] Clarke Hall, op.cit., p. 51.

[39] A.J. Shatter, *Family Law in the Republic of Ireland* (Dublin, 1977), pp. 220–21. Shatter states that some district justices have accepted the contention that this rebuttable presumption applies until the child's fifteenth birthday.

[40] Kennedy Report, p. 68.

[41] *HOPE* Report. p. 33.

[42] The Criminal Justice (Legal Aid) Act, 1962, did not require that an accused person be informed of his or her right to legal aid. In 1976 the Supreme Court held, however, that Healy's constitutional right to a fair and just trial had been breached because he had been convicted and sentenced without being informed of his right to legal aid and in the absence of legal representation.

[43] Committee on Criminal Legal Aid: Chairman — District Justice Tormey.

[44] A. Morris, 'The Children and Young Persons Act 1969 — before and after' in a publication by the British Broadcasting Corporation, *Signs of Trouble* (1976), p. 30.

[45] Parsloe, op.cit., pp. 180–1.

[46] Black Report, pp. 49–50.

[47] Parsloe. op.cit., p. 233.

[48] Black Report, p. 50.

[49] Morris, op.cit., p. 31.

[50] Grant, op.cit., p. 37.

Chapter IV

[1] In 1975, 37,028 males and 11,724 females in the 10 to 14 age group in England were cautioned for indictable offences. In the same year, 21,434 males and 2,376 females in a similar age group were found guilty of offences by the courts. Figures quoted by Wotton, op. cit., p. 166.

[2] A juvenile under 15 years who is found guilty of an offence which would be punishable by imprisonment if committed by an adult can be referred to an attendance centre or to a detention centre. A juvenile aged between 15 and 17 who is found guilty of such an offence can be referred to a Crown Court with a recommendation that he be sent to a borstal institution.

[3] D. Ford, *Children, Courts and Caring, a Study of the Children and Young Persons Act, 1969* (London, 1975), p. 27.

[4] The 1963 Children and Young Persons Act, s. 1, gave wider powers to local authorities in England than previously were available to provide facilities which had the aims of avoiding and reducing the need to take children into care and also to prevent, where possible, appearances before the juvenile court. The Children and Young Persons Act, 1969, s.12(2), took this a step further through supervision orders which may carry the requirement that juveniles comply with their supervisors. The 1969 Act thus legalised intermediate treatment as it had been described in the 1968 White Paper 'Children in Trouble', op.cit.

[5] The Lord Advocate still has the power to direct that a juvenile who commits certain offences, such as murder and assault endangering life, may be tried in the Sheriff Court or the High Court. The juvenile may also be referred to the sheriff from the hearing if he or his parents have disputed the grounds, or if it appears to the chairperson of the panel that they do not understand the grounds.

⁶ Social Work (Scotland) Act, 1968, ch. 49, as amended by the Criminal Procedure (Scotland) Act, 1975, and the Children Act, 1975, s. 31(1)

⁷ This may be held at an earlier date if either the child's parents or the local authority asks for a review. The second hearing has the same powers at the review as at the original hearing, which means that a requirement can either be varied or can be reduced or discharged outright.

⁸ The Social Work (Scotland) Act, 1968, s. 47, states that a child 'shall not continue to be subject to a supervision requirement for any time longer than is necessary in his interest'.

⁹ Both the juvenile and the reporter have a right to appeal from the sheriff's decision to the Court of Session by way of stated case on a point of law or in respect of an irregularity in the conduct of the case.

¹⁰ Valuable information concerning the law as it relates to the prosecution and disposal of juvenile offenders has been obtained for this section from a report commissioned by the Director of Public Prosecutions. D.C. Mitchell, *Young Offenders* (Dublin, 1977).

¹¹ A child is defined as being under 15 years of age, a young person as aged between 15 and 17 years.

¹² Children Act, 1908, s. 107.

¹³ Mitchell, op.cit., p. 29.

¹⁴ Probation Act, 1907, s. 1 (1). This corresponds with s. 107 of the Children Act, 1908.

¹⁵ A recognizance is defined as an obligation or bond acknowledged before a court of record or authorised officer and afterwards enrolled in a court of record.

¹⁶ However, where a juvenile has been convicted on indictment of an offence punishable with imprisonment, the court may in certain circumstances, in lieu of imposing a sentence of imprisonment, make an order discharging the offender conditionally on his entering into a recognizance, with or without sureties, to be of good behaviour and to appear for sentence when called on at any time during such period, not exceeding three years, as may be specified in the order. This provision applies to trial on indictment and not to a trial before the juvenile court.

¹⁷ Probation Act, 1907, s. 2 (1).

¹⁸ Probation Act, 1907, s. 2 (2), as amended by s. 8 of the Criminal Justice Act, 1914.

¹⁹ Criminal Justice Administration Act, 1914, s. 7 (1).

²⁰ McCarthy, op.cit.

²¹ The report was not published but information was obtained through personal communication with the Probation and Welfare Service of the Department of Justice.

²² Personal communication with the Probation and Welfare Service of the Department of Justice.

²³ Children Act, 1908, s. 63.

²⁴ Kennedy Report, p. 71.

²⁵ Ibid.

²⁶ Ibid.

²⁷ The interchanging of the titles Industrial Schools/Residential Homes and Reformatory Schools/Special Schools sometimes causes confusion. The legislation uses the terms Reformatory and Industrial Schools but the terms Special Schools and Residential Homes are now more generally in use.

²⁸ Except if 'the only common or reputed prostitute whose company the child frequents is the mother of the child, and she exercises proper guardianship and due care to protect the child from contamination'.

²⁹ Children Act, 1908 s. 58 (1), as amended by s. 10 of 1941 Act.

³⁰ Mitchell, op.cit., p. 38.

³¹ Kennedy Report, p. 76.

³² Ibid.

³³ Ibid.

³⁴ Mitchell, op.cit., p. 40.

[35] 1908 Act s. 57 as amended by 1941 Act s. 9. In the case of a youthful offender who is less than 15, it appears he cannot be brought back for another order.
[36] See the late Justice H.A. McCarthy's comments on this problem in Chapter II.
[37] J. O'Connor, *The Irish Justice of the Peace*, (London, 1915), Part II.
[38] Though Mitchell, op.cit., p. 59, suggests that the £10 limit does not apply to young people convicted of summary offences.
[39] Children Act, 1908, s. 101.
[40] Summary Jurisdiction Act, 1884, s. 7.
[41] Section 131 of the 1908 Act describes a 'guardian' as follows: 'The expression "guardian" in relation to a child, young person, or youthful offender, includes any person who, in the opinion of the court having cognizance of any case in relation to the child, young person, or youthful offender, or in which the child, young person, or youthful offender is concerned, has for the time being the charge of or control over the child, young person, or youthful offender.'

Chapter V

[1] Children Act, 1908, s. 21, s. 58, s. 59. Children Amendment Act, 1957, s. 2. Health Act 1953, s. 53.
[2] P. Moss, 'Residential Care of Children: A General View' in J. Tizard, et al., *Varieties of Residential Experience* (London, 1975), p. 21.
[3] CARE Memorandum, *Children Deprived* (Dublin, 1972), p. 25.
*This term refers to children placed privately for monetary reward but supervised by Health Boards under Boarding Out of Children Regulations, 1952.
[4] In addition to the research already cited, the following studies have been examined in the writing of this report:

M. Jordan, *Residential Care of Children*, unpublished M.Soc,Sc. thesis (University College, Dublin, 1967).
M. O'Connor, *Juvenile Offenders in a Reformatory School: a Sociological Study*, unpublished M.Soc,Sc. thesis (University College, Dublin, 1972).
V. Richardson, *Provision of a social work service for Children in residential care including study of the background and characteristics of children in long-term residential care in the City and County of Dublin*. Research in progress.
Children Coming into Care, 1978, Department of Health Report (1980).
Finding Parents for Children with Special Needs, A pilot study conducted by The Federation of Services for Unmarried Parents and their Children with financial support of The Medico-Social Research Board (Dublin, 1980).
Report on Residential Child Care in the South-Eastern Health Board Region, Assoc. of Workers with Children in Care (1974).
[5] Documentary evidence from *St Michael's Unit*.
[6] M. Hoghughi, *Troubled and Troublesome, Coping with Severely Disordered Children* (London, 1978), p. 205.
[7] (P. Finlay, 23 July 1979) Unreported judgement.
[8] Ibid.
[9] Ibid.
[10] *Report of the Commission of Enquiry into the Reformatory and Industrial Schools System*, 1936 op.cit., p. 19–20.
[11] Figures obtained through personal communication with officials of the Department of Education.
[12] Department of Education, *Statistical Report*, 1977–78, p. 88. (Figures cited for St Joseph's, Clonmel and St Ann's, Kilmacud, also come from this report, p. 88).
[13] *Task Force on Child Care Services, Interim Report*, p. 22.
[14] Ibid., p. 23.
[15] Ibid., p. 30.
[16] Ibid., p. 29.
[17] Figures given in the HOPE Report (p. 52) show that in a boys' hostel in Dublin the percentage of those known to be involved in delinquent activities was higher than

the percentage actually charged with delinquent acts. This is consistent with research on this aspect of youth behaviour in other countries, see Chapters I and II and W.A. Belson, *Juvenile Theft–The Causal Factors* (London, 1975).

*Figures taken from Annual Reports on Prisons for the years 1975–1978.
[18] CARE Memorandum, p. 93.
[19] Dáil Debates for May 1978.
[20] The Prison Study Group, *An Examination of the Irish Penal System* (Dublin, 1973), p. 42.
[21] E. Goffman, *Asylums, Essays on the Social Situation of Mental Patients and other Inmates* (London, 1968), pp. 25–6.
[22] B. Behan, op.cit.
    J. Boyle, *A Sense of Freedom* (London, 1977)
    F. Norman, *Banana Boy* (London, 1969).
[23] The Prison Study Group, op.cit., p. 40.
[24] Quoted by the Prison Study Group, op.cit., p. 2.
[25] Department of Justice, *Annual Report on Prisons and Places of Detention* (Dublin, 1978), pp. 52–55.
[26] Personal communication with the Probation and Welfare Service of the Department of Justice.
[27] Department of Justice, *Annual Report (1978)*, p. 17.
[28] Kennedy Report, p. 44. In fact the Kennedy Report suggested that only males of 18 years and upwards should be sent to St Patrick's
[29] Department of Justice, *Annual Report* (1978), p. 18.
[30] Cited in Osborough, op.cit., p. 92.
[31] Department of Justice, *Annual Report* (1968), p. 13.
[32] Department of Justice, *Annual Report* (1978), p. 18.
[33] Ibid.
[34] Department of Justice, *Annual Report* (1972), pp. 11–12.
[35] The Prison Study Group, op.cit., p. 72.
[36] Loughan House does not have any Visiting Committee since the time it was opened exclusively for young offenders.
[37] Department of Justice, *Annual Report* (1977), p. 59.
[38] Cited in CARE, *Who Wants a Children's Prison in Ireland?* (Dublin 1978), pp. 15–18.
[39] M. Hoghughi, 'Probing the Flaws in Security', *Community Care* (28 Sept. 1977), p. 16.
[40] Ibid.
[41] Kennedy Report, p. 10.
[42] Ibid., p. 40.
[43] Task Force Report, p. 29.
[44] Ibid.
[45] Kennedy Report, p. 30.
[46] *Children First Newsletter*, Nos 12, 13 (1978), pp. 15–18.
[47] D.B. Cornish, and R.V.G. Clarke, *Residential Treatment and its Effects on Delinquency*, Home Office Research Studies (London: H.M.S.O., 1975), p. 32.
[48] R.D. Vinter, G. Downs; and J. Hall, Juvenile Corrections in the States. Residential Programs and Deinstitutionalization Michigan, 1975.
[49] D. Romig, *Justice for our children an examination of juvenile delinquent rehabilitation programs* (Lexington, Mass., 1978).
[50] *Children First Newsletter*, p. 18.
[51] A.E. Bottoms, and W. McWilliams, 'A Non-Treatment Paradigm for Probation Practice', *British Journal of Social Work*, Vol. 9., No. 2 (1979).
[52] For a further exploration of this theme see: S.R. Brady, *The Effectiveness of Sentencing: A review of The Literature*, Home Office Research Study, No. 35 (London, 1976). D. Lipton, R. Martinson, and J. Wilks, *The Effectiveness of Correctional Treatment* New York, 1977). D.F. Greenberg, '*The Correctional Effects of Corrections: A Survey of Evaluations*' in D.F. Greenberg (ed.) *Corrections and Punishment*, Sage Criminal Justice System Annuals, Vol. 8 (Beverly Hills, 1977).

[53] Hoghughi, op.cit., p. 17.

[54] For detailed discussion and examples see K. Jones, 'The Development of Institutional Care' in *New Thinking about Institutional Care* (London, 1967), pp. 7–16.

[55] Tizard et al, op.cit., p. 5–6.

[56] Ibid.

[57] S. Millham, et al, *Locking Up Children* (1978), p. 92.

[58] Ibid., p. 153.

[59] Ibid., p. 186.

[60] Hoghughi, op.cit., p. 17.

[61] Kennedy Report, p. 40.

[62] First Interim Report of the Interdepartmental Committee on Mentally Ill and Maladjusted Persons, *Assessment Services for the Courts in Respect of Juveniles* (Dublin Stationery Office, August 1974). Second Interim Report of the Interdepartmental Committee on Mentally Ill and Maladjusted Persons. *The Provision of Treatment for Juvenile Offenders and potential Juvenile Offenders* (Dublin Stationery Office, August 1974).

[63] Task Force Report, p. 30.

[64] For early discussion of the effects of institutionalisation see Goffman, op.cit., but for qualification and refinement of the thesis see Tizard et al, op.cit., and Taylor, Walton and Young, *The New Criminology* (London, 1973).

[65] CARE Memorandum, p. 69.

[66] This Commission of Enquiry was organised by the Prisoner's Rights Organisation. The Commission was jointly chaired by Sean McBride, Nobel and Lenin Peace Prize-winner, and Dr Luke Halsman, Chairman of the Committee on Decriminalisation in Europe.

[67] Central Council for Education and Training in Social Work, Discussion Document, *Training for Residential Work* (London, 1973), p. 15.

[68] J. Dunham, 'Staff Stress in Residential Work', *Social Work Today* (July 1978), p. 18. Dunham quotes these responses from an article 'Burned Out' by C. Maskach in *Human Behaviour*, Vol. 5.

[69] R. Reid, 'An Exploratory Study of the Burned Out Syndrome', *The Social Work Profession* (Western Michigan University), quoted in Dunham, op.cit., p. 18.

[70] N. Tutt, *Care or Custody* (London, 1974), p. 110.

[71] G. Wright, 'A Model of Supervision for Residential Staff', *Social Work to-day*, Vol. 9., No. 45. (25 July 1978), p. 20.

[72] CARE Memorandum, p. 70.

[73] Central Council Report, *Training for Residential Work*, p. 12.

[74] S. Millham et al., *After Grace — Teeth* (London, 1975), p. 191.

[75] Ibid., p. 193.

[76] Tutt, op.cit., p. 155.

[77] Extracts from the Civil Service Commission regulations for the competition for appointment to the position of Prison Officer (Male) (Established). See Appendix D for further details on the recruitment of prison officers.

[78] CARE, *'Who Wants a Children's Prison in Ireland?'*, p. 24.

[79] Association of Workers with Children in Care (AWCC), 'The Professional Role', *Discussion Document* (Kilkenny, 1977), p. 2.

[80] R. Page, and G.A. Clarke, *Who Cares? Young people in Care Speak Out* (National Children's Bureau, 1977). This quotation is taken from an article of the same name concerning the book in *Social Work Today* (4 October 1977), p. 14.

[81] Association of Workers with Children in Care, *Discussion Document*, p. 2.

[82] Talk given by P.D. Brennan, Director of The School of Social Education, Kilkenny, to the Eastern Region of the Association of Workers with Children in Care, 3 May 1978.

[83] C. Payne, 'Residential Social Work', Ch. 12 in A. Vickery and N. McCaughan (eds) *Integrated Social Work Methods* (London, 1977).

[84] Present position re courses in the Republic of Ireland:
- a diploma course, one year full time, Kilkenny
- a three year part-time course, Cathal Brugha Street

- a three year part-time course, Sligo Regional College
- an induction course, Lota, Cork.
- a course being set up in Galway

[84] As from December 1980 there will be no Child Care Course carrying a professional recognition.

[85] The Social Work Education Consultative Committee (SWECC) is a fully constituted body whose membership consists of (i) a representative of each training course in social work, nominated by the institution providing the course, (ii) a representative from the various fields of social work service as nominated by the professional associations (Irish Association of Social Workers; Association of Workers with Children in Care), (iii) members with specialised knowledge in the field of social work training who are co-opted onto the Council.

[86] Including those by C. Debuust, 'The standpoint of experimental psychology and clinical psychology' in *The Effectiveness of Punishment and other Measures of Treatment* (Strasbourg: Council of Europe, 1967), and L.T. Wilkins, 'Survey of the field from the standpoint of facts and figures', in the same publication.

[87] According to officials in the Department of Justice, on 31 October 1979 about 80% of those contained were from the Dublin area.

[88] In the adjournment debate in the Seanad, Wednesday, 15 February 1978.

[89] CARE, *Who Wants a Children's Prison in Ireland?*, p. 31.

[90] The Minister for Justice stated in the Dáil that the total capital cost to date of Loughan House amounted to £1,236,000, (Dáil Debates for 16 May 1980)

[91] Task Force Report, p. 30.

[92] HOPE Report, p. 51.

[93] Task Force Report, pp. 29–30.

[94] The Department of Social Welfare is also involved where children's allowances and allowances for dependent children under the various income maintenance schemes are concerned.

[95] *Report of the Public Services Organisation Review Group*, 1966–69, (the Devlin Report as referred to hereafter) (Dublin, 1970), pp. 56–7.

[96] Devlin Report, p. 89.

[97] NESC Report, No. 29.

[98] Devlin Report, pp. 144–5.

[99] School Attendance Department, County Borough of Dublin, *Annual Report for Year Ended 30th June 1973*.

[100] Page and Clarke, op.cit., p. 15.

[101] Millham et al, op.cit., p. 43.

[102] Ibid. pp. 43–4.

Chapter VI

[1] Task Force Report, p. 10.

[2] Ibid, p. 16.

[3] Ibid., p. 17.

[4] T. Ward, 'Scratching as we are at the Frontiers of Social Science' p. 9. A paper presented at a special child care projects training day organised by the Department of Health, Welfare Division on 9 May 1979. The focus of the training day was on *Intermediate Treatment*, its possible contribution in Ireland and the training requirements of staff in special child care projects.

[5] Ward, op.cit., p. 3.

[6] Ibid., p. 5.

[7] Objectives as stated in document drawn up by Department of Education, 1977.

[8] These points were made by Brian Doolin at a meeting entitled 'Children's Rights' held by the Irish Council for Civil Liberties at Earlsfort Terrace on 18 January 1979.

[9] Personal Social Services Council, *A Future for Intermediate Treatment* (June 1977), p. 37.

[10] Department of Health and Social Security, *Intermediate Treatment–Planning for Action*, Reports of two Study Groups (May 1977), p. 5.

[11] Department of Health and Social Security, *Intermediate Treatment in Action*, a pamphlet for use in conjunction with the film of the same name presented by the Social Work Service Development Group, 1978.

[12] *Intermediate Treatment in Action*, p. 8.

[13] *In The Year of The Child–Barnado Child Care Services* (Essex, 1979) and *Report of The Working Party on The Future Development of The I.S.P.C.C.* (Unpublished, Dublin, 1977).

[14] Misuse of Drugs Act, 1977, s. 28.

[15] M. Ahern, Submission on *Development of Youth Work* to Youth Advisory Committee, Department of Education (1 June 1978), p. 7.

[16] Ibid., p. 2.

[17] Hope Report, p. 47.

[18] See H. J. Parad, *Crisis Intervention* (New York, 1965).

[19] Black Report, p. 9.

[20] Irish National Teachers' Organisation, *The Educational Needs of Disadvantaged Children*, Report of a Special Committee (October 1979).

[21] B. Murphy, and T. Morrissey, *A Study of Youth Employment in North Central Dublin* (Dublin, 1978).

[22] Ibid., p. 123.

[23] Personal communication with Fr Paul Lavelle, Killarney St., Dublin 1, March 1980.

[24] N. Hazel, *Family placement–a hopeful alternative*, a paper read at the A.P.S.A. conference, 1978, pp. 364–5.

[25] Ibid., pp. 365-7.

[26] In 1971 it was estimated by Seamus O'Cinnéide that at least 20% of the population were poor. In a recently-published book, he up-dates this estimate to 1975. Having established a 'poverty line' which, he suggests 'errs on the side of conservatism', he estimates that about 825,000 people or 27% of the total population live below the poverty line. See S. O'Cinneide, 'Poverty and Inequality in Ireland' in V. George, and R. Lawson, (eds), *Poverty and Inequality in Common Market Countries* (London, 1980), p. 144.

[27] Association of Garda Sergeants and Inspectors, *Discussion Paper on Proposals by the Association to Combat Crime in Ireland* (Dublin, 1980).

[28] Ibid.

[29] *Recommendations of the Inter-Departmental Committee on Dublin Inner City* (Dublin, May 1979), p. 25.

[30] G. Caplan, *Principles of Preventive Psychiatry* (New York, 1963), pp. 31-2.

[31] Government Green Paper, *Development for Full Employment* (Dublin, 1978), p. 17.

[32] S. Holland, *Rutland Street*, p. XIV, Introduction by Mr T. A. O'Cuilleanain, Chairman, Steering Committee of the Rutland Street Project.

[33] *Black Report*, pp. 9 and 5.

Select Bibliography*

M. Ahern, Submission on *Development of Youth Work* to Youth Advisory Committee, Department of Education (1 June 1978), 169

Association of Garda Sergeants and Inspectors, *Discussion Paper on Proposals by the Association to Combat Crime in Ireland* (Dublin, 1980). 181, 182

Association of Workers with Children in Care (AWCC), 'The Professional Role', *Discussion Document* (Kilkenny, 1977). 143, 144

Barnado Child Care Services, *In The Year of The Child* (Essex, 1979). 167

B. Behan, *Borstal Boy* (London, 1958). 9, 119

W. A. Belson, *Juvenile Theft—The Causal Factors* (London, 1975). 115

R. Boshier, and D. Johnson, 'Does Conviction affect Employment Opportunities?', *British Journal of Criminology*, No. 14 (1974). 11

A.E. Bottoms and W. McWilliams, 'A Non-Treatment Paradigm for Probation Practice', *British Journal of Social Work*, Vol. 9., No. 2 (1979). 132

J. Boyle, *A Sense of Freedom* (London, 1977). 119

S.R. Brady, *The Effectiveness of Sentencing: A review of The Literature*, Home Office Research Study, No. 35 (London, 1976). 132

W. Buikhuisen and F.P.M. Dijksterhuis, 'Delinquency and Stigmatization', *British Journal of Criminology*, No. 11 (197), pp. 185–7; 11

G. Caplan, *Principles of Preventive Psychiatry* (New York, 1963). 182, 183

CARE Memorandum, *Children Deprived* (Dublin, 1972). 74, 104, 105, 110, 116, 135, 139, 140

CARE, *Who Wants a Children's Prison in Ireland?* (Dublin 1978). 125, 126, 127, 142, 148

Census of Population, Vol. I (1979), 3, 9

Central Council for Education and Training in Social Work,

*The numbers at the end of each entry above show the pages on which the work is referred to in *Youth and Justice*..

Discussion Document, *Training for Residential Work* (London, 1973). 137, 140

Children Coming into Care, 1978, Department of Health Report (1980). 105, 106, 107

Children in Trouble (London, 1968). 56, 164

W. Clarke Hall, *The State and the Child* (London, 1917). 71, 72, 74

Commission of Enquiry into the Irish Penal System (Dublin, 1979). 136

D.B. Cornish, and R.V.G. Clarke, *Residential Treatment and its Effects on Delinquency,* Home Office Research Studies (London: H.M.S.O., 1975). 131

Dáil Debates, 117, 118

C. Debuust, 'The standpoint of experimental psychology and clinical psychology', *The Effectiveness of Punishment and other Measures of Treatment* (Strasbourg: Council of Europe, 1967). 147

Department of Education, *Statistical Reports* (Dublin). 112

Department of Health and Social Security, *Intermediate Treatment-Planning for Action,* Reports of two Study Groups (London, 1977). 164

Department of Health and Social Security, *Intermediate Treatment in Action* (London, 1978). 165, 166

Department of Justice, *Annual Reports on Prisons and Places of Detention* (Dublin). 117, 120, 121, 122, 123, 124, 125

E. Doleschal and N. Klapmuts, 'Towards a New Criminology' in C.R. Dodge (ed.) *A Nation Without Prisons* (Lexington, 1975). 48

J. Dunham, 'Staff Stress in Residential Work', *Social Work Today* (July 1978). 137

K. Elmhorn, 'Study in self-reported delinquency among school children in Stockholm' K.O. Christensen, (ed.), *Scandinavian studies in Criminology,* Vol. 1, (London, 1956). 2

M.L. Erickson and L.T. Empey, 'Court records, undetected delinquency and decision-making', *Journal of Criminal Law, Criminology and Police Science,* No. 54 (1963), 2

E. Fahy, 'Borstal in Ireland', *Hermathena,* Trinity College, Dublin (1941). 24, 25

Federation of Services for Unmarried Parents and their Children, *Finding Parents for Children with Special Needs* (Dublin, 1980). 107

A. Flynn, N. McDonald and E.F. O'Doherty, 'A Survey of Boys in St. Patrick's Institution: Project on Juvenile Delinquency', *The Irish Jurist*, Vol. 2 (1967). 7, 39, 41, 43, 44, 47

D. Ford, *Children, Courts and Caring, a Study of the Children and Young Persons Act, 1969* (London, 1975). 83

V. George and R. Lawson, (eds.), *Poverty and Inequality in Common Market Countries* (London, 1980). 180

E. Goffman (ed.), *Asylums, Essays on the Social Situation of Mental Patients and other Inmates* (London, 1968). 119, 135

Government Green Paper, *Development for Full Employment* (Dublin, 1978). 183

J. P. Grant, 'The Children's Hearing System in Scotland: Its Strengths and Weaknesses', *The Irish Jurist* (1975). 66, 82

D.F. Greenberg, 'The Correctional Effects of Corrections: A Survey of Evaluations' in D.F. Greenberg (ed.) *Corrections and Punishment*, Sage Criminal Justice System Annuals, Vol. 8 (Beverly Hills, 1977). 132

I. Hart, 'A Survey of some Delinquent Boys in an Irish Industrial School and Reformatory', *Economic and Social Review*, Vol. 7 (1969–70). 12, 42

I. Hart, *Factors Relating to Reconviction among Young Dublin Probationers*, Economic and Social Research Institute, Paper No. 76 (August 1974). 7, 41, 42, 45

I. Hart, 'The Social and Psychological Characteristics of Institutionalised Young Offenders in Ireland', *Administration*, Vol. 16 (1968). 7, 38, 44

N. Hazel, *Family placement–a hopeful alternative*, a paper read at the A.P.S.A. conference, 1978. 177, 178, 179

M. Hoghughi, 'Probing the Flaws in Security', *Community Care* (28 Sept. 1977). 128

M. Hoghughi, 'Provisions for Extreme Children,' *Children First Newsletter*, No. 12–13 (1978). 130, 132, 133

M. Hoghughi, *Troubled and Troublesome, Coping with Severely Disordered Children* (London, 1978). 109

S. Holland, *Rutland Street — The Story of an Educational Experiment of Disadvantaged Children in Dublin* (Oxford, 1979). 45, 46, 47, 184

Hope Report *Out in The Cold* (Dublin, 1979), p. 12. 3, 71, 76, 115, 148, 149, 170

Interdepartmental Committee on Mentally Ill and Maladjusted Persons, (1st Interim Report), *Assessment Services for the Courts in Respect of Juveniles;* (2nd Interim Report), *The Provision of Treatment for Juvenile Offenders and potential Juvenile Offenders* (Dublin, August 1974). 134

Irish National Teachers' Organisation, *The Educational Needs of Disadvantaged Children,* Report of a Special Committee (October 1979). 173

K. Jones, 'The Development of Institutional Care' in *New Thinking about Institutional Care* (London, 1967). 132

M. Jordan, *Residential Care of Children,* unpublished M.Soc,Sc. thesis (University College, Dublin, 1967). 107

T. Kellaghan, *Evaluation of an Intervention Programme for Disadvantaged Children* (Windsor, 1977). 45

Labour Party, *Crime — a Challenge to us All* (London, 1964). 55

Legislation and Services for Children and Young Persons in Northern Ireland; Report of The Children and Young Persons Review Group (Belfast, December 1979). 40, 41, 47, 80, 173, 188, 189

D. Lipton, R. Martinson and J. Wilks, *The Effectiveness of Correctional Treatment* (New York, 1977). 132

H.A. McCarthy, 'The Children's Court' *Christus Rex,* vol. 1-2 (1948). 71

H.A. McCarthy, 'The Supervision of Delinquents in Society' in B.G. MacCarthy (ed.) *Problems of Child Welfare* (Cork, 1945). 31, 32, 33, 34, 89, 98

J.W. Mack, 'The Juvenile Court', *Harvard Law Review* (1909). 53

F.M. Martin, and K. Murray, *Children's Hearings,* (Edinburgh, 1976). 66

C. Maskach, 'Burned Out', *Human Behaviour,* Vol. 5. 137

S.L. Millham, R. Bullock and P.F. Cherrett, *After Grace — Teeth, A Comparative Study of the Residential Experience of Boys in Approved Schools* (London, 1975). 140,156,157

S. Millham, R. Bullock and K. Hosie, *Locking Up Children* (Westmead, 1978). 133

D.C. Mitchell, *Young Offenders* (Dublin, 1977). 85, 86, 95, 96, 97

A. Morris and M. McIsacc, *Juvenile Justice* (Heinemann, 1978). 53

A. Morris, 'The Children and Young Persons Act 1969 — before and after' in a publication by the British Broadcasting Corporation, *Signs of Trouble* (1976). 78, 79, 82

P. Moss, 'Residential Care of Children: A General View' in J. Tizard, et al., *Varieties of Residential Experience* (London, 1975). 103, 104

B. Murphy, and T. Morrissey, *A Study of Youth Employment in North Central Dublin* (Dublin, 1978). 10, 11, 174

National Economic and Social Council (hereafter referred

to as NESC), *Towards a Social Report*, No. 25 (Dublin, 1977). 3, 4, 5, 10

NESC, *Some Major Issues in Health Policy*, No. 29 (Dublin, 1977). 151

NESC, *Population and Employment Projections 1986: A Reassessment*, No. 35 (Dublin, 1977) 3

F. Norman, *Banana Boy* (London, 1969). 119

S. O'Cinneide, 'Poverty and Inequality in Ireland' in V. George and R. Lawson, (eds.), *Poverty and Inequality in Common Market Countries* (London, 1980). 180

J. O'Connor, *The Irish Justice of the Peace*, (London, 1915). 98

J. O'Connor, 'The Young Offender', *Studies* (Spring 1963). 71

M. O'Connor, *Juvenile Offenders in a Reformatory School: a Sociological Study*, unpublished M.Soc,Sc. thesis (University College, Dublin, 1972). 107

N. Osborough, *Borstal in Ireland*, (Dublin, 1975). 21, 23, 24, 25, 123

R. Page and G.A. Clarke, *Who Cares? Young people in Care Speak Out* (London, 1977). 143, 155

H.J. Parad, *Crisis Intervention* (New York, 1965). 171

P. Parsloe, *Juvenile Justice in Britain and the United States* (London, 1978). 51, 60, 79, 80

Personal Social Services Council, *A Future for Intermediate Treatment* (London, 1977). 164

B. Power, 'The Young Lawbreaker', *Social Studies*, Vol. 0, No. 0 (Oct., 1971). 38, 41, 43, 44

P. Priestley, D. Fears and R. Fuller, *Justice for Juveniles. The 1969 Children and Young Persons Act: A Case for Reform?* (London, 1977). 55, 59

Prisoner's Rights Organisation, *A Survey of Fifty 12-16 Year Old Male Offenders in The Sean MacDermott St-Summerhill Area* (Dublin, 1978). 12, 39, 40, 43, 45

Prison Study Group, *An Examination of the Irish Penal System* (Dublin, 1973). 48, 118, 120, 124

Recommendations of the Inter-departmental Committee on Dublin Inner City (Dublin, May 1979). 182

Report of the Commission of Inquiry into the Reformatory and Industrial School System 1934–1936, (Dublin, 1936). 26, 27, 28, 29, 30, 110

Report of Commission of Inquiry on Mental Handicap, (Dublin, 1956). 44

Report of the Committee on Children and Young Persons (London,

1960). 54, 55

Report of the Committee on Children and Young Persons, Scotland (London, 1964). 60, 61, 62

Report of the Committee on Reformatory and Industrial Schools, (Dublin, 1970). 7, 8, 9, 26, 34, 35, 39, 40, 44, 69, 71, 74, 92, 93, 95, 96, 110, 122, 129, 130, 134, 135

Report of the Departmental Committee on Training and Protection (London, 1928). 60

Reports of the Garda Commissioner, (Dublin). 1, 13, 14, 20

Reports of the General Prisons Board, Ireland, 1877–1927, (Dublin). 20, 21, 22, 23, 52

Report of the Public Services Organisation Review Group, 1966–69, (Dublin, 1970). 149, 150, 151, 152

Report on Residential Child Care in the South-Eastern Health Board Region, Assoc. of Workers of Children in Care (1974). 107

Report of the Working Party on The Future Development of The I.S.P.C.C. (Unpublished, Dublin, 1977). 167

V. Richardson, *Provision of a social work service for Children in residential care including study of the background and characteristics of children in long-term residential care in the City and County of Dublin.* Research in progress, U.C.D.(Dublin, 1980). 107

D. Romig, *Justice for our children an examination of juvenile delinquent rehabilitation programs* (Lexington, Mass., 1978). 131

D. Rottman, 'Crime and Law Enforcement' *Towards a Social Report,* NESC, No. 25 (Dublin, 1977). 3, 5, 6

D. Rottman, 'The Changing Pattern of Crime in the Republic of Ireland' *Journal of The Statistical and Social Inquiry Society of Ireland,* Vol. XXIII, part v (1977–8). 1

Viscount Samuel, *Memoirs* (London, 1945). 53

Seanad Debates. 148

School Attendance Department, County Borough of Dublin, *Annual Reports.* 15, 153, 154

M. Schur, *Radical Non-Intervention* (Prentice Hall Inc., 1973). 49

R.D. Schwartz and J.H. Skolnick, 'Two Studies of Legal Stigma', Social Problems, no. 10 (1962). 11

P. Shanley, 'The Formal Cautioning of Juvenile Offenders', *The Irish Jurist,* Part 2 (Winter 1970). 68

A.J. Shatter, *Family Law in the Republic of Ireland* (Dublin, 1977). 74

Social Work and the Community (London, 1966). 62

Task Force on Child Care Services: Interim Report (Dublin, 1975). 35, 113, 114, 115, 129, 130, 134, 135, 148, 149, 158, 159

I. Taylor, P. Walton and J. Young, *The New Criminology* (London, 1973). 135

The Child, the Family and the Young Offender, (London, 1965). 56

J. Tizard, I. Sinclair and R.V.G. Clarke, *Varieties of Residential Experience*, (London, 1975). 132, 133

N. Tutt, *Care or Custody* (London, 1974). 138, 141

R.N. Vaughan and B.J. Whelan, 'The Economic and Social Circumstances of the Elderly in Ireland: A Preliminary Report', ESRI seminar paper, 7 December 1978. 16, 17

A. Vickery and N. McCaughan, (eds.) *Integrated Social Work Methods* (London, 1977). 145

R.D. Vinter, G. Downs and J. Hall, *Juvenile Corrections in the States. Residential Programs and Deinstitutionalization* (Michigan, 1975). 131

T. Ward, 'Scratching as we are at the Frontiers of Social Science' unpublished paper to a Department of Health training-day on *Intermediate Treatment*, (Dublin, 1979). 159, 160

B. Waugh, *The Gaol Cradle: Who Rocks it?* (London, 1876). 52

D. West and D.P. Farrington, *The Delinquent Way of Life* (London, 1977). 2, 11, 43, 50

L.T. Wilkins, 'A Behavioral Theory of Drug Taking', *The Howard Journal of Penology and Crime Prevention*, Vol. II (1962-65). 49

B. Wooton, *Crime and Penal Policy* (London, 1978). 72, 73

G. Wright, 'A Model of Supervision for Residential Staff', *Social Work to-day*, Vol. 9., No. 45. (25 July 1978). 139

Subject Index

217

Biographical notes on the Editors

Helen Burke, chaired the staff-student working party which produced *Youth and Justice*, lectures in social policy in University College Dublin. After taking her primary degree in Political Economy and Social Science in University College Dublin in 1958, she was awarded a fellowship by Florida State University in 1958 and there she trained as a social worker and took her master's degree in Social Welfare in 1960. She taught in Queen's University, Belfast before returning to University College Dublin, where she gained her Ph.D in 1976.

Currently chairwoman of the Department of Social Administration, University College Dublin, she chaired the social policy committee of The National Economic and Social Council from 1974 to 1980. She served as a commissioner for law reform from 1975 to 1977, chaired the 1977 working-party which drew up plans for the re-organization of the Irish Society for the Prevention of Cruelty to Children and has been president of that society since 1979.

Dr. Burke is married and has three children.

Claire Carney, lecturer in Social Science at University College, Dublin since 1968, is chairwoman of the Department of Social Work and Applied Social Studies. Having obtained a BA and a Diploma in Social Science at University College Dublin, and subsequently qualifying as a professional social worker at the Institute for Medical-Social-Work, London, Claire Carney was awarded a Ph.D. by the National University of Ireland in 1978. She worked first in the Mater Misericordiae Hospital, Dublin and subsequently was Director of the social work department of the National Medical Rehabilitation Centre.

Currently chairwoman of the Social Work Education Consultative Committee for Ireland, Dr. Carney is monthly correspondent for Ireland to the Directorate General for Employment and Social Affairs in the Commission of the European Communities. She is also a member of the Council for Social Welfare, a committee of the Catholic Bishop's Conference.

Geoffrey Cook was educated at the Universities of Bristol (B.A.) and Manchester (M.A. Econ.) and has been successively a social worker, lecturer and researcher. After a period at University College Cork he moved to University College Dublin as lecturer in social policy and administration. He has also been a CARE council member and for one year was secretary of that organization. His research interests extend from juvenile justice systems to housing policy and social security policy, among other areas of social policy analysis.

222